INTELLECTUAL TRADITIONS IN ISLAM

INTELLECTUAL TRADTIONS in ISLAM

Edited by

FARHAD DAFTARY

I.B.Tauris
LONDON • NEW YORK
in association with
The Institute of Ismaili Studies

Published in 2000 by I.B.Tauris & Co Ltd
Victoria House, Bloomsbury Square, London WC1B 4DZ
175 Fifth Avenue, New York NY 10010
website: http://www.ibtauris.com

in association with the Institute of Ismaili Studies
42–44 Grosvenor Gardens, London SW1W 0EB

In the United States of America and in Canada distributed by
St Martins Press
175 Fifth Avenue, New York NY 10010

ISBN 1 86064 435 X

A full CIP record for this book is available from the British Library
A full CIP record for this book is available from the Library of Congress

Library of Congress catalog card: available

Typeset in ITC New Baskerville by Hepton Books, Oxford
Printed and bound in Great Britain by WBC Ltd, Bridgend

To the memory of

NORMAN CALDER

1950–1998

JOHN COOPER

1947–1998

The Institute of Ismaili Studies

The Institute of Ismaili Studies was established in 1977 with the object of promoting scholarship and learning on Islam, in the historical as well as contemporary contexts, and a better understanding of its relationship with other societies and faiths.

The Institute's programmes encourage a perspective which is not confined to the theological and religious heritage of Islam, but seek to explore the relationship of religious ideas to broader dimensions of society and culture. They thus encourage an interdisciplinary approach to the materials of Islamic history and thought. Particular attention is also given to issues of modernity that arise as Muslims seek to relate their heritage to the contemporary situation.

Within the Islamic tradition, the Institute's programmes seek to promote research on those areas which have, to date, received relatively little attention from scholars. These include the intellectual and literary expressions of Shi'ism in general, and Ismailism in particular.

In the context of Islamic societies, the Institute's programmes are informed by the full range and diversity of cultures in which Islam is practised today, from the Middle East, Southern and Central Asia and Africa to the industrialized societies of the West, thus taking into consideration the variety of contexts which shape the ideals, beliefs and practices of the faith.

The publications of the Institute fall into several distinct categories:

1. Occasional papers or essays addressing broad themes of the relationship between religion and society in the historical as well as modern contexts, with special reference to Islam, but encompassing, where appropriate, other faiths and cultures.
2. Works exploring a specific theme or aspect of Islamic faith or culture, or the contribution of an individual figure or writer.
3. Translations of poetic or literary texts.
4. Editions or translations of significant texts of a primary or secondary nature.
5. Ismaili studies.
6. Proceedings of conferences, catalogues and bibliographies.

This book falls under the category six listed above. In facilitating these and other publications, the Institute's sole aim is to encourage original, interesting and mature thought, scholarship and analysis of the relevant issues. There will naturally be a diversity of views, ideas and interpretations, and the opinions expressed will be those of the authors.

Contents

Preface

The transformation of Islam into one of the great civilizations of the world has been the subject of many studies in recent decades. As Islam spread outside the Arabian peninsula, its birthplace, it became enriched by the intellectual contributions of a multitude of individuals, communities and cultures in regions that eventually comprised the Muslim world. Indeed, by the 10th century, the Islamic civilization was already characterized by a diversity of literary and intellectual traditions in various fields of learning such as theology, law, philosophy, literature, mysticism, arts and natural sciences, while Islam as a religion had been elaborated in a plurality of expressions and interpretations. To discuss the significance of these issues, a seminar entitled 'Intellectual Traditions in Islam' was organized by The Institute of Ismaili Studies at The Mellor Centre, Churchill College, University of Cambridge, during 14–20 August 1994.

The genesis of this collective volume lies mainly in this seminar, with a few exceptions. Professor M. Mahdi's contribution is based on a talk he delivered in 1990 at an earlier seminar organized by our Institute in Oxford; and Professors M. Arkoun and A. Sachedina decided to submit new, unpublished papers, in place of the presentations they made in Cambridge. My own contribution constitutes an expanded and revised version of my talk at the Cambridge seminar.

It is with much sadness that we have to record the death in 1998 of two of our authors, John Cooper and Norman Calder. John (Yahya) Cooper had a long standing collaboration with our Institute and also for several years taught courses on Islamic theology and philosophy, with special reference to Shi'i Islam, to our graduate students. Norman Calder was an eminent scholar of Islamic law and Qur'anic studies, and by the time of his premature death he had already made important contributions to his chosen fields of specialization. It is in recognition of the scholarship of these deeply missed colleagues that this volume is dedicated to their memory.

The essays in this book, with the above-noted exceptions, were originally transcribed from tapes and then edited. All the authors, except John Cooper, had the opportunity to check, correct and revise the edited versions of their papers. The system of transliteration used in this book is that of the new edition of *The Encyclopaedia of Islam* with the usual modifications. However, diacritical marks have been dispensed with except for 'ayn and hamza, while they are retained in the 'glossary' and 'bibliography'.

Dr A. Esmail, whose keynote address appears by way of introduction to this volume, played a key role in conceptualizing the intellectual structure of the Cambridge seminar. The Institute's publications editor, Kutub Kassam has been involved in every stage of this book's production from its inception; the final product owes much to his indefatigable efforts and meticulous editorial suggestions. I would like to record here a special debt of gratitude to him. Thanks are due also to Hamid Haji for having originally translated Professor Arkoun's paper from French into English. Finally, I would like to thank Julia Kolb who prepared the typescript of this collective volume for publication.

F.D.

Notes on the Contributors

MOHAMMED ARKOUN is a leading contemporary Muslim intellectual and Professor (Emeritus) of Islamic Thought at the Sorbonne, Paris III. He is also a Senior Research Fellow at The Institute of Ismaili Studies, London, a jury member of the Aga Khan Award for Architecture and Editor of *Arabica*. Amongst various awards and distinctions, Professor Arkoun has been appointed Officier of the Légion d'Honneur and Officier des Palmes Académiques. Professor Arkoun is the author of numerous books in French, English and Arabic, including *Aspects de la pensée Musulmane classique* (Paris, 1963), *L'Ethique Musulmane d'après Mawardi* (Paris, 1964), *L'humanisme Arabe au IVe/Xe siècle* (2nd ed., Paris, 1982), *Lectures du Coran* (Paris, 1982), *Pour une critique de la raison Islamique* (Paris, 1984), *L'Islam, morale et politique* (Paris, 1986), *La Pensée Arabe* (4th ed., Paris, 1991) and *Rethinking Islam* (Boulder, 1994).

NORMAN CALDER (1950–1998) was Senior Lecturer in Arabic and Islamic Studies at the University of Manchester. He read Oriental Studies at the University of Oxford and received his doctorate from the School of Oriental and African Studies, University of London. A scholar of Islamic law, Dr. Calder analysed early Islamic legal texts in numerous studies. His publications include *Studies in Early Muslim Jurisprudence* (Oxford, 1993) and more than twenty studies on the Qur'an, *tafsir* and aspects of Sunni and Shi'i thought, published in collective volumes and learned journals.

JOHN COOPER (1947–1998) was the E.G. Browne Lecturer in Persian Studies at the Faculty of Oriental Studies at the University of Cambridge, and a Visiting Lecturer at The Institute of Ismaili Studies, London. He was educated at the University of Oxford and the traditional Islamic centres of learning in Qumm, Iran, where he spent six years studying Islamic philosophy, theology and jurisprudence. John Cooper had excellent knowledge of Arabic and Persian, and his publications include numerous translations of classical and modern texts such as al-Kulayni's *al-Usul min al-kafi*, and al-Tabari's *Tafsir* under the title *Commentary on the Qur'an* (Oxford, 1987), vol. 1. He was Editor of *The Significance of Islamic Manuscripts* (London, 1992) and Co-editor of *Islam and Modernity* (London, 1998); his shorter translations and studies of Shi'ism appeared in a number of collective volumes.

FARHAD DAFTARY is Head of the Department of Academic Research and Publications at The Institute of Ismaili Studies. A scholar of Ismaili studies, he is General Editor of Ismaili Heritage Series, and Ismaili Texts and Translations Series, published by The Institute of Ismaili Studies. He is the author of *The Isma'ilis: Their History and Doctrines* (Cambridge, 1990), *The Assassin Legends: Myths of the Isma'ilis* (London, 1994), *A Short History of the Ismailis*, Islamic Surveys (Edinburgh, 1998), and Editor of *Mediaeval Isma'ili History and Thought* (Cambridge, 1996). His books have been translated into Arabic, Persian, Urdu and a number of European languages. He has contributed numerous articles to *The Encyclopaedia of Islam*, *Encyclopaedia Iranica* of which he is a Consulting Editor, as well as several Persian encyclopaedias of Islam; his shorter studies have also appeared in collective volumes and learned journals.

AZIZ ESMAIL was formerly the Dean of The Institute of Ismaili Studies, London, of which he is now a Governor. Dr Esmail was for several years a Lecturer in Philosophy and Religion at the University of Nairobi in Kenya, and subsequently held academic positions in several universities in America, including the University of Chicago and the Center for the Study of World Religions at Harvard University. His publications include *The Poetics of Religious Experience: The Islamic Context* (London, 1998) and contributions to collective volumes.

ALICE C. HUNSBERGER is Visiting Research Fellow at the Institute of Ismaili Studies. She was previously Adjunct Asssistant Professor in Religion and Philosophy at Hunter College, New York, where she twice received the College President's award for excellence in teaching. Dr Hunsberger received her PhD and MA from Columbia University and her BA from New York University, all in Persian, Arabic and Islamic Studies. Dr Hunsberger has presented papers at numerous academic conferences and is the author of *Nasir Khusraw: The Ruby of Badakhshan* (London, 2000).

HUGH KENNEDY is Professor of Middle Eastern History at the University of St. Andrews. A scholar of early Islamic history, Dr Kennedy's publications include *The Early Abbasid Caliphate: A Political History* (London, 1981), *The Prophet and the Age of the Caliphates* (London, 1986) and *Muslim Spain and Portugal: A Political History of al-Andalus* (London, 1996); his shorter studies have appeared in *The Encyclopaedia of Islam* as well as in learned journals.

OLIVER LEAMAN is Professor of Philosophy at the Liverpool John Moores University, and a Visiting Lecturer at The Institute of Ismaili Studies, London. A scholar of medieval Islamic philosophy, Dr Leaman is the author of *An Introduction to Medieval Islamic Philosophy* (Cambridge, 1985), *Averroes and his Philosophy* (Oxford, 1988), *Evil and Suffering in Jewish Philosophy* (Cambridge, 1995), *Key Concepts in Eastern Philosophy* (London, 1999), Editor of *The Future of Philosophy* (London, 1998), Co-editor of *History of Islamic Philosophy* (London, 1996), 2 vols, and *History of Jewish Philosophy* (London, 1996). Dr Leaman's shorter studies have appeared in *Companion Encyclopedia of Asian Philosophy* (London, 1997), *Encyclopaedia of Philosophy* (London, 1998) and in other collective volumes and learned journals.

MUHSIN MAHDI is a leading contemporary scholar of Islamic

philosophy and literature, and the James Richard Jewett Professor (Emeritus) of Arabic at Harvard University. Professor Mahdi has published numerous monographs as well as editions and translations of classic Arabic texts. His publications include *Ibn Khaldun's Philosophy of History* (London, 1957), *Al-Farabi's Philosophy of Aristotle* (Beirut, 1961), *Alfarabi's Book of Religion and Related Texts* (Beirut, 1968), *Alfarabi's Book of Letters* (Beirut, 1969), *The Thousand and One Nights (Alf Layla wa-Layla) from the Earliest Known Sources* (Leiden, 1984), and *Orientalism and the Study of Islamic Philosophy* (Oxford, 1990).

ABDULAZIZ SACHEDINA is Professor of Religious Studies at the University of Virginia, and a Visiting Lecturer at The Institute of Ismaili Studies, London. A scholar of Islamic legal tradition, ethics and political Islam, he has studied in India, Canada and the traditional Islamic centres of learning in Iran. Professor Sachedina is a core member of the 'Islamic Roots of Democratic Pluralism' project in the CSIS Preventive Diplomacy Programme and a key contributor to the Programme's efforts to link religion to universal human needs and values in the service of peace. He is the author of *Islamic Messianism: The Idea of Mahdi in Twelver Shi'ism* (Albany, N.Y., 1981), *The Just Ruler* (al-sultan al-adil) *in Shi'ite Islam* (Oxford, 1988), *The Prolegomena to the Qur'an* (Oxford, 1998), *The Islamic Roots of Democratic Pluralism* (Oxford, 1999), and has contributed numerous articles to learned journals.

ANNEMARIE SCHIMMEL is a leading German scholar of Islam and Professor (Emeritus) of Indo-Muslim Culture at Harvard University, and Honorary Professor at the University of Bonn. Professor Schimmel has received numerous literary awards and distinctions including the Giorgio Levi Della Vida Award in Islamic Studies (1987), the Friedrich Rückert Medal for outstanding translations (1965), the Peace Prize of the Union of German Booksellers (1995), the Grand Order of Merit from the German government, and the Hilal-i Imtiaz from Pakistan. She has published more than fifty books on Islamic literature, mysticism and culture, and has translated Persian, Urdu, Arabic and Turkish works into English and German. Professor Schimmel's books include *Gabriel's Wing: A Study into the Religious Ideas of Sir Muhammad Iqbal* (Leiden, 1963),

Mystical Dimensions of Islam (Chapel Hill, 1975), *The Triumphal Sun: A Study of the Works of Jalaloddin Rumi* (London, 1978), *Islam in the Indian Subcontinent* (Leiden, 1980), *And Muhammad is His Messenger* (Chapel Hill, 1985), *A Two-Colored Brocade: The Imagery of Persian Poetry* (New York, 1992) and *Deciphering the Signs of God: A Phenomenological Approach to Islam* (Edinburgh, 1994).

spirit of the age, to open new horizons, new possibilities of thinking and feeling, of being and acting, how is one, then, to
understand the responsibility of the intellectual to society? These
are questions about the place of the intellectual in culture and in
society. There are similar questions which concern the mind of
the individual. What is the place of the life of the mind within the
personality? What is its relationship to feeling? What is its relationship to character? What is its relationship to faith? What role
does intellectual life have in the development of personal identity and character? What relation does it have to the ordinary joys,
affections and sorrows of life, to friendship and love, and not least,
to one's relationship with God? What place does it have in the
individual's participation in society? To what extent does intellectual consciousness, which is often a critical consciousness, enable
such participation, and to what extent does it impede it? And how
exactly does the individual relate to the society through his intellectual activities?

These are questions, then, to do with the intellect. Now take
the second concept that is present in the title: that, namely, of
tradition. What traditions is one to cherish or to uphold in a world
in which an individual is exposed, as is the case nowadays, not to
one group of traditions but to a multitude of them? The world of
today is characterized by a pluralism of traditions. Numerous traditions criss-cross, overlap and jostle one another. Furthermore,
modern electronic media and communications have made diverse
traditions of the world uniquely, immediately and instantaneously
available at various parts of the globe. How might one maintain
anchorage in particular historical traditions in such circumstances?
Which thread among these traditions relates to which one, such
that the threads might somehow constitute a fabric that one can
call one's own? And where, therefore, is one to find a sense of
belonging, or what is called 'authenticity' or 'identity' (words about
which I have a series of other questions)? These are some of the
vexing and uncertain issues that surround the very concept of
tradition. Beyond them there lies a more fundamental question.
And that question, which is a contemporary one, is not only about
which traditions to call one's own, but about the likelihood of any
traditions surviving at all in a world which is changing rapidly under
one's very eyes. In a sense, one might ask: what is the future of the

past? What future does the past have in a world which is changing so fast – a world saturated with the instantaneous culture of global communication? What role does history have here? And if there is no past, if the past has no future, what is one to think about the present and the future?

Now, let me clarify what I mean by this. I am not talking about public or objective time here, but what we might call subjective time. For objectively, there is always a yesterday, a today and a tomorrow. There is the time of the clock; but there is also, in the life of a society, what we might call historical time – the mode of time in which one is related to, and bears a kinship with, one's ancestors and with the inheritance of an age, a legacy which one carries forward into the future. And this is true not only of society, but also of the individual, because the individual has a life history. The importance of life history, not so much in the public, observable form, but in its subjective mode, becomes especially pronounced at certain critical junctures in life, for instance, old age as well as youth. Where old age is blessed with wisdom, one looks back at the course of one's life as the only course that it could have taken, with the feeling that it was as it ought to have been. One finds a new relationship with one's parents, free of the wish that they should have been different. More generally, one might cherish, at this stage, the sense of a connection with bygone ages, a kinship with history and with distant forefathers which is at the same time a relationship that is to come. For the passing generation gives its lifeblood, part of its soul, to the generation which is yet to come. In this way one closes, as it were, the circle of life history.

Youth is another stage in the life history where the same negotiation, a very difficult, delicate negotiation, between what has gone on in one's life and what is to come, occurs. And what is particularly important at such a time is the relationship of the individual life history to the traditions that are outside it – in a word, to culture. The young man's or woman's relationship to traditions is one of either dependence or defiance. Youth has two opposite yearnings: a yearning to be told what to do and a yearning to tell whoever tells him what to do, to get lost. You will notice that I am using slightly milder language than may be heard in practice. What, however constitutes dependency? What is involved here are not only issues to do with family. They also appertain to the whole question of education, of schooling and the place of the school, as an institution, in society.

There are two models of the school, located at opposite ends of a spectrum. One is that of a military camp; the other of a playing field. The school which is based on the model of a military camp is the sort of school to which most of us gathered here probably went. This is not unlike the model of the public school in England, although the public school has its own grim kind of playfulness. This particular model of education treats with the utmost seriousness the maxim that the child is the father of the man. What it proposes is that the child must be more adult than the adult himself, that he must bend before the objective imperatives of learning. He must learn to make of his life a sustained devotion to duty, a consistent obedience to objective rules. The other type of school, which is the contrary model of education, takes seriously, perhaps too seriously, the adage that 'all work and no play make Jack a dull boy'. Modern liberal theories of education carry this maxim very far indeed, to the point where what it really means is 'all play and no work make Jack a smart boy'. Its central premise is that discipline is something to be avoided at all costs. Now, this is the trend of education which shuns traditions altogether so as to give the child the privilege, as it claims, of 'finding himself,' of creating his own knowledge, of forming his own opinions, in the absence of external discipline or constraint. We in our time have been so conditioned, so accustomed to notice the defects of the formal model of education, now widely considered 'oppressive,' that we are as yet little aware of the grave deficiencies of that model which places all its emphasis on the self rather than on society. It should become obvious, when we ponder on this problem, that education is only a microcosm of the culture of the society at large. The model of education I am criticizing leads to what I might call the tyranny of self-absorption. And one often finds among people who come from that particular regime of education a longing, a yearning for a system that will tell them what the world is like, what their place in the world is, and what one is supposed to do in the world.

In a nutshell, this longing is a quest for objectivity: that is to say, for a relationship to an objective order. Now, an objective order is accessible, especially for the young man or woman, through two channels. One is work, the other is culture. Work – a profession or occupation – gives one a firm relationship to a world of ideas, skills and tools. It is significant that throughout history, a majority of men and women have always found their identity in work, whether in hunting animals, in tilling the soil, in raising children, in making machines work, or in all those sundry occupations of an economic, political or organizational kind that enable these other kinds of work to proceed. They have always left to a minority, to higher institutions as it were, the task of complementing the satisfactions to be got out of basic, physical work. Thus, for most of history, political work was left in the hands of rulers; religious life was left in the hands of priests, rabbis and '*ulama*; and culture was entrusted to poets, artists, writers, philosophers and scientists.

In the modern world this relationship has altered. It altered about three centuries ago with the Industrial Revolution when the unit of work shifted from the family home, the farm and the shop to the factory. Traditionally, the shop was a family-orientated affair. It was in a way an extension of the community. But the factory is not an extension of the community, and modern work has proceeded from this point onwards on a separate track from activities in a family, and in a community. Thus, it is very common nowadays to hear people say, 'I find my social satisfaction outside work and not in work itself.' Accordingly, the types of self-expression available in each sector of life differ widely among themselves. This development has many sources, all of which are characteristic of modern history. They include the automatization and rationalization of work which went hand in hand with the rise of modern commerce and industry. The twin consequences of this was a differentiation of society into distinct sectors, and a corresponding differentiation of the individual personality into a multiplicity of roles.

As a result of these historical changes, the ethos of modern work is strictly apart from opportunities for self-expression now available in the secular Western world only in the cinema, the concert hall, the theatre, or else in pubs or cafés. But these institutions too – institutions like the theatre and the concert hall – are less communal than was true in the past. One may recall, for instance, the fact that chamber music was largely played in homes and not in concert halls; or that the opera was an event where people came to meet and talk. If you look at copies of *The Times* in England for example, from the last century, you will occasionally find in them complaints about opera singing which was so noisy as to make it impossible for the audience to talk to one another, and so enjoy themselves. Today, however, all such activities have become markedly impersonal, rather than communal.

In the Third World, two tendencies or trends may be found. On the one side, there is a greater prevalence of forms of art and recreation which are communal or social. There are, for instance, the rousing and rumbustious forms of music like Qawali performances, which are fundamentally communal, and where the social, the spiritual and the artistic seem to go together. Another religio-political form of self-expression is nowadays to be found in activities centred on the mosque, religious schools or *madrasas*, and theological colleges. Some of these institutions are taking over a large amount of the functions of culture and communal solidarity in Muslim societies. This is a phenomenon which demands some explanation.

One of the reasons for this trend has to do with the inroads of modernity, which causes the alienation provoking the search, in turn, for social forms embodying what are seen as moral spiritual values. There is also, of course, the problem of education. In the West at least there is a wide availability of opportunities not only for education but for education to be followed by work – opportunities, in other words, for the acquisition of skills and a chance to exercise those skills. When education is denied altogether, or having been acquired appears irrelevant or fruitless, when one is denied what competence one has and the sense of belonging that comes when that competence is exercised, then there is an enormous sense of *anomie* and moral vacuum among the young people affected by this trend. I think what is happening in the Islamic world is but a variant of what is happening in the Third World at large, in African and Asian countries, though not necessarily as much, perhaps, in the Far East.

One of the problems of modern history has been the rise of totalistic ideologies. In the Muslim world, the only major ideology which for a time seemed to be capable of mobilizing the society, and in particular its youth, was nationalism, which was usually combined with a degree of real or ostensible socialism. These ideologies were seldom successful in ensuring social justice and solidarity, and hence were succeeded by a period of gathering disillusionment. There is, therefore, a hiatus in these societies: a hiatus in meaning, a crisis of meaning. It has often been said that the rise of 'fundamentalism,' or what is called 'Islamic fundamentalism' in these countries, is something that is best explained by politics. But beneath the political problem, there lies the cultural problem. One must, therefore, look at culture, and not just at the political issue in order to understand the matter fully. For regardless of whether an ideology is religious or secular, it is intended to relate the self to society and to a picture of the cosmos at large. Ideologies represent the human need for a unifying doctrine – something that will tell people, firstly, what the world is like; secondly, what man's place in the world is; and thirdly, what the principles governing human actions or conduct in the world are to be. Ideology is thus a total phenomenon. It answers several of those great questions that Kant asked about the order of things, such as 'What is man?', 'What is my place in the world?', and above all, 'What shall I do?' This last question, it will be noticed, is that of ethics.

Within ideologies, there is a distinction to be made between what the psychoanalyst Eric H. Erikson once called, respectively, *totalism* and *wholeness*. 'Wholeness' may be defined, negatively, as an absence of disconnection or fragmentation. It represents a sense that one is connected to the universe; that one is connected to fellow human beings; and that within oneself, the various parts are interconnected, giving a unity to the personality. Totalism, which in some respects is preferable to the term fundamentalism, denotes a unifying system of thought which spells out everything, dictates everything, and makes, moreover, a very sharp distinction between its own world and other worlds, between what is deemed to belong inside and to lie outside its own sphere. Totalism insists that what belongs outside must not be let in, and what belongs to itself must not, at any cost, be left out. This rigid separation of the inside and the outside is a dichotomy found in all totalizing ideologies. It is present in the West's image of Islam as antithetical to everything for which Western civilization stands, and it is equally present in the absolutist definition of Islam, which opposes itself entirely to the culture of modernity.

It is important to realize that this totalistic definition of Islam is a modern one. Although it invokes history, it is not itself based in history. Historically, Islamic thought, or Islamic culture, was a composite phenomenon. It was a product of many cultural influences, a river into which many a tributary flowed. It had a certain central unity, some central integrity, which is very difficult to define. For instance, when we look at art across the Islamic world, it has a sufficient commonality, and a sufficient distinctiveness, to justify our calling it Islamic. Yet the diversity is considerable, and the influences from all the corners of the globe are also quite extensive.

Before going further, I would like to add several points of clarification. Often enough, when people say that they are looking for a Judaic answer to the problems of the world today, or a Christian answer, or an Islamic solution, what they seem to be saying is that they wish the tradition in question to continue. But there is every difference in the world between tradition and the desire for tradition, between what I call *tradition* and *traditionalism*. The idea of tradition is not a child of tradition. The idea of tradition, which is traditionalism, is born, so to speak, out of wedlock. It emerges from a divorce between ideals and the society in which those ideals are supposed to reign. It is the product of a divorce between past and present. In fact, traditional societies are the one kind of society which are singularly free from the idea of tradition. In the Islamic world, for instance, there is considerable talk, which has been going on now for an odd fifty years or so, about the Muslim 'tradition', the Muslim 'heritage,' and so on. These are peculiarly modern preoccupations, however. The German philosopher Martin Heidegger has a lucid image to describe something analogous to what I am speaking of here. A hammer in the hands of an artisan is a very different thing from a hammer in the hands of a repair man. In the hands of the artisan, when the hammer is in working order, it is almost an extension of his body. It is part of him and it is part of the workshop, hence a part of the economy of which that workshop is in turn a part. The moment the hammer breaks, when it no longer works 'naturally,' it becomes an object of scrutiny. It is separated from its function, and when one now looks at the hammer, one looks at it as an object, as a tool, whereas the artisan was probably using it almost unconsciously when it was working. If the economy runs into a problem and the workshop encounters difficulties, it becomes an object of attention, whereas formerly it was not. In the same way, tradition becomes an object of anxiety, nostalgia and attention when it ceases to work, not when it is actually at work. Therefore, it is not in traditional societies that one gets the idea of tradition. It is not in traditional societies that you get the attitude of mind or the cast of mind that I have here called traditionalism.

The measure of a traditional age lies in the amount of life that it is able to take for granted; and the amount, by contrast, that it cannot take for granted, or is no longer able to take for granted. In the distance that separates these two kinds of society lies the distance between the world which was once dominated by Athens, Jerusalem or Mecca, and the world dominated by Washington, Tokyo, by post-imperial London and Paris, and by all those cities in the rest of the world which are satellites of these metropolises. And even when societies which revolve around the modern cities seek to recapture the spiritual dominion of Jerusalem or Mecca, what they display, in so doing, is not their closeness or proximity to those ancient cities, but rather their nostalgic distance from them.

Let me move on now to some very general observations. I began by saying that each of the concepts that we have in the title of this seminar is not a topic but a question: that the life of intellect is a question, that the idea of a tradition is a question, indeed the idea of Islam itself raises a question. What is meant by Islam, and what is the relationship of the past and present in Islam? One of the functions of the seminar is to define these questions more sharply, because in these matters more than half the battle is accomplished by asking the right kinds of questions. Let us remember that for nearly the first four centuries of Muslim history, the nature of Islam was contested between different interpretations which had not yet hardened into fixed and compartmentalized positions. The notion that Islam had spelled out literal answers to every question to be encountered in history, and that the only impending task was to put it into practice, to effect it, is a misconception. What actually happened in history was, first of all, the fact of the tremendous expansion of Arab rule over large parts of the world, in historical terms an astonishingly brief spell of time. That rule raised all kinds of questions about governance, about ideas and values, about law and the organization of society. It also provoked considerable variation and dissent. From the beginning, there was a great divide over the question of authority, as to how the Islamic dominions were to be legitimately governed in a spiritual and temporal sense (the distinction between these two realms was not really made till much later). There is, I think, increasing evidence to show that the Shi'i viewpoint on this issue, which located authority in the *ahl al-bayt,* the Prophet Muhammad's family, began very early, not withstanding the orthodox Sunni view as well as the view of Western Islamicists who had greater access to Sunni than to Shi'i sources, and whose view was correspondingly shaped. So there was a period of ferment and formation, and that is why one may appropriately call this period, to which I have assigned a loose and necessarily arbitrary date, the formative age of Islam.

From the historical vantage point where we now stand, all the societies that originated from the Mediterranean region – I refer to all societies and not just Muslim societies, leaving out the great civilizations of India and China which have a very different history – appear to share a triple heritage. One is the heritage of a monotheistic faith, which believes in revelation inscribed in a scripture. Hence the term 'societies of the book', used by Mohammed Arkoun. The second mainspring of their culture is Graeco-Roman. Ancient Greek culture was not, of course, monotheistic. It was based on poetry and philosophy, on ritual and, of course, the theatre. The third major heritage of the modern world is that of the Enlightenment which took place in Europe in the 18th century, with the preceding events of the Reformation and the Renaissance. We must not forget the very close kinship in this context between the Judaic, Christian and Islamic societies. All of them are founded on a concept of revelation; all trace the foundation of their meaning back to the written word, even in Christianity, in which the Logos, the Word of God, is not a book, but the person of Jesus. But one only learns of Jesus through the Gospels, which then is the word that gives access to the figure of Jesus. In the case of Islam, of course, the primacy of the Word is wholly central.

It is relevant, in this connection, to make a few general obser-vations on the Qur'an. On the one hand, the Qur'an is a historical response to a historical problem. The tendency to read the Qur'an solely as a transcendent text tends to leave out the fact that it was a response to real historical events of the time. Yet, in answering the dilemmas of immediate history, contemporary history, what the Qur'an does is to place its response in a larger, a grander statement of the condition of man in the universe. In this sense, the Qur'an is an immensely integrating text. It integrates, gathers together all meanings under the aegis of the concept of the One God. The concept of the unity of God gathers together all the meanings that would otherwise be scattered. That is the way in which the Qur'an addressed the issues of the day, and the issues that pertain to the human condition at large. If we simply look at the very notion of what the Qur'an calls signs, the *ayat*, the con-text in which one is familiar with that term is in the designation of the verses of the text. But the same term is used in the Qur'an for the phenomena of nature. Again, the Qur'an treats history, the fate that befell former nations, as 'signs' of divine providence. It thus effects what I might call a textualization of the universe. It shows the entire universe as a text, of which the Qur'an is the central, shining paradigm. It converts the signs and marks of ex-istence into a map. It integrates diverse facets of the world as we experience it – as the Prophet Muhammad's contemporaries ex-perienced it – into a unitive, all-encompassing meaning.

Another topic which I would like to comment on very briefly in this connection is that of symbolic language. The specific point I have in mind is that there is a certain difference between sym-bolic religious language on the one hand, and ideological religious language on the other. There is a certain distinction to be made between spiritual religion and ideological religion, between sym-bolic faith – which keeps everything open, which fosters a plurality of meanings, because symbolic meaning cannot be tied down in a dogma or a formula – and a system of closed meanings. So, this contrast between the openness of the symbolic mode and the clo-sure of ideological religion is something which, I think, is well-worth keeping in mind. One can talk about this in the con-text of the other faiths as well, but here I am confining my remarks to Islam.

The second component of the triple heritage was that of Greek philosophy, which contributed a specific discipline of reason. In speaking of reason, one must remember that the Qur'an itself represents a rationalization at work, because it combats myth. Owing to its symbolic language, there is in the Qur'an the notion of the supernatural, of supernatural beings like angels, jinns, and so on. But it is nonetheless quite parsimonious about the concept of miracles. The Qur'an mentions the Quraysh as demanding a miracle to be sent down from God as a proof of the prophethood of Muhammad. However, it resolutely repudiates the expectation of such a miracle, and refers instead to the signs of God in the natural universe and in human history. There is thus a certain distancing from magic and miracle, and a rationalization which corresponds to the transformation of social structure brought about by the preaching of the Prophet. In Greek culture, philosophy emerged with Plato and Aristotle as the preferred pathway to truth. The ideal of reason had the same pre-eminence in ancient Greek society that God-fearing piety has in the monotheistic faiths. For that reason, when in the first few centuries following the Prophet's death, Muslim intellectuals came into contact with the philosophical tradition initiated by the Greeks, they were forced to wrestle with the differences between, on the one hand, the traditions of monotheistic faiths, which were embodied in the *shari'a* and based on the authority of scripture, and on the other hand, what the Greeks had said about reason as the gateway to truth. And what is most interesting about the efforts of the few, but towering, intellectual giants in all the three faiths, beginning with the Islamic domain, who studied philosophy, was the nature of the reconciliation that they tried to achieve between them. This reconciliation involved something which has not been emphasized sufficiently, what I would call political theology: the theology of life in a community or society. What philosophers like al-Farabi, Ibn Sina and Ibn Rushd were emphasizing was the unity of truth. Given this unity, the paths of reason on the one hand, and of tradition, based on authority and revelation, had to be both distinguished and related.

The intellectual path in the thinking of these philosophers, who clearly echoed Plato in this respect, is one that only an elite with the requisite intellectual aptitude can pursue. For the masses the same truth needs to be couched in terms of imagination – figurative language, parables, metaphors, symbols, stories, narratives. Furthermore, in this view, the Prophet is uniquely gifted not only at perceiving the truth, but in being able to relate it to the masses – in other words, in being able to couch it in the language of creative imagination, which is the only language that can mobilize people and recruit them into the service of the order of the body politic, while ensuring their own well-being and happiness. To this end, the philosophers disapproved of any attempts to expose the masses to philosophy. For they thought that this was something that would create havoc – undigested reason among people who cannot master it would cause them to lose their faith and attachment to traditions, without giving them the comforts or solace of the way of reason. That was one particular response to the issue of the relationship between philosophy and the traditions of monotheistic faiths.

The third major development in history relevant to this question is that of the Enlightenment. Here, reason came to mean something quite distinct. To an extent, the Enlightenment harked back to the classical philosophical heritage. But the operative model was that of modern science. The science of Newton provided the model for all human knowledge and all human activity. The philosophers of the 18th century associated religion in Europe, among other things, with the corruption of the clergy and the power of the Roman Catholic Church. The reaction to what was seen as the history of religious oppression and obscurantism came from several quarters. There was the intellectual revolution of the Enlightenment, but earlier on there had been the Reformation launched by Martin Luther. It was, I think, one of the most important events in human history when Luther translated the Bible into the vernacular. For it gave to the ordinary man access to the scripture which had previously been monopolized by the clergy. Finally, the rise of the nation state was also crucial in all these developments, because the nation state broke the unity of Christendom, just as in the present century the abolition of the Sunni *khilafa* in 1924 by Kemal Atatürk and the formation of the Arab states with the retreat of the British and French powers in areas of the Middle East, also had a great influence on the way that Islam is understood today.

All these three traditions – that is, the traditions of monotheistic faith, Greek philosophy and the Enlightenment – have come under explicit or implicit pressure and questioning in the contemporary world. There are many reasons for this. Here I will confine myself to alluding only to a few of them. One is the fact that in the modern world the very awareness of a plurality of cultures makes it very difficult for any one culture to believe in itself to the exclusion of others. It poses the danger, or to put it more mildly, the challenge, of relativism. Relativism says that all doctrines, all ideas and values can be explained by reference to time and place. But if all ideas and values are to be thus explained, one's confidence in upholding a single culture or tradition is seriously dented. It is this dilemma which is partly reflected in the controversy currently raging in England, for instance, over whether schools ought to teach world religions in a neutral tone, that is, without advocating any normative religious positions. Is then the function of religious education to provide facts or is it to inculcate belief? There are those who will say that to inculcate belief in a young child is a form of indoctrination. There are those, by contrast, who will insist that the neutral way of teaching religion, that is, of imparting only facts about religion, is anything but religious education.

Another central issue of our times concerns the relation of the individual to society. In the late modern West, the dominant model, which is the model of the market, dictates attitudes towards culture. Culture, in this way of thinking, becomes a supermarket of ideas, values and doctrines, where one chooses according to taste, not according to objective essence – where the desire of the individual is the final arbiter of choice. Thus, if I choose to live a particular life, it is not because I am justified in believing in the objective rightness or suitability of that particular option, but because I so desire it. For freedom goes hand in hand with desire, and it is one's desire which eventually dictates what is right and what is wrong. Now this model presupposes a different conception of selfhood than the models which it has displaced. And although at one level it may be felt as liberating, it also harbours a potential for moral crisis. For, when morality is predicated on choice, that means there is nothing else but choice to dictate what the morality of the age shall be. A society based on this notion is more in the nature of an association than a *Gestalt*, a whole bigger than the sum of the parts. In earlier cultures, community came first and individuals second; individuals drew their lifeblood, as it were, from society. But in the contemporary world, society is seen as the product of individual decisions to band together, to come together in random groups, and that in itself constitutes one of the major cultural and intellectual dilemmas of the present age.

In answering, or in at least asking these questions, in exploring these issues, which represent the need of the hour in the world today, the monotheistic faiths have a great role to play. But this role will be effective only under certain conditions. One of these conditions is the growing need for a genuine mutual appreciation between the faiths which share a common origin, what we call the Abrahamic faiths. Attention to this common heritage, the Abrahamic heritage, which is a source of shared issues and problems, is especially important for Muslims who live as minorities in the Western world. The second condition is that to engage with the contemporary world means to take it seriously, which means to understand it, not to dismiss it. The theological rhetoric which says that the modern world is the antithesis of what the Islamic tradition teaches us – in other words, the rhetoric which sets Islam and the modern world as separate, opposing blocs – is a maladaptive rhetoric. Engagement does not mean surrender; for criticism too is a form of engagement.

One of the great mistakes that Protestant Christianity and Protestant Christian theology made in recent history was to take on board virtually all the concepts of the modern age. When the age passes, so do its concepts. If Protestant theology becomes too strongly wedded to the modern concept of modernity, it will find itself left behind, because it will have succumbed to the drift, the fashion, of a particular age. It will have abdicated the critical distance, which is the gift of prophecy, from the world in which it operates. How Islamic theology may engage with the modern world without becoming a prisoner of the modern understanding of modernity is one of the major challenges facing Islamic thought today. How it will meet this challenge is anybody's guess at the moment. It is something that still awaits the verdict of history.

2

Intellectual Life in the First Four Centuries of Islam

Hugh Kennedy

In the first four centuries of Islam, two main political issues and processes emerged which form, I think, the essential background to the development of Islamic culture. The first great issue to confront Muslims, and to fuel political debate and discussion among them, was that of the leadership of the community. The question of whether the Prophet Muhammad himself gave instructions about the succession to the leadership is a matter of dispute among Muslims, but it has to be agreed that there was not a general consensus on the nature of the leadership after the Prophet. Broadly speaking, two traditions or points of view developed in the early centuries of Islam over the crucial issues of who should lead the Islamic community, how they should be chosen, and what powers the leadership should enjoy.

One point of view suggested that the leadership of the community should be inherited by the *ahl al-bayt*, the family of the Prophet himself; this was usually but not always defined as the descendants of his daughter Fatima and her husband ‘Ali b. Abi Talib, who was also the Prophet’s cousin. There were those who thought that the Prophet’s family should be more broadly defined;

nevertheless, all adherents of this viewpoint felt that the leadership should remain in his family. Consequent upon this was the
idea that the leadership was chosen and sanctioned not by man
but by God, and that it should therefore have religious power and
authority to interpret the Qur'an and the *sunna*. The idea of a
divinely sanctioned leadership – to call it 'absolutist' is to misunderstand the term – seems to have developed from South Arabian
traditions of monarchy and hierarchy; this may have inclined people from the South Arabian tribes to look to this kind of
charismatic, divinely sanctioned leadership as the natural way for
the Muslim community to progress. But there was an alternative
model of leadership that was much more limited and essentially
developed out of the idea of the tribal shaikh. The tribal shaikh
comes from a leading group within the tribe, but he is chosen,
usually from the members of the leading family, for his qualities
of secular competence, leadership in battle, decision-making,
advice-giving and so on, a leadership which is, in fact, chosen not
by God but by the members of the community. Not surprisingly
this idea of a limited leadership chosen by men perhaps found
favour with those members of the new Muslim community who
came from a North Arabian tribal background and were used to
such a style of very limited monarchy. I do not want to go into all
the details of the development of these ideas, but I think that it is
worth making the point that much of early Islamic political, intellectual and cultural life was concerned with debating questions of
leadership within the community.

The questions of who was to be leader, how he was to be chosen, and what sort of powers he was to have, were central to early
Islamic intellectual life; and there were serious political issues to
be debated, for early Islamic politics were in a sense experimental. This is a very rare situation in human societies; for most
societies, when they are adopting or developing political models
and organizing their affairs, tend to look backwards to past paradigms for points of reference on how to proceed in the future. In
the Western European political tradition, for example, there is a
tendency to look to the good old days of king so-and-so, or to
some point in the past when conditions were supposedly perfect,
and then to extrapolate or develop from that point. But the advent
of Islam made the ideals of the past irrelevant. This was a new

dispensation, a new society, that had to forge new rules, new ways of doing things. This accounts, I think, for the very vigorous political debate which is characteristic of early Islamic society, and much of the intellectual life of the community is concentrated on issues of this sort.

The second major issue is, of course, the question about the spread of Islam, whether Islam was to be a religion confined to the ruling elite, a religion of the dominant ruling class, or whether it was to be a universal world religion. Here again there were different points of view and we see the gradual breaking down of the original hierarchical idea. In the period of the Rashidun, the rightly-guided or orthodox caliphs (632–661) – the word 'orthodox' has to be used with great care because every group believed they were orthodox and rightly believing – it was essentially only the Arabs who were Muslims. During the period of the Umayyads (661–750), non-Arabs were converting to Islam in increasing numbers and changing the nature of the Islamic community – from a community of conquerors, who were essentially a small minority living off the taxation on the land that they had conquered, to a community which was broadening its base. In fact, many of the disturbances of the Umayyad period were linked to this broadening of the Islamic community and the increasingly vociferous demands of the new non-Arab converts, the *mawali*, to have a share in the decision-making and to be accepted as fully equal members of the Islamic community. The issue of the status of non-Arab Muslims thus became another key political talking-point, and the debate became entangled or intertwined in numerous ways with the discussion about leadership, with a tendency for many new Muslims to look to the *ahl al-bayt* and to their representatives, as a way of overcoming their disabilities.

The Abbasid period (750–1258) saw, with the rapid progress of conversion, the breakdown of the idea of the Islamic community as simply an Arab community. Interesting work has been done recently on conversion in Islam by an American historian, Professor R. Bulliet. Using historical data from biographical dictionaries, mostly from Iran, Bulliet suggests in his *Conversion to Islam in the Medieval Period* (Cambridge, Mass., 1979) that it was in the period from about 800 or possibly 850 AD through to the year 1000 that the vast majority of the people of Iran, and by extension, those of

Syria and Egypt, as it were, the core lands of Islam, were converted to the new religion. By the year 1000, he suggests, the process of conversion was almost complete, although there were still non-Muslim populations in Iran, Egypt, Syria and so on. But the spread of Islam destroyed the unity of the caliphate. It is a paradox: the very success of the religion in attracting new converts, in spreading to all areas from Spain to the Indian subcontinent, destroyed its political unity, because there now emerged local Muslim elites and ruling groups who were non-Arab, and whose family and cultural links were within the areas they came from, but who nevertheless were devout Muslims. And while they were prepared to accept the authority of the Qur'an and the *sunna*, and the authority of the Prophet and sometimes his descendants, they were not prepared to accept the authority of the Abbasid caliph at Baghdad. Thus, the caliphate broke up as a process of evolution of local Muslim communities gradually breaking away and distancing themselves from the political control of the centre. It was more like – I think this is a viable analogy – the way in which the British Commonwealth developed several identities as new generations emerged, than a model of rebellion against the caliphs and a striving for independence. It was against the background of these two great issues, which dominated the thoughts of the early Islamic community, that Muslim intellectual life developed.

The early Muslim intellectuals were preoccupied with problems that were related to the spread of Islam. One of these was, of course, that for the first generation of Muslims the memory of the Prophet's deeds and words was, if not fresh in their minds, at least came from personal contact; even for the second generation of Muslims there was a feeling of direct rapport with those who had known the Prophet. But as time passed, direct personal contact with the generation of the Prophet was lost. Intellectuals had, therefore, to start thinking about, firstly, how they were going to preserve and record the utterances and deeds of the Prophet and of his Companions, the founders of Islam, and increasingly as time went on, how they were going to separate the genuine Prophetic Traditions (*hadith*) from those that for one reason or another had crept into the Islamic canon. I think it is easy to misunderstand the appearance of the new Traditions. I suspect that deliberate forgery, as we would understand it, was extremely rare. It is more a question of people filling in the gaps and developing Traditions to explain or support points that they felt were part of the Islamic faith, rather than people actually trying to falsify the record; the first was a much more common process than the second. Secondly, there was the need to explain the great mass of the Qur'an and particularly the *sunna* and all sorts of Prophetic Traditions to people who came from backgrounds that were very different from that of the Arab society in which Muhammad had lived; things that were quite obvious to the Companions of the Prophet, like the meaning of Arabic words, which required codifying and explaining to people who might come from Spain or north-eastern Iran, with no knowledge of Arabic and completely different cultural backgrounds. Consequently, a whole series of sciences were developed in order to solve these problems, and it is on the development of the Muslim sciences that most of the intellectual life of the early Islamic centuries is concentrated.

Take the science of grammar, for example. At one of those cultural sessions reported from the court of the Abbasid caliph Harun al-Rashid (786–809), there was a famous jurist, basically a tax lawyer of the period, by the name of Abu Yusuf. When he attacked, as these people were always doing, one of his rivals, the grammarian Abu'l-Hasan 'Ali al-Kisa'i (d. 805), with the accusation that the study of grammar was useless, the caliph is said to have replied that grammar is what he wanted to know in order to understand the Qur'an and poetry. Grammar was a vital tool for understanding and interpreting the Qur'an; without it one could be easily led into error and misunderstanding. Now, for the bedouin of the desert that might be one thing, but for people who had grown up in a non-Arab environment it was important to have books where these things could be explained. So you get the development of a very complex formal grammar in Arabic, above all associated with the 9th-century figure of Sibawayhi (d. ca. 796), but there are numerous others as well. Anyone who has ever tried to master classical Arabic will know that the structures imposed on it make it a complex language. As a spoken language Arabic comes naturally to people who have grown up with it. But if you attempt to analyse the speech patterns and how they work, it is something of an organizational nightmare; you have to invent immensely elaborate rules and careful formal grammar. And so it

was that the study of classical grammar became one of the main
fields of intellectual activity and a major constituent of early Islamic culture, because for early Muslims grammar was useful – in
fact, it was more than useful; it was vital if they were to understand
the basis of religion.

Take another example which may appear to some of us today
as bizarre, that is the science of genealogy. Here again, as in the
case of grammar, there was a great movement to systematize and
explain everything. The great figure in this connection is Ibn al-
Kalbi, from the late 8th century. He compiled a vast schema which
assigned all the Arabs, or at least all the significant Arabs of the
period of the Prophet and immediately afterwards, to their tribal
origins. He attempted to catalogue who belonged to which tribe
and how the various tribes were related; to construct a vast genealogical tree which would lead downwards from the two fathers of
the Arabs from the north and the south; and to explain how all
the groups that existed at this stage were, in fact, related in the
tribal structure. This was a very artificial exercise in the sense that
there was much confusion and dispute amongst the Arabs themselves over which groups certain tribes belonged to. But again, as
with the science of grammar, it was an attempt to explain and
systematize for the benefit of the people who were not familiar
with the way the Arab society worked. It is also rather more than
that, because in early Islamic society, or in the first two centuries
of Islam, the question of stipends and state pensions was closely
related to the role one's fathers, grandfathers and ancestors did
or did not play in the Islamic conquests. It was therefore very important to know who was related to whom and who was descended
from whom, in order to be assigned to the right group and receive the correct pension. So the science of genealogy – which in
the West today is a hobby which interests but a few people – had a
very useful function in early Islamic society. It answered questions,
it put people in their right place, and, as with grammar, a very
elaborate formal scheme was constructed so that everyone knew
where they were.

The same thing was gradually done with poetry, which is closely
connected with the study of grammar. If we want to fully
understand the Qur'an and the Prophetic Traditions, we have to
immerse ourselves in the language and thought of the Prophet's

contemporaries. Thus, the poetry of pre-Islamic Arab society and of the early days of Islam came to have a very important role in Muslim intellectual life. There are other reasons too: people got genuine pleasure out of poetry and song, but this leads again to the need to explain the poems to people who were unfamiliar with them. We therefore get the science, as it were, of commentaries on poems, explaining what these often quite obscure pre-Islamic poets meant, and great collections of poems to introduce Arabic poetry to people who came from a different cultural background and were not familiar with it. The *Kitab al-aghani*, the great book of songs compiled in the 10th century by Abu'l-Faraj al-Isfahani, who was descended from the Umayyad caliphs, represents in a sense the culmination of this process. It gives selections of poetry, but it also discusses biographies of the poets, long accounts of pre-Islamic battles, desert conflicts that happened three-and-a-half centuries earlier, the names of the warriors and how they were all related – such details are lovingly recreated in order to put everyone in their slot and explain what is going on in this field.

Another aspect of the systematization of learning was the study of history. Historical writing in Islam came in only gradually because of the need, originally, to record the life of the Prophet himself and then, of course, the events of the Islamic conquests. The earliest genres of historical writing are typically the compilation or compositions of individual traditions and anecdotes, what the Arabic sources call *akhbar*. The typical *khabar*, in the singular, is a short prose anecdote about two individuals meeting and what they said to each other, or who was the first person to climb the walls of Damascus – this is a classic type of *khabar*. There are many anecdotes of people who had either known the Prophet or had played a part in the conquests, in addition to the numerous anecdotes of the life of the Prophet himself by the people who knew him. But in the initial state, these are simply atomistic, individual, short paragraphs, so to speak, of history. What we get in the Abbasid period, when it became apparent that these materials had to be arranged in a logical and coherent order, is the compilation of chronological histories in which all the individual anecdotes are put together in the right place and order. The Abbasid editors of the 7th and 9th centuries were often as confused

as we are about some of the material they handled. They had information from a variety of sources, especially from the period of
the conquests after the death of the Prophet; all sorts of little
stories about how particular regions had been conquered, and so
on. They had extensive details, but they did not really have much
of a chronological structure, a framework to put these details in.
Thus, the first stage of historical writing is often the verbal report-
ing of these anecdotes; the second stage is the collection of the
anecdotes; the third, and intellectually most challenging and developed stage, is the ordering of the anecdotes to make a consistent
or at least a comprehensible narrative. Just as grammar, genealogy and poetry are systematized in the Abbasid period, so too
history is systematized to cater for the great thirst for knowledge
about early Islam, especially from the newly-converted peoples.

It is characteristic of this intellectual activity that it was overwhelmingly conducted by non-Arabs, in many ways because they
needed to know things that were, like grammar, more apparent
to the Arabs. In the case of history, the great name is al-Tabari
who died in 923 and whose 'History of the Prophets and Kings'
(*Ta'rikh al-rusul wa'l-muluk*) became the definitive work of early
Islamic historiography. In fact, a part of al-Tabari's achievement
was not just to collect all the traditions of early Islamic history,
but to put them within a structure of world history as he perceived
it, from Adam to his own day. He attempts in a very ambitious
intellectual scheme to integrate the Old Testament narratives with
the histories of the Persian kings and what he could recover of
the histories of the kings of South Arabia, though he had problems with that. He says at one point that the Persian kings are the
most important because you can work out the succession of rulers, meaning you have a reliable framework. South Arabia is more
difficult because there are a multitude of names but we are not
sure how they all fit together. He also makes at least some allu-
sions to the history of the Roman Empire, though in a much more
limited fashion compared to his perceptions of Eastern history.
Al-Tabari's history of the early Islamic state is one of the great
monuments of early Islamic intellectual life, and for anyone who
is not familiar with classical Arabic, it can now be appreciated in a
complete English translation. I am not suggesting that it should
be read in its entirety, but rather that it should be savoured because

it gives us some idea of the complexity of the information and the vividness of the anecdotal eyewitness accounts or purported eye-witness accounts, which remind us, at the same time, of the immense labour that these people underwent.

There are other genres of Islamic sciences as well, the science of *tafsir*, the explanation of the Qur'an, the science of Islamic law, and so on, none of which will be examined in any great detail here. I want instead to move on from the Islamic sciences to the non-Islamic sciences or the intellectual disciplines from outside. But first I should make the point that the overwhelming bulk of early Islamic intellectual life is concerned with the Islamic sciences, including such things as history, grammar and poetry, because they are fundamentally there to explain Islam. The sciences that come from outside the Islamic tradition were very much the oc-cupation of small groups or coteries of intellectuals at this stage, in the first four centuries; they gradually made a wider impact on Islamic thought, but not really until after the period we are look-ing at. The non-Islamic sciences we are concerned with are, above all, philosophy, medicine, astronomy and astrology. All these sci-ences, as they were brought into the Islamic tradition, were based on translations made ultimately from the Greek, often in the 9th century. The key name here is that of Hunayn b. Ishaq al-'Ibadi who died in 873. Working sometimes under the patronage of the Abbasid caliphs and their courtiers, people like Hunayn trans-lated numerous texts of the Greek literature into Arabic. This process of translation began certainly around the year 800, or possibly shortly earlier, and it was often translation at one remove. In fact, Hunayn knew Greek and translated directly from it, but many other scholars did not. Much of this classical learning had originally been translated into Syriac, a language which is a liter-ary version of Aramaic, the common language of the Near East in the years before the coming of Islam. Syriac is simply a written, formalized version of a dialect of Aramaic, but it became the main literary language. So this material was translated from Greek into Syriac by local Christians and then translated, again, usually by local Christians or sometimes by Jews, from Syriac into Arabic, and thus it went through two removes. Subsequently, it often went through another stage, particularly in Spain where it was trans-lated from Arabic into Latin; and so it does, as it were, a complete circle of the Mediterranean and comes back to dominate, and in some ways to haunt, the early universities of Western Europe – but that is another story.

The great movement of translation, patronized by the Abbasid caliphs, brought much of this information to the attention of Arabic-speaking intellectuals. The Muslims were seeking useful knowledge and they translated only what they believed to be of practical use to them. Just as the Islamic sciences developed because people needed to know certain things, so they chose from the classical Greek heritage what they believed to be useful. Philosophy was required as a technique for analysis of arguments and logic, but it was really logic that they were interested in more than abstract or general philosophy; and above all it was the logic of Aristotle (Aristutalis) that came to be the key text. They were interested in medicine for obvious reasons and translated medical texts like that of Galen (Jalinus) on medicine or Dioscorides (Diyusquridis) on the uses of plants – works which they believed had an obvious value in Arabic. They regarded astronomy and astrology as practical sciences, astrology especially because, as elsewhere in the medieval world, many people in the Islamic lands firmly believed in the influence of the planets and the importance of doing things at the right time; and along with astronomy came mathematics. But they were not really interested in the history of the classical world, about which the Muslim intellectuals remained on the whole quite ignorant. None was interested in Herodotus or Thucydides, who are among the great monuments of Greek learning, nor was anyone interested in Greek poetry, theatre and drama. In many ways, the aspects of the Greek classical heritage that we find today perhaps most striking and appealing were of no interest to the Muslims at all; they never seem to have been translated and they certainly never caught on.

Thus, there was an influx of foreign learning which was taken up by groups of intellectuals who at various stages were concerned to explain and develop it in Arabic. Medicine is the most obvious and perhaps the least controversial of these sciences. There is a long tradition of medical literature from the Abbasid period onwards, and the anecdotes of the caliphs are full of reports of their illnesses, what their doctors told them, the deaths of caliphs, why they died, and so on. The medical literature is very developed, but whether the medicine did anyone any good is, of course, another matter; like most pre-modern medicine it probably did as much harm as good, but nonetheless it was a product of this intellectual activity. Philosophy in terms of logic was much slower to develop, and all through the early Islamic period it was very much a minor pursuit. The question of how much philosophy should be involved in the analysis of religious texts was clearly an important issue. Astronomy and astrology, too, developed fairly slowly with their own specialist literature. It is not really until the 11th and 12th centuries that these studies become more widespread as major areas of intellectual activity. In sum, it is the Islamic sciences which I think are the key to the overwhelmingly important part of the intellectual life in the early centuries of Islam. These, the so-called foreign sciences, seem to have been given disproportionate weights by the historians of Islamic thought, whereas they were always minority interests.

I want to say just a little in conclusion about the circumstances of intellectual life. Who were these people? What sort of intellectual environment did they live in and what were the practicalities of their intellectual life? The first point I have already stressed is that certain subjects were studied because they were perceived to be useful. That does not mean that people were not interested in knowledge for its own sake – but basically the subjects that were chosen for study were those considered to be useful. The second point is that there was no structure of intellectual life, for there did not exist an academic profession as such. There are isolated examples, such as the Abbasid caliph al-Ma'mun in the early 9th century founding the Bayt al-Hikma, the House of Wisdom, where people seem to have been given pensions, and of poets receiving large sums of money from caliphs for composing flattering poetry. But these examples are very much the exception; most of the people who worked on these sciences were not professionals in the sense of being professional intellectuals. Knowledge of the law could, but did not necessarily, lead to an appointment as a *qadi* or judge; besides, not everyone wanted to be a *qadi* and the literature is full of examples of people declining judgeships. The institution of the *madrasa*, which paid salaries to individuals for developing and teaching Islamic sciences, is something that does not seem to appear, at least on any significant scale, before the

11th century.

Thus, in the first four centuries of Islam there was no institutional framework for intellectual life; rather, the people who engaged in these activities either had private incomes or lived off the revenues from their lands. We know, for example, that the historian al-Tabari had estates in his native Tabaristan, the area just south of the Caspian Sea, and though he lived in Baghdad most of the time, he got people to bring the revenues from his estates to Baghdad at the time of the *hajj*, and he lived off the proceeds of this income – he was a gentleman scholar in an old-fashioned way. Other people were much less fortunate or less well off, but there was much book selling and copying of manuscripts about which we have extensive information. We have an anecdote from a rather obscure scholar called al-Akhbari who died in 1037; he said that in his life he had made 25,000 *dirhams* from copying Arabic poetry, particularly the poems of al-Mutanabbi (d. 955), a poet who became enormously popular throughout the Middle East; he would copy these volumes and sell them for about 150 to 200 silver *dirhams* each. It cost him, he said, five *dirhams* in paper and three nights' work to produce one of these books, so when he was short of money he would dash off a copy to order, and that provided an income for him. We have another example of a mathematician called Ibn al-Haytham who lived by making a copy of Ptolemy's *Almagest* and a copy of Euclid every year, for which he was paid 150 gold dinars, which was enough to live on.

All the available anecdotes make it clear that Baghdad was very rich in these 'unofficial' intellectuals, people who were keenly interested in books, book selling, book copying, book dealing, as well as in reading and collecting the Prophetic Traditions. But there was, as already mentioned, as yet no structure of academic career or anything similar. To be sure, some people like *qadis* made money out of their learning; bureaucrats too who worked for the government had to be able to write properly. The development of calligraphy was partly a response to demands for clear and elegant Qur'ans, and partly a response to the need of governments for elegant decrees, official correspondence, etc. It was in the Abbasid period that Arabic calligraphy developed from the rigid and what must have been very time consuming Kufic script of the early Qur'ans to the much more fluid, fluent writing that appeared from the 10th century onwards. The bureaucrats had to know good classical Arabic as well, because they had to be able to express themselves elegantly and clearly. A good knowledge of Arabic grammar and a skilful calligraphic hand could get the individual – particularly if he could put some poetry into it at crucial moments and remember a few old proverbs to brighten it up – career qualification to work for the government. But one is constantly reminded by the large number of people who pursued these interests on an 'unofficial' basis.

It is worth noting too that the tools of the trade are important in understanding this great volume of early Islamic intellectual life, in which the importance of paper can hardly be overestimated. In a sense the introduction of paper, which came into the Islamic world from the early Abbasid period onwards, probably from China, was as important as the introduction of printing was in Western Europe and throughout the world from the 16th century onwards, because paper was inexpensive and it was easily accessible for writing. Before paper, one could either use papyrus which was accessible and cheap but could only be produced in certain areas such as Egypt, and it was rather fragile and perishable; or one used parchment, made from the skins of animals, the classic writing material of Western Europe all through the Middle Ages. Parchment has great advantages; it lasts for a very long time and it is very difficult to tear, burn or destroy. That is why it was used particularly for the Qur'ans and why so many of the 7th and 8th century Qur'ans have survived, at least in fragments. But Arabic and Muslim intellectual life as a whole was carried on paper because it was cheap and easy to obtain. It was also very fragile, in the sense that it could be burnt and destroyed in all sorts of ways, and that is why we are so often dependent on later copies of important works. At any rate, without the invention or importation of paper, early Islamic cultural life would never have developed the richness and the diversity that it did.

Now, all these things are rather like nuts and bolts of a civilization; perhaps they do not belong to the higher ranges of philosophy, but I do think that in explaining how intellectual life worked in this early ambience, it is crucial to get some grasp of the environment. I have, therefore, tried to convey an outline of how I see Islamic intellectual life developing in this early period.

3

Scientific and Philosophical Enquiry: Achievements and Reactions in Muslim History

Oliver Leaman

One of the most important features of Muslim history is the rapid expansion of the Islamic empire after the death of the Prophet Muhammad. This led to the extension of the empire into parts of the Middle East in which a variety of civilizations had been established for a very long time. The new Muslim rulers found themselves thrust immediately into contact with people who had relatively sophisticated ideas about theology, medicine, astronomy and mathematics, and they had to come to some decision as to what their attitude was going to be to this kind of learning. They could have rejected it as the products of ways of thought which are based on religious and cultural beliefs that are just wrong, and so basically not worth studying. Alternatively, they could have worked out how to incorporate some of this material into their own way of looking at the world. As we know, the trend was to follow the latter policy, and as a result an extremely rich symbiosis of cultures and religions took place, one which produced great scientific and philosophical riches.

There were basically two motives for using the discoveries and theories which were present in the Middle East at that time, and later on in Persia and India. One was the need to argue with the people of other religions and persuade them to become Muslims. It would be convenient to think that the familiar adage, 'There is no compulsion in religion', made it necessary to debate with non-believers before they could be brought to Islam, but this is unlikely to have been the whole story. It probably was not feasible to force everyone to convert to Islam, nor was it particularly in the interests of the new empire that everyone should have done so. There was no problem in having a diversity of faiths and cultures within the empire, provided that the leading role of Islam was acknowledged. Nonetheless, it would have looked distinctly embarrassing if the new faith was unable to defend itself with the same degree of sophistication and skill as the existing religions, and this made it necessary to use the methodologies of the older religions to show how Islam constituted an improvement on what had gone on before the Prophet revealed the final message of God.

The other motive for using the science and philosophy of local cultures was probably a practical one. Some might suggest that when the Muslims first came to the Christian world, for example, they were motivated by the Prophetic Tradition, 'Seek knowledge, even though it comes from China', in their attitude to the cultures which they found around them. This is far-fetched, even if we discount the fact that this *hadith* is really more about religious than secular knowledge anyway. One imagines that when the Muslims came to Syria, Iraq and later on Persia, they found out that those peoples had a comparatively high standard of living. They were relatively healthy and literate with a high standard of education, and naturally the Muslims wanted to learn how they had achieved this state of affairs and what use could be made of the knowledge which had led to it. This resulted in a great deal of interest in the early Islamic world for the scientific, medical and philosophical discoveries which were all around them. There seems to have been great initial enthusiasm for the cultural products which were so ubiquitous, and academies of translation were developed employing scholars to translate manuscripts from Greek and other languages into Arabic, often via Syriac by Christians.

Let us return to the earlier motive for interest in foreign culture, the need to be able to match the level of sophistication of
the local community. What that community had was a large corpus of philosophical works, especially those of Aristotle, which
went into detail on the nature and status of different argument
forms, and which were clearly of great use in working out how to
analyse and address competing theoretical views. Aristotle puts
on a formal basis the variety of arguments which are available to
thinkers, and his system of classification was taken even further
than he took it himself by the Alexandrian tradition, which ended
up classifying every literary product, even poetry, as some sort of
argument. The existence of a series of rhetorical techniques allowed one to present ideas clearly, persuade an opponent that
one view was valid and its contrary not, and put one in a position
of authority in a culture where the expression of ideas was an
important part of life. One might have thought that the original
enthusiasm for philosophical techniques would have waned once
the attempt to convert the local population had largely succeeded;
but it did not, because there then arose the necessity to persuade
Muslims of a particular party outside one's own, those subscrib-
ing to different theological schools or political viewpoints, that
they ought to abandon their views and adopt the correct line.
And as we know, the early centuries of the Islamic empire were
riven with much political discourse, upheaval and dissent.

It is strange to think of philosophy as having a practical value
in this sort of way, but there certainly seems to have been some
demand by people for rhetorical material with which they could
persuade others of the validity of a particular position, of the de-
sirability perhaps of changing their position and accepting a
different one. What could be more useful for this debate than
philosophy? Philosophy is all about the ability to debate, the techniques of debating and the principles of valid argument. So
philosophy came to be quite popular – and not just at the level of
the important philosophers – in the Islamic world from al-Kindi
all the way to Ibn Rushd (Averroes), and many others beyond
that period of Peripatetic thought. We know that al-Farabi, Ibn
Sina (Avicenna) and Ibn Rushd were all very important thinkers
by any stretch of the imagination, but it is also important to look
at those thinkers who were not so important as philosophers but

whose works were probably much more widely read – people like
Abu Sulayman al-Sijistani, for example – whose works were much
more popular and consisted of the sayings of philosophers, apho-
risms, witty asides, and so on. One assumes that these works, which
are more of the *belles-lettres* genre often called *adab*, more literary
than philosophical and more pedagogical than theoretical, had a
much wider circulation than the rather demanding commentaries on Plato, Aristotle or Plotinus.

So there is some evidence that philosophical literature was quite
widely read in the first few centuries of the Islamic empire, and
there is certainly much evidence of great scientific work also taking place, first of all in the Middle East and later, of course, in
Andalus in Spain. It is said that during the time of the great civilization in Andalus, anybody in Europe who wanted to know
anything scientific had to go to Andalus, and there are many accounts in Latin literature of how a particular problem remained
unsolvable, until somebody turned up from Andalus and suddenly
the problem was solved. Thus, Islamic Spain had a reputation for
several hundred years of being the real high point of philosophical, scientific, technical and mathematical knowledge. It was a bit
like the position of America today where some of the most important universities are located. But just as we should not concentrate
only on the great philosophers but also on the thinkers who were
not so original but were probably more widely read, we should
not concentrate so much on the great mathematicians, astronomers and medical scientists, but also examine those discoveries
and developments which were surely of much greater importance
to most people's lives, that is, the work of the engineers, the crafts-
men, the people who were actually developing machinery to
irrigate fields or were involved in town planning.[1] These techni-
cians and practical people are the people about whom we know
much less than the great mathematicians and astronomers. They
had far greater impact upon the lives of ordinary people, and it
was they who gave Andalus as a civilization such a glorious image
in the rest of Europe, because people would go to Spain and they
would see beautifully irrigated fields, towns laid out in a rational
pattern, and some sort of sanitary system which worked much
better than anything elsewhere in Europe. So, although we do
not know who most of these people were, we should acknowledge

their contribution to what was taking place.

One of the interesting features of the development of science and philosophy in the Islamic world is precisely this incorporation of alien elements, the interest in things which came from outside of the Islamic world, from the older civilizations of Greece, India and Persia. There was definitely a move to say that Muslims should take the best of the ancient sciences, the ancient philosophers, scientists and mathematicians, to use and develop those forms of knowledge so as to improve their lives and ability to know about the world in which they lived. Of course, that was not an entirely smooth process. There were people at the time who were opposed to that approach or who thought that the philosophers and the scientists ought to be careful about the way in which they brought in work from outside Islam, because it was argued that work which was carried out without the benefit of religion or without the benefit of Islam, might well have something wrong with it. For example, there was a concern that if the philosophers were so enthusiastic about Plato, Aristotle and other Greek thinkers who were not Muslims, then they were developing a philosophy based on pagan thought. Now there was a way around that, and some philosophers like al-Farabi invented stories whereby the Greek thinkers were presumably originally taught by some of the prophets. But this use of the 'first sciences' obviously was a bit of a problem in the sense that, from a religious point of view, one would expect 'Islam to be the answer', to quote a slogan which is popular at the moment. One would expect that in the Qur'an and other religious works there would be the answers to all the various questions which one would pose. It should, therefore, not have been necessary to go to pagans of great antiquity to find out about the world. How could non-Muslims know something that Muslims did not already know, or so the argument went. As it is often suggested, this might seem like some form of obscurantism, but it is not really so. It was the argument that Muslims could solve theoretical problems by using the Islamic sciences of grammar, law and *hadith*; and hence the sort of Greek philosophy which was so warmly embraced by many Muslim thinkers appeared to be an alien competing methodology.

The contrast here should not be seen as a contrast between the people who wanted Greek philosophy, mathematics, medicine,

progress and truth, and the obscurantists who were frightened of
these alien influences. The opposition did not unfold in that fashion; it was between people who thought that Greek philosophy
and science presented the way forward within the Islamic world,
and those who thought the Islamic sciences, the traditional sciences which had grown up within Islam as a religion, were
sufficient in and of themselves. This is not a contrast between those
who supported reason and those who did not. Reason is needed
just as much to determine what the law says on a particular topic
as it is required to work out whether an Aristotelian argument is
valid or not. The argument was about the different ways in which
reason might be employed. The philosophers and many of the
scientists argued that the Greek approach to science and philosophy represented something of a paradigm of how to conduct
science and philosophy. For them, Greek thought represented a
brilliant earlier period in which great philosophers and scientists
flourished, whose discoveries they sought to incorporate into their
approach to the world. Just because Plato and Aristotle were pagans and lived a long time ago did not mean that Muslims should
have nothing to do with them. On the other hand, there were
those thinkers who argued that Plato and Aristotle, interesting
though they were, did not possess the profundity which was available in the Islamic sciences as a whole. And when we think about
the points of view of people who were listening to these debates
more than a thousand years ago, it is not obvious which side is
more rational since both used reason in attempting to win people
over to their opinion. Both sides were, in fact, entirely rational.

This was a dispute about who would sort out the theoretical
problems of the Islamic world. Would it be the philosophers inspired by Greek science and philosophy, or would it be the 'ulama
and the fuqaha, the traditional Islamic scholars and jurists? It must
have been quite a debate, and certainly from the accounts we have
it was, because people's positions and livelihood were on the line.
If falsafa or philosophy was the way forward, then this made the
'ulama and the fuqaha naturally feel a little diminished in significance, and vice versa. This struggle went on for many years in the
Islamic world, and it is important to see that there was a whole
variety of different stages, and degrees of reception and opposition,
to philosophy and science coming from without. It was not one

general attitude but a whole variety of complicated attitudes which had a variety of different results.

Basically, the issues surrounded one very important question: how much is it acceptable for one to borrow from a culture which is not one's own? How far could Muslims incorporate secular knowledge in their own culture and still maintain that culture? This is not so distant from the debates which one has nowadays. The philosophers obviously thought, or at least they argued, that it does not matter where thoughts come from. They argued that there were many different points of view, and that ordinary Muslims, who know nothing about science or philosophy but who just perform their religious duties, have access to the truth, the very same truth that the philosophers and the scientists have access to, but in a different way. A very common example related to medicine. The philosophers, many of whom were doctors as well, gave this sort of an analogy: If you are not a doctor and you are ill, the very worst thing to do, they argued, was to read about your disease, because you do not know how the human body works; the worst thing to do is to work out by yourself what is the matter with you. It is even more serious if you use what you have read to determine the nature of your ailment and its appropriate remedy. What you should do is go to the doctor who will hopefully cure you. It was not the ordinary patient's job to treat himself or herself because they just did not have the expertise, and they needed to go to somebody who did.

Now that represents the nature of the relationship between the ordinary believer and the philosopher. The ordinary believer is not used to think abstractly; he is not really expected to think about how the world was created, whether it was created from nothing, whether it is eternal or can come to an end, and whether God really knows about what we are doing now. Is it really possible to think of God listening to our prayers? What is the nature of the afterlife? The ordinary believer is not supposed to think about these things, otherwise he or she is going to get very confused and possibly lose his or her faith eventually. It is like the patient who has a sore throat and starts to look up the medical book to read about it, then thinks that he has got meningitis or something equally serious and unlikely. This is not what we are supposed to do. We are to follow the principles of our religion in the way that religion sets them out, and leave to the philosopher the theoretical work of finding out, or of actually delving into, the mysteries of the creation of the world and of God's knowledge of us.

There are two different perspectives on the same truth, so the argument went. For example, Greek philosophy, which tended to think with Aristotle that the world is eternal, is compatible with the way in which most Muslims would think of God having created them. God said 'Be!' (*kun*), and as a result the world was created, probably out of nothing, *ex nihilo*. Most Muslims might think of an afterlife in corporeal ways, and perhaps most philosophers would be rather critical of that idea, but that is acceptable because there are different versions of the same truth, perfectly appropriate for different people. Now, one might think that kind of attitude is terribly patronizing. Does it not mean that the philosophers claim to know how things are and the ordinary people do not? As long as they go often to pray, pay the *zakat* and observe the various tasks which they are supposed to as Muslims, then it is best to leave these people to do as they please. They do not really understand what is going on, whereas the philosophers do, and it is therefore perfectly all right to have these two different systems of knowledge and belief running together.

Of course, the philosophers were not quite that patronizing, although sometimes they did describe these issues in a rather elitist way. They said that there are some people who are interested or skilled in discussing different issues. For example, some people at the end of a hard day's work like to read philosophy, while others like to indulge in relaxing activities. Now, religion has to be capable of bringing all these people together in a particular way, because the aim of religion is to make the truth accessible to everybody in the community, however educated or ill-educated. The humblest person in the community is brought nearer to God by a faith which is capable of inspiring everybody in the community, and this, according to the philosopher, is represented by the excellence of the Prophet Muhammad. The Prophet is taken to be the most perfect politician in the sense that he was able to get his message across to everybody. The Prophet not only had the theoretical knowledge which the great philosophers and scientists had, but he also possessed the ability to get this message across to the most humble, the most illiterate person who was least interested in theoretical enquiry. Muhammad was able to get his message across to everybody in the community, and that is what religion is all about. A religion is an institution which is capable of moving everybody in the community nearer to God, nearer to the truth.

That means, of course, that people have to be addressed in different ways. To the people who are simple, who do not have time for theoretical reflection or who are just looking for some very simple, straightforward rules in accordance with which they can organize their lives, one talks in simple terms, giving them simple rules. To the people who are more interested in intellectual enquiry, who know something about science and technology, about the way in which the world works from a theoretical point of view, one speaks rather differently. They want to know the answers to much more complex questions. But the excellence of any religion and of any prophet depends upon his ability to frame his message in a way which is capable of gaining, to put it in current political terms, the widest possible constituency. The philosophers argued that Muhammad was the supreme Prophet because he, as compared with Moses or Jesus for example, was best able to get over his message to the widest possible number of people in the community.

The Prophet Muhammad was, thus, taken to know all the theoretical knowledge which originally the philosophers acquired through Plato and Aristotle. But he was able to combine that theoretical knowledge with an understanding of how people should behave, how they should live, and so on. Obviously, there are different levels of the message for different levels of people, and any religion has to cater for everybody. One might wonder why, but presumably the answer is that since God created people at different levels of ability, it would be very unfair if salvation was going to be reserved only for those of a fairly refined disposition. If God created some people with more intelligence than others, if He created people who are sighted and those who are blind, people who are interested in theory and people who are practical, then there must be a path to salvation which is common to all these peoples, otherwise God would be unjust. So the philosophers argued that Islam promotes a particular message which all people – ordinary people and philosophers, scientists and practical people

– can accept at different levels and in different ways. This was
their argument against those who maintained that Islam really
should not incorporate all these foreign materials. Their argument basically was that if this information is useful, if the scientific
discoveries were true, if the philosophical techniques were valid,
then they have to be used.

The sort of philosophy I have been describing here belongs to
the Peripatetic school which really went into a rapid decline about
800 years ago in the Islamic world, until its revival in the 19th
century. The other form of philosophy which was very much practised in the Islamic world, the Ishraqi or Illuminationist
philosophy, is still very vigorous, especially in Persia. But the type
of philosophy which I have been describing was transmitted to
Western Europe and became very influential in the development
of philosophy and science for several centuries. There are two
interesting problems here. One is how far can an Islamic philosophy or science borrow from outside of Islam and incorporate what
it finds to produce something which is specifically Islamic? The
other issue is that here is the case of a very powerful intellectual
civilization which disintegrated a long time ago, and it has proven
so far impossible to recreate it. It was possible a thousand years
ago to create a civilization which was a combination of Islam and
science, philosophy, poetry and literature, and a variety of other
fields and traditions of learning as well. Is it possible to recreate
that in a specifically Islamic way? And what sort of issues arise in
accomplishing that?

Now, we might well say that this civilization in the past was not
specifically Islamic anyway. It just occurred within a part of the
world in which Muslims were predominant or in which there were
quite a few influential Muslims, but really there was nothing specifically Islamic about it. There just happened to be at that time a
number of people, Muslims in many cases, who worked in what
are now called the Islamic languages, and who happened to produce great philosophical and scientific works; but there was
nothing specifically Islamic about it. Thus, the central issue is how
far should Islam relate to modernity in producing a specifically
Islamic version of how things should be now. We might argue
that there are certain common features in the art, philosophy and
science of Muslim societies which do make them specifically

Islamic. What might these features be? One feature which is very important, which was a common ingredient of much of Islamic philosophy and science, is a concern in the broadest sense with the spiritual, with the fact that this world is not the whole of reality, it is temporary and transient, that we are a microcosm of a much greater macrocosm which we can only see in so far as there is a reality behind that which is before us. Again, one might say that there is nothing Islamic about that, since all religions have that view. I think most religions do have that perception, but the way in which it is described and articulated, the forms in which the sense of the spiritual is produced, was done in a specifically Islamic sort of way by using Arabic and other Islamic languages, using imagery from the Qur'an, examples from the *hadith* and techniques from Islamic law. In a sense, this was a very Islamic way of going about doing things. And the whole notion of science as a purely technical way of solving problems, which might be regarded as a Western paradigmatic science, certainly seems not to be there to the same extent in what we might call Islamic science. There was a developed notion among Muslims that science was not just a technical answer to people's problems, but that it was an aspect of God, a spiritual aspect of the universe. It was not just a case of turning a switch on to make a thing work; there was more to it than that – it operated in a far wider theoretical perspective.

If there is going to be a way of incorporating modernity, modern science, modern culture in the Western sense, within Muslim societies, I think that the spiritual aspect of philosophy and science which was there explicitly a thousand years ago, has to be reinvented and reconnected with the techniques of modern philosophy and science. What is specifically Islamic about that? Is this not just what many religions aspire to do? But the way in which the Muslims present their way of spirituality will obviously be tinged by the language with which they express themselves and that will frequently be a specifically Islamic way of phrasing a point. And maybe if we compare these ways of talking about philosophy and science, and the need to reincorporate more spirituality, perhaps we could find Christians, Jews, Buddhists, Hindus and adherents of other faiths, who would say very much the same thing. An Islamic response needs to be presented in a certain way, from within an Islamic context. Does this mean that there is a unique

4

The Rational Tradition in Islam

Muhsin Mahdi

1. HISTORICAL PERSPECTIVES

The rational tradition in Islam can be studied and looked at in various ways. The main danger is not to expand the tradition so much that it would cover almost everything in Islamic history and culture, because whenever Muslims engaged in thought and whatever direction their thinking may have taken, they had to use reason, and by doing so they became, whether they wished it or not, part of the rational tradition, broadly considered. This is true not only of scientists and philosophers but certainly of many of the theological schools and the mystics too, because whenever they tried to express themselves or communicate their experience, they had to use reason and therefore connect somehow with the rational tradition.

In this very general sense, the rational tradition would cover almost any statement that is made by any Muslim at any time. In its most narrow sense, but perhaps not for us the most interesting sense, it would cover the so-called positive sciences which would be concerned purely with rational things and connections. Anyone who wants to study this field can easily look up the histories

43

of science and follow the research of the historians of science. The most interesting part of the rational tradition for us is where it comes directly in contact with, and tries to understand, the whole question of religion, the origins and structure of the religious community, where it stands today and what one can do about its organization. This normally takes the form of political philosophy, but that is only one part, perhaps the most interesting part, of the way in which the rational tradition tries to understand and deal with the phenomenon of religion and the religious community.

It is in this particular sense that one can say that the rational tradition is Islamic – otherwise one can ask what is so different about this tradition? It is possible to study mathematics anywhere, there is nothing Islamic about the venture. But this tradition also has something to do with religious tradition and a religious community like Islam. It is not only encouraged by the religious community – which can encourage or discourage all kinds of things – but it sees problems in the presence of reason in the community and tries to harmonize the relationship between reason and the so-called revelation. It sees conflicts and tries to mitigate them; it finds mysterious things in religion and tries to understand them or give a rational account of their possibility at least, if not a full explanation of religious dogmas or doctrines; and if it has a political or social dimension, it tries rationally to talk about and communicate certain ideas about how the community should be organized.

If we are not simply historians but live in the present and are trying to become conscious of the ways in which our minds work as we think about the rational tradition in Islam, it is important for us to remember that we hardly ever look at the Islamic tradition without any intermediary notions. Usually we begin with certain common notions that we hold about rationalism and what rational thought is, and whether we like it or not these happen to be modern European notions. That is the culture that we start with, because we study it in schools, and it is through the notions of this culture that we begin to think about the world, so to speak.

What is the most important 'cultural baggage' that we bring to our understanding of the rational tradition in Islam? It is undoubtedly what is normally called rationalism. If we read about rationalism in the current literature, even literature that impinges on Ismaili studies – let us say, through the works of the late scholar Henry Corbin (1903–1978), we find a general trend against rationalism. There is, indeed, an aspect of rationalism which is very strange and negative. I suppose it is a trend of thought which denies the very existence or importance of values, of anything that is not mathematical or physical more or less and is not part of positive science. It is opposed to all religions and religious institutions, all religious beliefs and dogmas. That is one extreme form of rationalism. The other extreme is expressed when people talk about fundamentalism, by which they mean that it is not rational. This is a sense of rationalism that is the exact opposite, which says that the most angelic good that a human being can have is to be rational about his ideas, his institutions, traditions and way of life, rather than blindly following whatever dogmas one has.

This conflict about rationalism and the notion of rationalism became central to European culture and history in the 17th and 18th centuries, during a period which is called the age of rationalism, the age of Enlightenment. It is almost useless to talk about the rational tradition in Islam without having some very basic notions of what it was, in the Europe of the 17th and 18th centuries, that was taken to be rationalism in the good and the bad sense. What were its salient features? That tradition began late in the 17th century through a dictionary – it was the age of dictionaries and encyclopaedias – by a man named Pierre Bayle (d. 1706) who called his work *A Critical and Historical Dictionary*. This dictionary was critical in the sense of being destructive, not constructive. It was an attempt to 'clean' religious traditions and dogmas of what they used to call prejudices that have surrounded the history of religions. The dictionary was not a rational attempt to justify religious beliefs. Rationalism is sometimes also understood in this positive sense, as for example when we say: 'He rationalizes, he is trying to give a rational account of something religious.' That is a constructive form of rationalism, an attempt to understand, to justify, to give reasons for something. But in the case of Bayle – as well as the famous *Encyclopaedia* in which the rationalism of the 18th century was embodied and to which the major thinkers of the time such as Diderot, Voltaire and others contributed – it was a destructive kind of rationalism. It was an attempt to show much of religion and religious ideas to be merely prejudices and without foundations.

These rationalists were not simply against the idea of religion. There was also the idea of what to do about the religious society that existed then. We should remember that we are in France, not in England where toleration had already been a tradition for a long time. France, where this rational tradition developed, was a country that was still strongly religious, monarchic and absolutist; in fact, it was a model of the absolutist monarchic tradition. The French had just emerged from a long period of religious wars between the Catholics and the Protestants, and the Catholic Church was one of the mainstays of the monarchy in France. The question of the rationalists was what to do with their society which was strongly religious. Then they developed the strange notion of the 'republic of letters' ruled by the 'men of letters'. In short, by a few 'enlightened' people, who are supposed to use the law of reason and are equal among themselves, would rule society and spread their notions against religion in society as a whole. These people were to be the new 'priesthood', if we can think of that as an analogy; they would design what was good and what was true, what was bad and what was false; they were the ones who were to judge and condemn the obscurantist prejudices of society. We see how easily this situation can lead to the substitution of one public dogma for another, of a new dogmatism for another. Those who know anything about the French Revolution know how fanatical and intolerant a society can become to religion when it begins to believe in such notions.

Next, they entertained strange notion of public opinion. Religion, as far as the multitude is concerned, is obviously a collection of beliefs and opinions. But unlike in England where public opinion had a very positive sense and could be built upon, developed and improved, among the rationalists in France at that time public opinion was simply rejected. In short, public opinion had to be totally replaced. It was not understood as semi-enlightened and in need of clarification, but as utterly blind and in need of a new enlightenment. New ideas had to be substituted for the old ones by these 'men of letters', the enlightened few who were supposed to become the new rulers. They were to form the opinions of the public. In reality, they became, analogically, just as militant as the religiously militant people anywhere on the globe in their vocabulary and their methods. A few rationalists even thought of themselves as capable of changing the community in general as Christ and his apostles, few as they were, had meant to do.

There is a famous letter written by Voltaire in 1760 to de Lambert, one of the leading contributors to the French *Encyclopaedia*, which is blasphemous because it basically compares the philosophers, *les philosophes* as they called them in French, to the apostles of Christ. 'Would it not be possible,' he asked, 'for half a dozen enlightened people to succeed in changing society the way a dozen disciples of Christ did it before?' This is an important social aspect of the rationalist movement in Europe. Think of Marxism, for instance, how it started and what it was. Again two or three people had the intention of changing society completely. Their notion was to subject everything to the order of reason and not to let prejudices rule humanity any more. Their vision of man was purely naturalist, concerned only with this world. The rationalists, as such, had no notion that one might think about the world to come, and the political dimension soon became revolutionary in terms of society. The French Encyclopaedists such as Voltaire and Diderot were not political revolutionaries in the sense that they were happy with a kind of limited monarchy, but it did not take long for some real revolutionaries to surface and claim that they would destroy all the churches, get rid of the Catholic Church and establish a society on the basis of reason and solely of reason.

Finally, one of the more interesting aspects of the French Encyclopaedists and the rationalists was their thinking about the relationship between reason and imagination. Those who know the works of our late departed colleague Henry Corbin, know how important is the question of the relationship between imagination and reason. The Encyclopaedists thought of themselves as the disciples of the great English philosopher Francis Bacon (d. 1626), who had contributed some ideas about the organization of the sciences for an encyclopaedia in English called *The Chambers Encyclopaedia*, which is still published today. It was Bacon's idea that there are three human faculties: memory, imagination and reason. His organization of the three was to start with memory, the idea being that the impressions that come to the mind from

outside – he and others were materialist in this sense – are separated first by memory, which leads to history. Then there is
imagination which imitates, or as the Encyclopaedists used to say,
counterfeits what comes from the senses, and that leads to poetry. Finally, there is reason which examines, compares and digests
these impressions. But the French Encyclopaedists changed this
arrangement: they started with memory, then went to reason and
finished with imagination. Their explanation was that Francis Bacon was only talking historically, whereas they wanted to think of
knowledge in its real metaphysical sense, and for them the level
of reason is above that of imagination. Imagination only imitates
and counterfeits, it does not think or distinguish, it does not relate, and therefore it cannot be the basis of true knowledge or
true science. They knew, of course, about something called faith
– the Catholic Church had made sure that they knew it existed –
but it does not occur in the arrangement of their *Encyclopaedia.*

Having in a way, or to some extent, briefly clarified the kind of
problems that we have to think about in relation to rationalism,
we must begin by asking ourselves how the rational tradition arose
in Islam in the first place. How was it precipitated, so to speak?
We have heard a lot about this question, about the rise of rationalism in Islam and its relation to prophecy, the sacred book,
revelation and similar matters; but the central question which
seems to have started the debate was – and I do not think I exag-
gerate – the claim to rule. Who has the claim to rule the Muslim
religious community after the departure of the Prophet
Muhammad? One should never forget that the origin of Islamic
religious thought, or *kalam*, is this very question of who has the
right to rule? Is it by the Prophet's designation of an imam or is it
by election? If it is a process of designation, there is no choice
because the ruler is designated, just as in the case of the Prophet
there is no choice because God Himself chooses the Prophet. But
if the leader is to be elected, as the majority of the Muslim community, unlike the Shi'is, thought should be the case, then what
are his qualifications? Can just anyone be picked out and made
the ruler? And that begins the whole process of rationalism in
Islam.

Obviously this leads to wider questions about God's justice,
man's duties to his community, and so on. But while this internal

debate was taking place, there came from outside through movements of various kinds, directly and indirectly, by way of
translations and personal contacts, a millennial tradition of theological, religious and rational thought that was already there. One
should never forget or underestimate the importance of this tradition. It was already there among the Greeks, the Indians, the
Persians and the Syriac-speaking Christians. Christian theology,
which already had a thousand years of history, dealt more or less
with some of the questions that were of concern to the Muslims.
The Christians were right there, living among the Muslims and
speaking their language. So one cannot simply say that this tradition did not exist or that it was not important. The difficulty in
trying to understand this process is always the fact that as it comes
in, it is in a much more developed stage than the indigenous one.
In short, while the Muslims were just beginning to think about
the problems of God's justice, divine attributes and so on, the
Christians had been thinking about them for almost a millennium.
The relationship at the beginning was unequal and it took some
time before Muslims could master these questions for themselves
and become able to do just as well, if not better, than the tradition that they received. In these matters, especially concerning
rational thought, one should always remember that in the formation of a tradition, people do not reinvent the wheel every time;
they have to start from the stage where things have developed
already and try to push them a stage further.

Within the tradition that came in, there was a central important strand called Neoplatonism, which was significant for all the
revealed religions. Neoplatonism was the intellectual baggage, so
to speak, that came through Greek, Syriac, Christian and Jewish
thought, and tried to make room for a God beyond reason. The
idea of God is not just something that is hard to understand, or
which would take time for one to know. God is simply above and
beyond reason; He cannot be touched by reason which is a stage
below, the product of that higher being called God. This could
be expressed mythologically in many different ways. The founder
of the Neoplatonic school, Plotinus, lived in the 3rd century, but
we are speaking now of Muslims in the 7th and 8th centuries. So
five centuries of philosophic thought were in part dominated by
this school, which somehow the revealed religions, especially

Christianity, found very attractive. They found it easy to understand and to build their intellectual baggage, so to speak, around this idea, because in the Bible and the Qur'an one reads many things about the divinity that cannot be simply understood rationally, or which would take long, convoluted, rational arguments to make sense of. It was much simpler to say that all this belonged to that centre of the divinity that was not approachable through reason. In addition, Neoplatonism provided the revealed religions with support for the idea that the divinity is active. That is the important thing about the divinity; it is not just a mind, it is something that does things. In Greek it is called *ergon*, deed, rather than *logos*, speech. The divinity is not only above reason, it is also something that acts and causes things to be.

The first impact among Muslim theologians was therefore of Neoplatonism. In Islamic thought, the recovery of Plato and Aristotle came much later. It took a century or two to translate their works and try to understand them. Also, and this is part of what precipitated things, the secular powers, especially the Abbasid caliphate in Baghdad, now had mundane needs. As a vast empire, it needed communications, bridges and hospitals, which depend on mathematical and medical knowledge. These mundane sciences had to be encouraged, developed and supported. We must remember that in Greek and medieval philosophies, these sciences had never been separate in our modern sense. No one would learn just biology and nothing else; it was necessary to study philosophy as part of a medical education, mathematical studies or physics. Ultimately, the entire early Near Eastern tradition of thought, including philosophy and science, became incorporated, absorbed and thought about in the Muslim community along with the problems it generated.

How did the community, or the various parts of the community react to this tradition? Initially, as far as anyone knows, there was a single global theological school, the Mu'tazila. Within that were all kinds of factions and wings consisting of mystics, atomists, pure rationalists, historians, traditionalists, and so on. But it seems that by the 10th century, it was impossible to incorporate the entire Greek–Christian tradition under one umbrella and, therefore, there seems to have been a break up. It was a scenario in which too many things were moving and struggling with one another, and not really getting along any more. The most famous illustration of this is the thinker and theologian Abu'l-Hasan al-Ash'ari (d. 935–6), who decided to break with the general school of the Mu'tazila and founded what then became the standard Sunni theological school. But other than that, and more interesting for us perhaps, is that at the other extreme some more or less pure rationalists, who were in many ways like the European Encyclopaedists, also broke away. The famous figure here is that of Abu Bakr Muhammad al-Razi (d. 925 or 935), the physician who, among other things, had a famous debate with an Ismaili philosopher, Abu Hatim al-Razi (d. 934). The former al-Razi claimed to know more than Galen, the greatest physician of the past. Like the Encyclopaedists, he opposed all forms of human authority in matters of knowledge, even that of the Prophet. Abu Bakr al-Razi thought that all reasonable men are equally able to look after themselves and their own affairs, since they are equally inspired. He believed in something one could call global inspiration, that every person has the potential of being inspired, and he therefore opposed any special kind of inspiration. According to Abu Bakr al-Razi, the Prophet had no business to claim a special connection with the divinity. We all have a connection with divine reason in our own way, depending on how good we are in our knowledge, in our studies and so on. So everyone is able to know the truth, to know what earlier men taught, and equally able to improve on it, exactly as the Encyclopaedists thought. Like them, al-Razi believed in progress, but his notion of progress was not our notion of progress, which is in the moral sense. We think that society somehow develops and becomes better morally; but previously the notion of progress was limited to what one might call the sciences and the arts, to advancements in human knowledge.

Unfortunately, the only real documentation we have of the debate between the two Razis is from the side of Abu Bakr al-Razi's Ismaili opponents who defended the need for prophecy (*nubuwwa*), and yet in his heart that is what Abu Bakr al-Razi really thought. He was opposed altogether to prophecy, to particular revelations and to the divine laws, and he engaged in serious criticism of religion in general. He thought that organized religion was a device employed by evil men to establish a kind of tyranny over mankind, and that it led to conflicts and wars. This is exactly

what the Encyclopaedists thought of religion, that it was of evil
origin and meant to oppress human beings, to create fear among
them, to exploit their innocence and credulity, to perpetuate their
ignorance, and to prevent them from learning and understanding. Abu Bakr al-Razi even speculated about the demonic origins
of prophecy. There is a long tradition of this idea among the
Greeks, among some Muslims if they can be called thus, and in
the Orientalist studies of Islam.

As for the school of al-Ash'ari, which I have mentioned already,
it developed a certain atomistic structure to defend God's power.
The atomistic world does not have its inner structure but it em-
phasizes God's activity at every point. The Ismaili philosophy that
developed in the 10th century modified the whole philosophy of
Plotinus, Neoplatonism, in directions that would then make sense
of some of the basic religious doctrines that had existed before.
The mystics went in the direction of both, serving the ennobled
God and getting to know Him personally, whatever that means,
through religious activity, piety and prayer, rather than through
reason or rational knowledge.

Out of this came what we normally think of as the main tradition of Islamic rationalism – 'Islamic' not in the sense of Abu Bakr
al-Razi or the Encyclopaedists but in a more strict and particular
sense, in the tradition of people like al-Farabi and Avicenna (Ibn
Sina). This tradition is obviously not the same as the theological
or mystical traditions, but it has an understanding of non-rational
phenomena which does not exist among people like Abu Bakr al-
Razi or the Encyclopaedists. In short, we have somehow to think
of the rational tradition in two terms: one that may be called extreme rationalism in which anything that is religious is denied as
non-existent or is explained as being simply there to rule and corrupt society, and the other rationalism which more or less dedicates
itself to trying to make sense – perhaps not rational in the narrow
sense – of the non-rational phenomena of prophecy, revelation,
the divine law and the problems that cannot easily be subjected
to the laws of pure reason.

Of course Islamic philosophy was more than that: it was very
closely connected with the sciences. None of the traditions just
mentioned, such as Neoplatonism, Ismaili philosophy or any
strand of *kalam* or theology, had much to do directly with the

scientists, with mathematics, physics or other similar sciences. But the main trend of Islamic philosophy – traced through Avicenna (d. 1037) who was a great physician, al-Farabi (d. 950) who was a great mathematician and musician, Averroes (d. 1198) who was a great physician, and so on – was very close in a very practical sense to the sciences. The other side of this tradition was the attempt to somehow make intelligible, in a wider rational sense, phenomena that were admittedly beyond reason, that were not rational and could never be turned into something altogether rational.

The whole notion of extreme rationalism is to get rid of religion and have a society that is based purely on reason. But the main tradition of Islamic philosophy never thought that a society can be based purely on reason, or that something like prophecy or the divine law can be explained purely on the basis of reason. One can make rational justifications here and there, like the 'purpose of going to Mecca is because we need to travel and see the world', but that is not really the Islamic notion of going to Mecca; or that 'we pray because we need daily exercise', but God did not decree prayer so that people could exercise their bodies. That is not what is meant by justification; one would need to have a better understanding of the communal aspects of religion especially. In a way, I am pessimistic about the possibility of a purely rational organization of society. The only way society can be held together, the only way people can be encouraged to pursue virtues and avoid vices, which may not always be in their rational interests, is through something like a divine law, through a doctrine of reward and punishment in the hereafter. However, such a law may not be useful because it asks people to do things which are beyond immediate utility in this world.

So the dominant tradition of Islamic philosophy tried somehow to mitigate the possible conflicts between reason or rational knowledge and the givens of revelation. It is not necessary, say the philosophers, that there should be an unknowable God in order for us to have laws that are not completely rational or instrumental. The question of the nature of the divinity does not really always enter into the question of the law as they try to understand it. For instance, the man who started this tradition, al-Kindi (d. ca. 866), wrote about how one could miraculously bring a law and make contact with a divinity that would take an enormous number of years, centuries or millennia, for humans to reach. In short, one way to understand the divine law and its needs is to say that everything in the law, everything that the Prophet does, is ultimately rational in the sense that, if we had all the time in the world, if we could spend millions of years at it, we would eventually come to know how and why it was done. But we do not have this kind of time, we have to live in the here and now, we have to be part of a community, we have to do our duties, to do what is right and to avoid what is wrong. How are we to be in direct contact with the divine? There is a way of short-circuiting that search through prophecy. In short, for the time being, we have to take the word of the prophet because all those who have mystical contacts with the divine claim to have a way that is shorter, that is more effective than it would take us to know rationally. So there could be a doctrine of rationalism which says that it is not necessary for us to know everything that we need to know here and now.

Then there is the question of the political arrangement of the community. The rational tradition in Islam happened to be very political in the sense that it was really concerned not simply with doctrines as such, but with why there should be a religious community and the relations between a religious community and a non-religious one. This tradition was very strong among the Abbasids in Baghdad, in Persia, in Central Asia where Avicenna came from, in Andalusia and North Africa. It is not an accident that the Ismaili community tended to be centred in North Africa on the one hand, and in Central Asia on the other. The main issue in Andalusia was mysticism. There is the famous connection between Averroes (Ibn Rushd) and Ibn al-'Arabi (d. 1240) that Henry Corbin speaks about. Averroes met a man who said that his son seemed to receive divine inspirations and asked Averroes to talk some sense to him. Averroes was older and well known, and he told the father to bring the son to him. The young man was Ibn al-'Arabi. Averroes looked at him, was very impressed with the young man and said 'Yes?', 'Yes,' replied Ibn al-'Arabi. 'Yes?' asked Averroes again. 'No!' answered Ibn al-'Arabi. Averroes in many ways had just as much of a sense of something that is not quite rational, that is in the realm of the divinity, but the question was how to get there. Averroes thought the only way to get there was through increased rational knowledge. As one perfects it, one gets to its limit and then has a vision of what is beyond it. But Ibn al-'Arabi thought that the way was through practice and the teachings of those who had never studied anything in books. In fact, during his travels Ibn al-'Arabi met an old woman who did not know how to read and write, and who then became one of his teachers.

These are the two conflicting traditions. Behind Averroes there was the whole rational tradition. The genuine rational tradition never says that there is nothing beyond reason, because in almost every case the doctrine is that something must have generated reason, something must have been at the beginning, and that could not be the kind of reason that we know. Technically, the philosophers would say that it, the primary cause, combines essence and existence but that is not what is important. It is the doctrine of the source, that there is a source of this expanded notion of reason, but that the source itself cannot be reason as we understand it. If one likes, one can still call it reason, but it is not structured; it is more like a steel ball that breaks up to produce what we know as reason.

2. THE CONTEMPORARY SITUATION

In the remarks I made in the first section, I tried to explain that in my view the rational tradition can be divided into two extremes. One – of which I tried to give a major example in 17th and 18th-century European history through the Encyclopaedists whose prime Islamic representative is the physician Abu Bakr al-Razi – is the kind of rationalism that limits itself to a certain kind of reason and denies the existence of, the need to understand or justify, anything that is beyond this kind of reasoning. This is, as I have said, quite irrational because it denies certain realms of existence or experience that are obviously there.

This irrationality becomes even more obvious in the European case through the reaction of such concepts as existentialism and certain strands within Catholic thought, but I am not interested in going into that here. What I personally think of as true rationalism is the kind that understands and accepts the fact of the existence of things that are not quite rational, and this is the kind of rationalism that I think was the core of the Islamic philosophic tradition, especially through those whom I have spent a lot of my life studying – al-Farabi, Avicenna and Averroes. They begin, I think, with the notion of a religious community and they try to explain the advantages of a religious community over a non-religious community in terms of virtues and vices, of claims to rule, and so on. But they also see that there are certain tensions between reason or the attempt to understand things rationally, and the common view of the community. These tensions are partly an attempt by the leaders of the religious community to try to test the philosopher by asking questions such as: 'How can you explain the creation, or the world to come, or reward and punishment? How can you explain such matters as the creation of an individual soul and the survival of an individual?' The Islamic philosophic tradition, throughout its history, tried to tackle these questions, to speak about them intelligently and to make sense of them. Perhaps the person who did that most effectively and who, therefore, had a great deal of influence in later Islamic philosophy was Avicenna.

What I should like to try to do now – rather than give more details and explanations of these various attempts to meet the question of harmonization between philosophy in its broader, true rationalist sense and religion, revelation or divine reason – is to begin something that is quite central to understanding the background of modern Islamic thought, what called itself and what we should continue to call 'the new wisdom' (al-hikma al-jadida). For that we have to move from Andalusia and Baghdad to Isfahan of the 17th century. At the very time when rationalism was being developed in France, this new wisdom was emerging in Persia and from there it extended to Central Asia and the Indian subcontinent.

The new wisdom tried to integrate a number of strands from earlier Islamic thought: theology, mainly Mu'tazili theology, because now we are dealing with an Ithna'ashari or Twelver Shi'i community, and Mu'tazilism was traditionally associated with Shi'i theology from the 10th century onwards; philosophy, and by that was meant the entire tradition from al-Kindi through Avicenna, including some knowledge of the Andalusians but not much; and above all mysticism, personal experience and direct vision. Wisdom, true wisdom, now came to be understood as the completion of philosophy or rational thought, to be attained through private illumination, which could be in dreams or visions. The philosophic and theologic strands of the Mu'tazila are well known; but the main point was to incorporate the mystical strand. The Ithna'ashari community, which was then dominant in Isfahan in Persia, had been traditionally against mysticism, and it was through Nasir al-Din al-Tusi (d. 1274) that it had been somehow encouraged to originally move in that direction. By the 17th century, it was clear that mysticism had become part of the intellectual tradition of the Ithna'ashari community. This meant not only that the Shi'is did not want to have anything to do with al-Ghazali (d. 1111), who had attacked the Ismailis and the Twelver Shi'is in his writings, but also that Ibn al-'Arabi, Nasir al-Din al-Tusi and Avicenna became the great authors to study.

The two great thinkers of that period, of the new wisdom, the originators and founders of this school, Mir Damad (d. 1630) and his student Mulla Sadra (d. 1640), began again to tackle the central religious questions, but on a new basis. The problem of creation was constantly in their minds: was it created in time or eternal? How was Ibn al-'Arabi's mystical, partly anti-philosophic, anti-theological thought to be combined with the Aristotelians like Avicenna or the Illuminationists like Shihab al-Din Yahya al-Suhrawardi (d.1191)? This was a synthesis that they tried to develop. It was a tradition which, successful as it was, encountered a lot of difficulties with the *fuqaha*, the traditionalist Twelver Shi'is, who did not share their enthusiasm for these people and their ideas. In Safawid Persia, there was already this tension between the *fuqaha* on the one hand and the philosophers who were the purveyors of the new wisdom, a tension that can be observed throughout the modern-day Islamic Revolution in Iran.

But to my mind – again I am not expressing here the common notion but my own personal view – the new wisdom had a basic flaw, which was its fatal neglect of political and social problems. One may read all of Mir Damad and Mulla Sadra, but one will find hardly anything that deals with the Muslims as a community, with their political arrangements, with the relationship to their kings or with problems of reform. Obviously, like everybody else, they wanted to reform the community by making everybody a student of the new wisdom, by making everybody a kind of little philosopher, but that was quite irrational. When I raised this question in Iran in the 1970s, I was told that there is a book by Mulla Sadra on ethics; I have not seen the book yet but it is all that might exist by him on the subject. For Mulla Sadra, ethics obviously meant individual ethics, not as a way of life practised in the community but as a way of personal salvation – an old story among the Neoplatonists, I am sorry to say, and even a tradition that was partly encouraged by Avicenna. Earlier on, Nasir al-Din al-Tusi had tried to reverse the trend in his *Akhlaq-i Nasiri*, which has been translated into English (as *The Nasirean Ethics*, tr. G.M. Wickens, London, 1964). There is an attempt on his part to go back to al-Farabi, to think about the form of the state, the form of the community, and so on, but it was too little and too late. What happened in Islamic thought at this time is a kind of a replay of the development of Greek thought, which begins with a great deal of interest in the political and social thought of Plato and Aristotle, and ends up with Neoplatonism and hardly any interest in political, social or communal matters.

I am, therefore, quite happy to say that what has characterized the rational tradition from the beginning of the contemporary situation with thinkers such as Muhammad Iqbal (1877–1938), started with an attack against the new wisdom, to reform this kind of education which is a combination of philosophy, mysticism and *kalam*. The attack was aimed at this very point, perhaps the weakest point of the new wisdom, its lack of social and political norms, its emphasis on individual withdrawal rather than communal participation, on individualistic ethics rather than communal ethics, its inability as a tradition – a tradition that has gone on from the 17th century through to the present day, a tradition that is 200 or 300 years old and not a passing phenomenon – to speak intelligently about social, cultural and political problems at a time when Europe was experiencing a major intellectual and cultural transformation. By isolating itself from that development, and by so doing isolating in effect the only real, creative, active intellectual tradition in the whole of the Islamic community at that time, it isolated itself and therefore the whole Islamic community from developments in Europe, including the problems of domination by European powers.

It is, I think, useful to quote Iqbal's attack on the new wisdom.

There is some misunderstanding about Iqbal, who was a great poet and somebody of whom we should all be proud. Although he was a student of the new wisdom – his doctoral thesis dealt with the development of metaphysics in Persia – he was not really its disciple, despite the common view to the contrary. To quote from a letter he wrote in 1917:

> The present-day Muslim prefers to roam about aimlessly in the valley of Hellenistic/Persian mysticism, which teaches us to shut our eyes to the hard reality around us and to fix our gaze on what is described as 'illumination'.

This is not how we normally think about Iqbal when we read his poetry. He adds:

> To me this self-mystification, this nihilism that is seeking reality where it does not exist, is a physiological symptom giving me a clue to the decadence of the Muslim world.

This was Iqbal's reaction to the new wisdom, his reaction to that tradition from which, in a way, he must have emerged as a young man, which he must have studied like everybody else, such as Jamal al-Din al-Afghani (1839–1897) whom he admired so much. When Iqbal speaks of the Persian encrustation of Islam, he has only one thing in mind, and that is the tradition of the new wisdom. The new tradition that Iqbal followed was initiated by one of the students of the new wisdom, Jamal al-Din al-Afghani. With the recent publication of documents about Afghani, it is clear that he was not from Afghanistan; he was a Persian who had studied the new wisdom in Persia, and there are copies of the books that he studied and his annotations in the margins, which include Mulla Sadra and so forth. But his philosophic background is vague and no one has really clarified it. The general tendency from the evidence of these documents is to say that he was a student of Mulla Sadra, but I do not think that he was. I think he had tried very hard to go back beyond the tradition of the new wisdom, to Avicenna and al-Farabi, and to try to see the politico-social weakness of the new wisdom and somehow to make up for it by concentrating on the problem of the politico-social weakness of the Muslim world in his time, including the problem of Western domination. In Afghani's debate with Ernest Renan (d. 1892), he tried to put forward a theory of the rise of religion and the importance of the religious community. But Renan was in many ways one of those extreme rationalists who thought that sooner or later all religions would be gone and there would be secular societies based purely on reason which would have nothing to do with the dogmatic, backward prejudices that seemed to rule the world. Of course Renan was irrational in thinking like that, since nowadays religion is coming back with a vengeance, and not of the kind that he would have liked.

In a way, Afghani was much more sensible in talking to Renan and in defending the case for religion. He believed that human society without God and prophetic knowledge could not be a stable society. It is in a state of constant war with people fighting each other and individuals living in fear about their lives and futures. Yet suddenly in this kind of a community certain individuals, certain geniuses rise up, who are not only inspired but they are also fully rational. They have actualized reason as well as the contact with their divinity; they bring to societies, through divine mercy and revelation, the kind of law and order which gives human beings a sense of security, a sense of community, a sense of comfort and well-being, and a sense of their futures, both individually and as a community. So he had a defence which was certainly not of the new wisdom; his thinking on the origins of religion was much closer to the older philosophic tradition of a man like al-Farabi than it is to, say, Mulla Sadra.

But beginning with Afghani in the 19th century there is a trend which comes through some of his disciples who were concentrated in the Arab world and the Ottoman Empire, because he lived in Egypt for a long time and was very much involved in the political problems of these regions. There was a famous shaikh, the Imam Hamid 'Abduh, who became head of the new school in Egypt. He was a theologian and a jurist who had become a judge there, and under him two tendencies seem to have developed. One was represented by Rashid Rida, his student and biographer, who moved in the direction of what we now call conservatism, fundamentalism and Wahhabism. Even the Muslim Brothers (al-Ikhwan al-Muslimun) of today to some extent trace their origin to him.

On the other hand, there were students like Taha Hussein (1889–
1971) and others whom we normally associate with secular thought
in Egypt. One could ask questions about why this division took
place, why the unity of the school did not continue, and so on.
But this was exactly what happened. In short, their concern with
political and social problems seemed to lead to religion as well as
away from it, to people who would say: 'Well, if our problems are
secular, social and political, we have to talk politics and stop talking religion.' On the other hand, Rashid Rida and others were
saying that they were Muslims and wanted nothing to do with Europe. One often forgets that in 1936, Taha Hussein gave a series
of famous lectures at the University of Alexandria entitled 'The
Future of Culture in Egypt', in which he said that they were a part
of Europe, that the 'nonsense' about being Eastern made no sense
and that they must become like the Europeans. In short, this is
much like what Mustafa Kemal Atatürk (1881–1938) was trying
to do in Turkey.

Neither of these trends was intellectually very strong in the sense
that these were not major philosophers and they present us with
tendencies rather than philosophic positions which can be argued
about at length. But if one is discussing the fate of the rational
tradition in contemporary Islam, that is what actually happened
in at least one of the major centres of Islam. We could ask what it
is that drives people away from the Islamic community to extreme
Europeanization, to becoming a part of Europe? Is it perhaps that
the European cultural tradition is simply too powerful and will
thus inevitably exercise its magic, so to speak, on Muslim intellectuals? Perhaps the figure who would exemplify this would again
be Iqbal, because he could not be accused of not knowing the
Islamic tradition. Iqbal had obviously studied its history and its
philosophies. The question then is, what is his attitude to the
present and to the future? Where is the Muslim community in
relation to European culture? In a way Iqbal exemplifies this
situation quite well, an issue I should like to take up.

If one reads, let us say his major work, *The Reconstruction of Religious Thought in Islam* (Lahore, 1930), obviously one is impressed
with the passion and force with which he tried to reconstruct religious thought, to build it somehow at a time of decline. But the
question is, what was it being reconstructed on? What is the basis

on which he was trying to reconstruct it? My impression is that it was being reconstructed completely on the basis of modern European thought and modern European understanding of things, including religion. Iqbal certainly felt that the European thought of his time presented an infinite advance over traditional thought, over Greek and medieval thought in general, including religious thought. The notion was to reconstruct religious thought not only on the basis of one's own tradition, but also on fresh inspiration from modern thought and experience. We would all think that this is something quite reasonable, that one should get inspiration wherever one finds it.

The problem, I believe, is that Iqbal, especially during his stay in Europe, became enchanted with modern thought and experience to a degree far surpassing his allegiance to what he called 'free and independent enquiry'. As we read him, he quotes freely and with complete approval from authors like Alfred Whitehead, Bertrand Russell, Henri L. Bergson and Albert Einstein. He considered Immanuel Kant (d. 1804) as some kind of a prophet and speaks of the 'mission' of Kant, which he calls 'almost apostolic'. But this means more or less following the Kantian view which separates science, especially natural mathematical science, from religion, and considers religion – as Iqbal seems to have considered it in his book – as a kind of a 'higher poetry'. So religion is reduced to a kind of imaginative poetry. We are reminded of the Encyclopaedists who held that imagination simply counterfeits things. Iqbal accepted the distinction between nature and history in the way that modern thought has accepted it. He looked back at the Islamic tradition in the light of modern thought and forced religion to recede to the realm of personal experience and mysticism. So there was a strand of the new wisdom which continued in Iqbal despite his fervent political interest in an Islamic community in India.

What happened in the case of Iqbal is something that has happened amongst us as modern Muslims over and over again. We become enchanted with the modern West through our education and studies in modern European culture, and we try to look at Islam through this perspective. A few things then follow. One is that we praise everything that Muslims have done if it has had anything to do with science, because then we are proud of having contributed something to the modern world. In one place in *The Reconstruction of Religious Thought in Islam*, Iqbal talks with great delight of thinkers or trends which 'very nearly reach the modern'. He is delighted to see something of the kind. The modern West is very much given to the problem of history; history is very important to it. So what does Iqbal do? He looks at the Islamic tradition and *hadith* to find anything that has to do with history because that has now become a major problem for him too. Islam for him has to be understood as belonging to, and being relative to, a particular stage in history. Having taken on board this concept of history in modern thought, one eventually becomes some sort of a Hegelian in the sense that one begins to see the world as moving in stages, each stage having its own characteristics but being constantly bypassed by the next stage which is better and higher, and on and on.

If one looks at the world like this, the next question is where does Islam fit into this scheme of history? Islam gets pigeonholed; it becomes just one stage among many; it is a stage that has been bypassed by the Renaissance, by Albert Einstein (1879–1955), by the atom bomb and so on, which ultimately means that Islam is made redundant. We may continue to believe in Islam simply because we are Muslims or we like to be Muslims, and so on, but historically, universally, Islam is finished. According to this view, Islam was relative to a particular age, Muslim greatness was limited to the past, and that is it. One can continue to speak with pride of the Islamic origins of modern knowledge, but that does not get past the problem of Islam having been relative to a particular stage in history which has passed, which is over and which, in short, has very little to do with life today, unless somehow it has pre-given something that may look similar to what we call the 'modern'.

Think of the number of books and articles that Muslims have written to prove that Islam preceded the West in X, Y or Z, and ask why do they do it? Obviously they believe that what has happened in the West represents a higher stage and, therefore, anything that we have to contribute to that is good, and anything that we may have done that did not contribute to that was a waste of time because times have changed.

Iqbal went on to add that since he had to give Muslims

something to be proud of, and that there was a distinction between scientific advance and ethical advance, he ended up by
claiming that Europe today is the greatest hindrance in the way of
man's ethical advance. So again we have this kind of a notion,
very common in the Muslim world, that since Europe is at the
forefront of science and technology, whereas we are strong in ethics, we should have a combination of both. If somehow we can
integrate Europe's science and technology with our ethics, then
obviously we would be the ideal society. In this way, Iqbal wanted
to create something which he called 'spiritual democracy'. I must
admit, with some hesitation, that I feel this is some kind of a delu-
sion, and I often worry about what has happened to Iqbal's
homeland after all this. My explanation is that Iqbal's lack of real
thinking about the political and social problems of the time and
his talk of religion as higher poetry perhaps meant that modern
Indo-Muslim thought did not have the basis, the strength or the
power that would enable it to create what it always desperately
wanted, a genuine Islamic constitution. An Islamic constitution is
not created by considering religion as higher poetry. Religion must
be understood as something different in order to create an Islamic constitution.

The second and, I think, fatal error is the historical view of
Islam belonging to a particular period of history that has been
overcome and more or less bypassed by other stages, the notion
that we can always say: 'Well, it was great for its time, but what do
we do today?' This notion of Iqbal, which I am afraid is very common, is to be also found in an author who I always thought was
perhaps the greatest modern disciple of Iqbal, Fazlur Rahman
(1919–1988), who was my successor at the University of Chicago.
Fazlur Rahman wrote a book called *Islam and Modernity* (Chicago,
1982). I have the greatest respect for my late colleague, but one
thing that disturbed me was precisely this notion of trying to look
at Islamic law – something that concerned him very much – not
in terms of reform, because obviously Islamic law must be reformed
if we want to retain it, but in this Iqbalian sense of somehow explaining Islamic law through history, that it was something that
was fine at the time but today we have to change it. And to change
it in what terms? Is it to be in European terms, in modern terms,
in Protestant terms, in terms that mean the separation of church

and state, or this and that, as was partly attempted in Egypt by the secularists? Islamic law has always been subject to change. The fatal notion is to think of Islamic law, to say nothing of Islam as a whole, as simply a stage in historical development that is finished, as something medieval, something that was a great advance in its time but not in the 20th century. The question then is: what do we do as we approach the end of the 20th century? And I leave that question with you.

5

The Limits of Islamic Orthodoxy

Norman Calder

I will begin by setting out what it is that I am not going to discuss in this essay. The word 'orthodoxy' means 'right teaching'; but observing Islam, I am not in a position to judge between Sunnism and Shi'ism, to say whether one of them is orthodox and the other the non-orthodox tradition. What I think will be the case is that within the Sunni tradition, or within the Shi'i tradition, there might be some sense in which that tradition defines for itself a set of right beliefs and does not go very far beyond them.[1] The question I want to ask here is: what are the outside limits of 'right belief' for the Sunnis?

F.M. Denny, in his *An Introduction to Islam* (New York, 1985), claims that 'orthodoxy' is not the best term to use when characterizing Islam; it is better to use the term 'orthopraxy' meaning right practice. I do not think that this is true. From the point of view of a sociologist, it may well be true that in a given Muslim society there are practices which are rejected by that society. But I do not think that the practices of any particular Muslim society will represent orthopraxy, the focus of what it is to be a Muslim. In fact, theologically, it is clear that the Sunni tradition does not allow practice, works, to be taken into consideration in the definition of a Muslim. In order to achieve salvation as a Muslim,

66

one has to have right belief in some sense or another. If one has right belief, wrong actions are not a barrier to achieving salvation. One may go to Hell for a short time, but all times are short by contrast with eternity, and all Muslims, or all Sunni Muslims, who have faith – I am not quite sure where the limits lie here – are guaranteed eventual arrival in Paradise, perhaps after a period in Hell suffering the consequences of their bad deeds. But their bad actions do not stop them from being Muslims. The Muslim jurists are careful to distinguish between those who fail, let us say, to pray five times a day – they do not cease to be Muslim – and those who deny the incumbency to pray five times a day who might be apostates. So I do not think that Islam, either in its social practice, or in its theological and intellectual traditions, is a religion of orthopraxy; it is a religion of orthodoxy. There is a right teaching somewhere which we might find inside Sunni Islam defined in a particular way, and inside Shi'i Islam defined in a different way.

One of the places we might look to discover the right teaching of Islam is to those books which are called 'aqida or 'aqa'id in Arabic. The word means 'creed' and the books (often booklets or pamphlets or even sections within larger books of a different genre) set out the agenda of beliefs that represent being a Muslim. There is a genre of such works which have been produced by both the Sunni and the Shi'i tradition. To move away from Islam for a moment to the Roman Catholic tradition. The Roman Catholic Church has a creed, a set of beliefs, 'I believe in one God, the Father', and so on, which is recited every day at the Mass. It derives from a number of Councils which were held in the 4th and 5th centuries. In the first five centuries of Christianity, there was debate about what it was you had to believe to be a Christian, and finally at, say, the Council of Chalcedon, a form of the creed was agreed on, under the authority of that Council and the Pope who convened it. Since then it has stayed exactly the same. For the last 1500 years, the same creed has been recited in the Mass day after day, week after week, century after century. The Catholics achieved that kind of focus and continuity because they have a formal hierarchy consisting of the pope, cardinals, archbishops, bishops and priests, who can be summoned together in order to make final and binding decisions about the articles of faith and the mode of their expression.

Islam, by contrast, does not have such a system of authority. There has never been a council in Islam and there are no clearly articulated hierarchies. In fact, we cannot find a single Muslim (or Sunni) creed which is believed in by all Muslims. There are probably hundreds of Muslim creeds; certainly dozens can be found in, for example, the university library at Manchester. Each of these creeds is written by a particular jurist; so we can find the creed of al-Tahawi, the creed of Ibn Taymiyya, the creed of al-Ash'ari, and the creed of Abu Hanifa. We can look at them and ask: where is the right belief of Muslims? The answer, however, would seem to be that there is not one. There is al-Ash'ari's view about right belief, al-Tahawi's view, Ibn Taymiyya's view, and so on. Throughout Islamic history there are different creeds written out by different scholars. The significant creeds are those that emerge within a discursive tradition, through an informal, consensual acknowledgement of value that is quite different from the formal procedures of the Roman Catholic hierarchy.

The creeds that were thus produced in Islam had, of course, much in common, not least the components of the *shahada*, the belief that God is one and Muhammad is the messenger of God. But there were also more recondite beliefs – for the Sunnis, for example, that God has real attributes and the Qur'an is the uncreated word of God. These are central focuses of the creed; but how that creed is expressed varies from person to person. How high up on the agenda of faith a particular item is brought changes from time to time. Sometimes it may seem that an issue thought to be primary in one century is gradually displaced, moves towards the bottom of the list, and may fall off the list altogether. For example, the earliest Muslim creeds have a great deal to say about faith and works, whether works count towards faith. The issue was contentious, but in the end an established pattern of variation emerged. There seemed to be agreement that works count towards getting quickly to heaven (though God's mercy and the Prophet's intercession were also important), but they do not count decisively in the question of whether one can achieve salvation. For the Sunni tradition, faith alone guarantees salvation, and the limit of faith is *shirk* or polytheism. Those who avoid *shirk* will go to heaven eventually.

There remained significant and articulated differences about

THE LIMITS OF ISLAMIC ORTHODOXY   69

the definition of faith and its consequences, even within the Sunni tradition. The question, however, became unimportant and did not have to be expressed in every creed; it certainly was not expressed at all in some later creeds. But since the creeds form a tradition of literature, a continuous and authoritative tradition, the issue could always be revived, and be invested with a new significance. This is one of the patterns of flexibility that lies in the Muslim tradition; certain items on the agenda of faith move up and down the scale of importance, perhaps lose their significance, but may later recover and require re-expression, and must then be re-expressed in a manner that is not inconsistent with the decisive presence of a literary tradition.

Every Muslim agrees that God is one, but how does one express this? Ibn Sina or Avicenna, as he came to be known in medieval Europe, produced a philosophical definition of God as the necessary existent (*wajib al-wujud*), a phrase which did not immediately find acceptance in Sunni theological circles. However, through the influence of those scholars who admired the philosophers, and especially through the influence of Fakhr al-Din al-Razi (d. 1209) who was clearly fascinated by Avicenna's writing in spite of its dubious status as an articulation of right belief, the notion of God as the necessary existent became acceptable to Sunni Islam. In later creeds, even of the Sunni tradition, God is not only one but also the necessary existent.

Thus, there are patterns of development in the articulation of right belief, and there are acknowledged areas of dispute internal to the community. Both the agenda of relevant items and the way of expressing individual items may change with the passage of time. Where then precisely is orthodoxy? Does it lie in this or in that articulation of the creed, in this or in that century, in this or in that terminology?

Just to simplify things for the moment, let us say that it lies inside the discursive tradition of jurists who write creeds. As you see, I come back here to a set of ideas that I have already introduced in contrasting Islam with Roman Catholicism, that Muslims are caught up in a discursive process, an ongoing process of interpreting their own past. They seem not to – and this may be a great advantage – come down to established formulae that are going to last for 1500 years, but to provisional assessments. No matter how

vehement, forceful, elegant or sophisticated the articulation of
this or that scholar, no matter even how influential, it is not a
final articulation. The scholars of the community, in consultation
with one another and listening to one another, gradually develop,
change and move – though, perhaps, not too far. There is always
a core of belief which is there: the belief that God is one,
Muhammad is the messenger of God, and that God, in some more
or less mysterious sense, has attributes which can be named and
numbered.

The question of what Muslims meant by God's attributes was
always a difficult one, but it is not possible here to illustrate how
the scholars expressed their understanding of this belief. Possibly
even more difficult was the question of the Qur'an and its status
as, in some sense, the uncreated word of God. There is some evidence that, since the late 19th century, the question of whether
the Qur'an is the uncreated word of God has moved down the
agenda, perhaps indeed dropped off it. Many Sunni Muslims today do not even know that this was an important item of their
credal system. Indeed, some major writers have suggested that it
is not only unimportant but quite unnecessary to claim, in any
sense, that the Qur'an is the 'uncreated' word of God. And yet
that was one of the most important and top-ranking elements of
the creed at various times in the past.

We come back then to the general point that the creed is a set
of beliefs, elaborated in a discursive tradition by scholars, who are
committed to and engaged with the tradition as the core of orthodoxy. But what are the limits, the outside limits, of this
orthodoxy? When does one drop off the edge, as it were, and stop
being a Sunni Muslim? At this point, let me relinquish the question and try a different approach. For even if we concede that the
literary tradition of creeds represents the core of orthodoxy, there
is something unsatisfactory about the concession. Something
seems to have been left out: I mean the law. Islam, it seems obvious, is a religion of which the central theological feature is the
law, and yet the creeds scarcely mention the law. It is a striking
fact that many law books (both *furu'* and *usul*) contain expressions of creed, but the creeds do not contain expressions of law.
There is perhaps a significant symbolism in that fact, in the context
of our question about the outer limits of orthodoxy. Books of law

contain expressions of the creed, but not vice versa (unless of course some formulation of the injunction to obey God and his prophets be seen as just this).

If we are looking for a definition of orthodoxy, we ought to look for one which includes at least some reference to the law. So here I will draw a line under everything I have said so far, and start again from a different angle. From a purely abstract point of view, we might be able to categorize religious belief amongst all peoples at all times in terms of a limited number of typological headings. Let me make an effort in that direction. I shall even claim, for the limited purposes of this paper, that all possible forms of religious belief can be caught under the following five headings: scripture, community, gnosis, reason, charisma.

Some people claim that the way towards knowledge of God is through scripture, that God has revealed His own being through a set of written texts which we can call scripture or 'revelation'. Others claim that God's self-revelation to man is not through scripture, or not primarily through scripture, but through the community, that one particular community has been chosen by God and within that community correct belief will be articulated and preserved, because that community is guarded by God and preserved from error. A third group claim that the way towards knowledge of God is through 'gnosis' – I am using that word here to stand for mystic knowledge, as when a particular person, a holy man, claims that he can, through prayer, ascetic exercises or whatever, achieve direct communication with God. A fourth group claim that the way towards understanding God is by using reason, and that human reason is an adequate way to gain a complete knowledge of God. Perhaps the Islamic philosophers are an example of this point of view. Finally, there are communities which state that God has appointed, throughout the generations, one particular person to express and guard His message, claiming perhaps that this person has special charisma and knowledge of God, and that he is, in some sense, protected by God and given right belief.

Now, what I have done is set out five categories which, at least in theory, we can look upon as pure categories. Theoretically, there might be a religion which says that the only way God reveals himself to man is, let us say, through charisma, that is, through the choice of a particular man who is the leader of the community and who will tell the community about God and their duties towards Him. But in practice, most religions are mixtures of the five categories. Religions will both have a scripture which is God's revelation and, perhaps, a theory that inside the community there will always be right belief and, perhaps combined with that, a suggestion that there will be some people in the community with direct contact with God, mystically. All the great religious traditions of the world, like Hinduism, Islam and Christianity, in fact, have all five elements in various mixtures. And the same is likely to be true, within Islam, in relation to the two great orthodox traditions of Sunnism and Shi'ism. We can, further, usually pinpoint within a large religious tradition certain movements that correspond to particular items in that five-part epistemology that I have just presented. If we ask ourselves how we have knowledge of God, the question leads, I think, to this kind of epistemological typology, and I suspect that every religion could be analysed in terms of these five epistemological categories.

Within Islam, the Twelver Shi'a and the Ismaili Shi'a in their various forms are communities which lay stress on charisma as being, in various degrees, the highest and most important form of our achieving knowledge of God. Within Islam, there are two communities again, two sets of people, who lay great stress on reason as the means for our achieving knowledge of God. One is represented by the philosophers like al-Farabi and Avicenna. The other significant group is the Mu'tazila, a historical group who flourished in the 9th and 10th centuries, and for some centuries thereafter. They are rejected by the Sunnis because, in their view, the Mu'tazila overstress the role of reason. In an Islamic context, the term gnosis, refers, of course, mainly to the Sufis.

Where do the Sunnis lie in this epistemological spectrum? The reader will perhaps already sense the direction of my argument. I wish to claim that the Sunnis lie somewhere between scripture and community, or rather that they encompass both categories. By so doing, I go slightly against the way some Western scholars present Sunni Islam. In general, they seem to present Sunni Islam as a community which relies on scripture. But I think they have not taken enough note of what actually happens when Muslims are engaged in thinking about, expressing and developing their religion, and that we have here a religion whose major understanding of God is expressed through acknowledgement of what happens inside the community, the ongoing community. In fact, I wish to claim of Sunni Islam that it is more a religion of community than of scripture.

What are the major components of Sunni Islam? This religion states that at a certain point in history, God sent a prophet called Muhammad. He was not the first prophet, there were many prophets before him: Adam, Noah, Abraham, Moses, Jesus. In fact, there were many besides that familiar list, for it is said that there were 124,000 prophets altogether. Of these, some 300 (Ibn Qutayba says 315 in his *Kitab al-ma'arif*) brought a scripture of some kind. As a result of these prophets, and in particular the Prophet Muhammad, we have scripture or revelation. Divine intervention in history, manifested in God sending prophets to diverse human communities through the ages, culminated, and in some sense ceased, with the mission of the Prophet Muhammad. As a result of his mission, the whole of humanity – for his summoning the whole of humanity was one of the distinctive qualities of Muhammad's mission – was left with two bodies of texts, the Qur'an and the *hadith*. These are, for Sunni Muslims, the content, the manifestation, of revelation. These are the texts to which Muslims appeal when they are expressing and interpreting their faith.

These texts are the residue of salvation history. I use the term 'salvation history' here to indicate that part of history which is brought forward by a religious tradition as being somehow part of the definition of that religion. When young Muslims are brought up, they may be taught their local or national history at school, but as Muslims they are also taught about Adam, Noah, Abraham and all the prophets, as well as the life of Muhammad, at an appropriate level for youngsters. There are stories of the prophets for children and there are stories of the prophets for adults. These stories are the central components of salvation history for Muslims. As a result of salvation history (a history which has now come to an end because Muhammad was the last, the seal, of the prophets) we have revelation, scripture. The precise term is not important here. The reference is to a bundle of texts which constitute authority. Out of these, at least in theory, the Muslim community derives a theology and a system of law, both explained and justified by reference to the Qur'an and the *hadith*, through engagement in the exegetical process.

Some Muslims would say, with justification, that what they derive from scripture and revelation is, in fact, a way of life. And this is true in so far as the interpretation of scripture and revelation leads to the whole practical and historical experience of the Muslim community. But I want to focus here on the intellectual experience of the Muslim community and on that aspect of their faith which claims that out of revelation, that is, the Qur'an and the *hadith*, come the intellectual traditions of theology, law and exegesis. It is, in fact, possible to propose that the whole intellectual tradition of Sunni Islam can be encapsulated in a list of literary genres, these being the genres, the traditions of writing, through which the Sunni community has given expression to its understanding of its relationship to God and his Prophet. Rather schematically presented, the complete list (and I emphasize that I am referring here specifically to the Sunni community) is as follows: *qisas al-anbiya*; *sirat al-nabi*; Qur'an; *hadith*; *fiqh*; *kalam*; *tafsir* and *sharh al-hadith*

The *qisas al-anbiya* (literally, 'tales of the prophets') refers to a literary genre which offers a retelling of salvation history for Muslims. A continuation of this aim, but a different genre (different that is by the nomenclature of the literary tradition itself), is discovered in the *sirat al-nabi* literature. This offers a biography of the Prophet Muhammad. There are, of course, many different realizations of the tales of the prophets, as there are many realizations of the biography of Muhammad. Each generation rewrites these materials differently. Later generations draw upon and comment on the works of earlier generations. Each generation deals differently with the fact that some are intellectuals and some are five-year olds. For a five-year old, you tell the stories of the prophets and the biography of the Prophet Muhammad in a very different way from when you are dealing with people older, more educated or more intellectual.

The body of revelation in Islam is represented by the Qur'an and the *hadith*. Beyond these, and in some way exegetically linked to them, there are the great intellectual genres of *kalam* which is Islamic theology, *fiqh* which is Islamic law, *tafsir* which denotes commentaries on the Qur'an, and *sharh al-hadith* which denotes commentaries on *hadith* literature. The fact that the Muslim community produced commentaries not only on the Qur'an but also on the *hadith* is a reminder that both these sources have the status of revelation, both requiring to be interpreted in search of meaning and significance.

Now, if you go to any traditional Muslim library, and in particular to a Sunni Muslim library, I think you will find that a majority of the books in such a library, in so far as they relate directly to religion, can be accommodated under these broad generic headings. In order to make that claim absolutely certain, I would have to add a commentary on my own categories. For example, one of the problems facing the Muslim community was that of setting the limits on acceptable *hadith*. There are a great many collections of *hadith*, some of which are central and universally accepted, while others are recognized as of immense and undisputed importance, and there are still others which have a marginal status and are a focus of discussion. So, one feature of Muslim tradition is that it acknowledges an indeterminately large body of *hadith* literature. Associated with this body of literature is a method of critical assessment which, in turn, is embodied in literature. There is a range of books and types of book which offer views on how to pass judgements on *hadith*. The most important of these books are perhaps those known generically as books of *jarh wa ta'dil*, books that offer a methodology for categorizing the transmitters of *hadith*, and so permitting an assessment of the *hadith*s themselves. For the purposes of this paper, I want to bundle all the books of this type under the general heading of *sharh al-hadith*. Just as I want to classify here the many different types of book that deal with the Qur'an, including specialist studies of its vocabulary, literary style, the incidence in it of abrogation, or such large studies as al-Suyuti's overview of the Qur'anic sciences (*al-Itqan fi 'ulum al-Qur'an*), as all part of *tafsir*. This is not a resource of despair – for the genres of Islamic religious literature could be more discriminately analysed and categorized – but a matter of practical convenience.

My aim in delineating these genres and in proposing that they form the bulk of the contents of a traditional library, is to suggest that the limits of Islamic orthodoxy are expressed in this list. This is what Islam, or specifically Sunni Islam, in its broadest sense, is about. It is about everything contained in the *qisas al-anbiya, sirat al-nabi,* the Qur'an, *hadith, kalam, fiqh, tafsir* and *sharh.* Anything that is brought in under these headings and held inside the discursive tradition of Muslim literary experience belongs within the limits of Islamic orthodoxy. And these are discursive limits, for the question of what can be held inside these works is not fixed by reference to one work, or the works of one century, one school or one geographical region. The canon of literature which expresses the orthodox tradition of Sunni Islam is fairly clear in its central components – and even there such controversial and apparently irreconcilable figures as Ibn Taymiyya and Fakhr al-Din al-Razi must be held inside the tradition – but it offers almost limitless extension in the direction of minor and contested figures, who might always be drawn nearer or further from the centre as time and scholarship move.

In such a large tradition, where the centre is in debate and the boundaries are contested, is anything, one may wonder, excluded? Can this exploration of the limits of orthodoxy demonstrate that some particular belief or set of beliefs falls outside of those limits? Let us consider, for a while, *tafsir. Tafsir* is a term that designates, in one range of use, commentaries on the Qur'an. A work of *tafsir* will contain the whole text of the Qur'an, divided up into segments; the commentator will present a segment and then he will tell you what the segment means – except that he will not tell you what the segment means; he will tell you what the people before him said the segment meant. Works of *tafsir* characteristically consist of reports intimating that so and so said that this part of the Qur'an means such and such. One finds a very similar phenomenon, a similarly literary format, in works of *fiqh.* The single text is broken up by the operation on it of time and scholarship. The possibility of a single meaning is lost, the message is rendered into fragments, and all the fragments are brought into the present, because we find that a single verse of the Qur'an may have ten different scholars commenting on it with ten different views as to what it means. There will be limits, but there is a tendency, as time passes, for the meanings of the Qur'an to grow bigger. And there is also a tendency for Muslims not to comment directly. When a scholar writes a large *tafsir,* he explores the views of earlier authorities, including of course the views of the Prophet himself, the views of his Companions, the views of the next generations, until at the end, he might say 'And my view is ...' or 'My preferred view is ...', thus expressing preferences within the tradition rather than pinning down the meaning of the Qur'an. It almost never happens – in fact, I would go so far as to say that prior to the 19th century it does not happen – that a Muslim scholar sits down with the Qur'an and, using his own intellect, literary skills and imagination says 'I think it means X'. When such a thing did happen, the scholar in question usually became open to accusations of heresy.

One man who did this is, perhaps, the Bab, I mean Sayyid 'Ali Muhammad Shirazi (d. 1850), the founder of the Babi movement, and indirectly, of the Baha'i faith. The Bab wrote a *tafsir* of the *Surat Yusuf* (Sura 12) of the Qur'an. What he seems to have done is to express his opinion, at least in the end. There are, in his work, some vestiges of what might be called the orthodox technique, but in the end he simply used the Qur'an as a prompt to express his own religious experience. In the course of his lifetime, he was both perceived to be, and in the end claimed to be, the founder of a new religion. It was a deviation from orthodoxy, an abandonment of tradition, which is symbolized in his failure to acknowledge in his *tafsir* the experience of the community – I mean here the intellectual experience represented in generations of exegetical activity. It is perhaps odd, and it does not sound like the religion we so often hear about, and yet it is insistently the case: the intellectual tradition of Islam is one which makes it a requirement that each succeeding generation look at and take into consideration the work of the preceding generations. It is not a religion which, from generation to generation, goes back to the original words of scripture and revelation. When a scholar makes this attempt to go back to the original sources and to look at them with an unprejudiced eye (if there is such a thing), people are not sure about this and, as in the case of the Bab, he is liable to rejection.

Even when people are less radical than the Bab, they still get pushed aside. Consider the fate, for example, of those movements within Islam called the Zahiri and the Salafi. The terms can be translated, respectively, as Literalist (implying a return to the literal meanings of the revealed texts) and Primitivist (a return to the values of the early community). The terminology records the perception of the mainstream tradition in respect of these minor traditions. They were perceived to have a backward orientation, an orientation towards the verbatim words of scripture or the primitive community. The main tradition was represented by the great schools of law (Hanafi, Maliki, Shafi'i and Hanbali) and by the main theological traditions (Ash'ari and Maturidi). The Salafi thinker, Ibn Taymiyya, who lived in the 13th and 14th centuries, has had a tremendous influence on 20th-century Islam; but he had very little influence in the centuries after his death. In the 19th century his thinking was revived and discovered to be a good thing, although earlier he was not regarded as a good thing.

Let me return to my assessment of the contents of a traditional Muslim library. Those who are familiar with such a library may have noticed that there is one major literary genre, one that has a significant presence in a Muslim library, that is missing. It is the genre of *tabaqat* ('generations'), biographical works, and I missed it out deliberately because, in recalling it now, it helps to make my point. One of the most productive literary genres in Islam, the *tabaqat* literature, though it has many specialist divisions, conforms basically to a single format: it chronicles the transmission of knowledge through the generations. Whether dealing with jurists, exegetes, experts in *hadith* or with all types of scholar, such works offer a diachronic realization of Islam; an assertion that the essential message is preserved, not solely within the revealed texts, but in the teaching about these texts that is transmitted from generation to generation through the ages. The genre of *tabaqat* is an essential part of the religious self-expression of Muslims, and as such it tends to confirm what I have been suggesting, that Sunni Islam is a religion in which although everything in one sense is taken back to scripture, in another sense it is ongoing. It is a religion which seems to demand of its participants that appropriate acknowledgement be granted to the community as it develops through time (and as it is represented by scholars). Every later participation in the forms of literature – and it is through established literary forms and genres that thought takes place – every later statement of faith or assessment of meaning in the Qur'an, takes into account the earlier statements worked out by the community. The epistemological categories of scripture/revelation and community are always balanced inside Sunni Islam, and always balanced, I would say, in favour of community, not scripture.

This does not quite end the problem. I have not yet, as it were, reached the limits of orthodoxy. My first step is to suggest that the limits of orthodoxy are represented by what is, or what can be contained within, the broad literary tradition that I have identified in the preceding paragraphs. But this literary tradition contains references to other literary traditions. For example, it contains references to the writings of the Mu'tazila, to the philosophers, to the Sufis, and sometimes to the Twelver and Ismaili Shi'is. And it seems to me that we might attempt to define the limits of orthodoxy not only by saying that it is here, inside the literary tradition of the Sunni community, but also that it is there, in those aspects of the other traditions which seem to be necessary for the Sunnis to define their own position. There is a sense in which the preservation and recall of the Mu'tazili position on God's attributes constitutes the necessary ground of the Sunni position. Certainly, there are very few attempts to state the Sunni position on the divine attributes which do not explicitly recall the Mu'tazili position, making it the focus of fine distinctions which distinguish and clarify the Sunni position. The explicit acknowledgement of parallel and erroneous traditions is a part of the orthodox tradition. And the articulation of orthodoxy could not be achieved without a discursive exploration of the boundaries that separate the orthodox tradition from those traditions that are acknowledged to deviate from it.

What is at issue can be caught in the notion of 'intertextuality', a term that denotes the way that texts refer to other texts. The reference to other texts can be implicit – in the sense that a novel implies the existence of a whole genre of such things – or it can be explicit. The implicit references are more interesting but also difficult to assess. What is clear and immediately useful for our present investigation is the fact that inside this body of literature, that which constitutes Sunni orthodoxy, are numerous explicit references to that other body of literature, the works of the Mu'tazila, the philosophers, the Shi'is and the Sufis. In so far as such explicit references are helpful and accommodating, then these alternative traditions are being given a place in orthodox Islam, in this context Sunni Islam. In so far as they are explicitly rejected, we are approaching a definition of the boundaries of orthodox Islam.

Now, as far as I have ever been able to ascertain, in so far as the Sunni tradition mentions anything about the Ismailis, it is with clear and explicit rejection. One of the clearest boundaries of Sunni Islam is that which separates it from the Ismaili faith. It is just possible that, in the 11th century, when al-Ghazali attacked the Ta'limiyya, as he called the Ismailis of his day, he was moved by his sense of the strengths of their philosophy to build up parallel strengths in his depiction of Sunnism, but there has been very little subsequent acknowledgement of the Ismailis. Unlike, say, the philosophers, Ismaili writers do not become a significant part of the discursive move towards self-definition by later Sunni thinkers. It is also true that the Twelver Shi'is are not particularly referred to, and not particularly liked in general, within that body of literature. From a Sunni point of view, the basic Shi'i error, their refusal to acknowledge the historical succession to the Prophet Muhammad, is frequently acknowledged, and this is, of course, a fundamental part of the depiction of Sunni tradition. But the great tradition of Shi'i writers, whether on law, theology or philosophy, remains almost unacknowledged within the Sunni tradition. In fact, I would be tempted to say that the epistemological category of charisma, as I have defined it above, is very clearly outside the boundaries of Sunni Islam, except possibly at a popular level where it has tried to accommodate certain beliefs about the exceptional status of 'Ali b. Abi Talib, though these are in a Sunni context often assimilated to Sufism rather than Shi'ism.

The Sunni tradition of *kalam* refers to the Mu'tazila frequently and tries to derive a kind of shifting position in which certain of the views expressed by the Mu'tazila are more or less acceptable to Sunni Islam. Some scholars such as Ibn Taymiyya were extremely negative about the Mu'tazila; on the other hand, another Sunni theologian, Fakhr al-Din al-Razi, was much more accommodating. He found it necessary to cite, explain and clarify a great deal of the Mu'tazili tradition in order to assess its compatibility with the Sunni tradition. Unlike Ibn Taymiyya, he is not vehemently negative about this alternative tradition, but rather holds on to it, makes it a means whereby to discover and express the possibilities of Sunni Islam. In one other way the Mu'tazili tradition produced books that were accommodated inside Sunni Islam. A famous example is the Mu'tazili exegete, al-Zamakhshari (d. 1144). Although his *tafsir* contained Mu'tazili ideas, it contained also so much that was good, so much that was interesting to the Sunnis, that they began writing commentaries on al-Zamakhshari's work in which they took seriously what he had to say. Here then, at the boundary between Sunnism and the Mu'tazila, the line is not so clear. There is a sense in which the boundary is discursive, such that certain patterns of advance and retreat can be noted and mapped. The Mu'tazili tradition, in some way, is a part of the history of Sunnism and a permanent element in Sunni self-definition.

How about the philosophers? Al-Ghazali, famously, set out reasons why the philosophers were unacceptable to him, but in so doing established for them an important place on the defining fringes of orthodoxy. And not everyone agreed with all of al-Ghazali's strictures. Again, Fakhr al-Din al-Razi is an important figure here. Fascinated by the work and the arguments of Avicenna, he wrote a summary of the *Tanbihat wa'l-isharat*, Avicenna's last and possibly his most brilliant literary achievement. By that very fact of writing a summary, Fakhr al-Din indicated that he, a Sunni theologian, was taking on board at least some of what Avicenna had to say, and, indeed, many of the ideas and much of the terminology of Avicenna appear in Fakhr al-Din's *tafsir*. Thus, a great deal of philosophical terminology and thought crept into the Sunni tradition and became internal to that tradition. Of course, it was not absolutely internal, because other Sunni writers disliked the philosophers intensely, notably Ibn Taymiyya. So inside Sunnism we have a kind of 'yes' and 'no' with regard to both the philosophers and the Mu'tazila; and in that sense reason as an epistemological category has a significant place, albeit a highly qualified place, within Sunni Islam.

What about gnosis? Here, let me just say that, as far as I can see, from the 12th century onwards, slowly but insistently, there emerges an increasing quantity of favourable reference inside that body of Sunni literature to the literature representing Sufism. Again, it is Ibn Taymiyya who represents the opposition movement. He clearly felt strongly that the Sufis, in some respects, were a danger to Sunni Islam. But that negative evaluation was matched by more positive evaluations elsewhere, above all perhaps by a general tendency in the major juristic schools to acquiesce in the religious aspirations of the Sufi tradition. By the 19th century, there had emerged a long tradition of references and statements which indicate that Sunni Islam, as represented by that body of literature defined above, is at ease with gnostic literature, as represented by a long, continuous tradition of specialist works, beginning with figures like Abu 'Abd Allah al-Muhasibi, Abu Nu'aym al-Isfahani, Abu Talib al-Makki, al-Qushayri and others, and finally embracing Ibn al-'Arabi, who as *al-shaykh al-akbar*, 'the greatest shaikh', becomes a symbol of Sufi literature in its most sophisticated and, perhaps, its most dangerous form. In spite of this, he is, on the whole, approved of.

That last point may be illustrated very briefly by reference to a Hanafi juristic work of the 19th century: the *Hashiyat radd al-muhtar* of Ibn 'Abidin (d. 1842), which is a commentary on a commentary on an epitome of the law – the layered glosses of the work incidentally neatly illustrate the stress on continuity, on preserving the tradition, on acknowledging diachronic continuity, which I have already identified as an essential part of the Sunni religious experience. But here I want to note more specifically a couple of contexts in which Ibn 'Abidin makes explicit intertextual reference to works of the Sufi tradition. In a brief biographical reference to Abu Hanifa, founder of the Hanafi school of law, Ibn 'Abidin recalls the information, well-established by his time, that amongst those who followed the great imam in his juristic methodology were many of 'the noble friends of God,' including Ibrahim b. Adham, Ma'ruf al-Karkhi, Abu Yazid al-Bistami and other famous Sufis. In proceeding to make some remarks on these figures, Ibn 'Abidin mentions the works of Abu Nu'aym al-Isfahani and al-Qushayri. By citing these works, he establishes that they too belong to the constellation of authoritative sources that validly tell us about the experience of the (Sunni) Muslim community. He is telling his readers not only that some of the most important early mystics who were contemporary with Abu Hanifa learnt their law from him, but that the literature through which the Sufi tradition gives expression to its identity is acceptable to that tradition within and through which Ibn 'Abidin gives expression to his identity. Both the story (history) and the intertextual reference signal an alliance between the juristic school of Abu Hanifa and the mystic tradition as represented by even al-Bistami, who was often looked upon with suspicion because he held rather extreme mystic views. The story of Abu Hanifa's relationship with mystics was developed still further, with special reference to al-Shadhili, eponym of one of the most powerful mystic orders of the 19th century. And so we see that there developed a kind of narrative tradition, a set of stories, which signal the relationship between Sufism and Sunni Islam. In a different context, Ibn 'Abidin takes up the question of the acceptability of the teachings of Ibn al-'Arabi. It cannot be said that he offers an easy acquiescence in the problematic philosophy of the great mystic, but he does offer a kind of acquiescence, a modulated recognition that there is nothing essentially alien to Sunni Islam in the ideas of Ibn al-'Arabi, if correctly understood.

In conclusion, let me offer a final statement about the limits of orthodoxy in Sunni Islam. At an intellectual level, the limits of orthodoxy are represented by the contents of that set of books defined above as constitutive of a traditional Sunni library, together with such aspects of the alternative traditions (Shi'is, Mu'tazila, philosophers, Sufis, etc.) as are acknowledged in the primary set. My own, in this context necessarily broad, analysis of these books permits a kind of conclusion, namely that Sunni Islam is primarily a religion of community, scripture and gnosis, marginally of reason, and hardly at all of charisma. The primary elements are community and scripture (in that order I am sure), because they are the fundamental epistemological categories of Sunni literature. Gnosis has to be added and brought up to a primary position because, on balance, the body of Sunni literature acknowledges the religious validity of the Sufi experience, though its expression depends on a different set of literary texts. The totality of the experience available to a Sunni Muslim includes both the scholastic tradition or, if you like, the exegetical tradition represented in the former body of literature, and the mystic tradition represented in the tradition of Sufi literature.

In coming to these conclusions, I am conscious of a difficulty, namely that the situation I have described is not demonstrably true of the 20th century. As a university teacher, teaching 'religion' within a secular educational system, I am concerned not with the discovery or the evaluation of religious truth, but rather with the analysis of texts. In an academic context, it seems to me, I can say nothing about the existence or the nature of God, or the possibility of salvation. About the nature of texts and the arguments, about the beliefs and opinions that mould them, I can say at least a little. It is even possible, in this context, to formulate questions about religious experience which permit of answers that are within the sphere of academic analysis, answers that might be demonstrably true or false, or at least, more or less adequate to the situation analysed. In this context, students come from all over the world, including all parts of the Islamic world, to participate in this exercise of academic analysis. In proposing, year on year, to read with my students either this book or that, I can choose, without difficulty, texts which are a great pleasure for me to read and a great pleasure for them to read. They are the texts which constitute the intellectual heritage of Muslims throughout the world, and for non-Muslims too they are a part of the human heritage, a part which we too can share and enjoy, even if we do not have faith. Whether Muslim students come from Saudi Arabia, Malaysia or Africa, or even Iran with its predominantly Shi'i tradition, they are happy to read any work, from any of the literary genres that constitute Sunni Islam. But should I propose to read Ibn al-'Arabi, I would certainly meet with some resistance, with some intimation that this is not central to, or even perhaps is not, a part of the Islamic tradition. That is, there is a tendency for some contemporary Muslims to reject one major part of the historical experience of their community. This – and here I take off my academic hat and, with due apology, put on a judgemental one – seems to me on the whole not a very healthy tendency. I am inclined to think that if you have a rich, complex and varied tradition, the needs of the 20th century hardly indicate that it should be restricted, rather that it should be accepted in all its richness. Contemporary Muslims are, as it were, offered by their tradition a massive, complex, sophisticated heritage, a generous profusion of modes of religious fulfilment, and any step towards making that heritage smaller must be a bad thing.

If we ask why there is a tendency for at least some modern Muslims to make their heritage smaller, we will I think find that it goes back to a very great man and a very important thinker, Muhammad 'Abduh (1849–1905). He wanted to reform Islam and make it relevant to the modern world, and the method he chose was a method of rejection. It had some very positive results, but one of the things he rejected was the whole mystic tradition. He claimed that much mystic lore was nonsense, *khurafat*; he called upon his followers not to listen to mystics and to get rid of them. One can perhaps understand what he meant in terms of what mystic traditions were like, or how they appeared, in the late 19th century, but nonetheless it is not a particularly good point of departure for Muslims today trying to find their way forward as Muslims. Muhammad 'Abduh also, in fact, initiated a novel stress in the area of scripture versus community. I am inclined to say that the reality of the Islamic (Sunni) tradition is that they combine the epistemological characteristics of scripture and community, while laying greater stress on community. Muhammad 'Abduh implied that Muslims, in order to accommodate themselves to the 19th and 20th centuries, should go back to the beginning. The products of the great intellectual tradition were not to his mind so very wonderful; for him, much of what these jurists and theologians had produced was of little value, they could be safely and wisely discarded. The community should go back and start all over again with the Qur'an. The relevant juristic hero for Muhammad 'Abduh was not Abu Hanifa, Malik, Shafi'i or even Ibn Hanbal, great figures though they all were; it was Ibn Taymiyya. And his usefulness was that he offered a scourge for the intellectual tradition and a banner for revivalism; he represented, *par excellence*, the Salafi (Primitivist) tendency in Islam.

Now, perhaps Muhammad 'Abduh was right; perhaps this was a necessary way forward, a retreat the better to advance. But on the whole, I would be inclined to say that, at that point of transition, Islam started to become a smaller tradition; and that, in some respects, sadly, Muhammad 'Abduh is the cause of a smaller, more limited Islam than that which was on offer before, and which remains on offer inside not simply the Sunni scholastic (exegetical) tradition, but also inside those other traditions which the Sunni tradition hauls in its wake – the precious baggage, the inescapable burden, of experience.

6

Intellectual Life among the Ismailis: An Overview

Farhad Daftary

The purpose of this paper is to present an overview of the intellectual activities of the Ismailis during medieval times. A major Shi'i Muslim community, the Ismailis have had a complex and colourful history dating back to the middle of the 8th century. It was at that time that the earliest groups identifiable as Ismailis separated from the rest of the Imami Shi'is. The early Ismailis laid the foundations of intellectual traditions which were further developed during the Fatimid and subsequent periods in Ismaili history. In the Fatimid period (909–1171), when the Ismailis possessed a flourishing state of their own, they elaborated a diversity of intellectual traditions and institutions of learning, making important contributions to Islamic thought and culture.

I shall concentrate here on selected areas of intellectual activity which were of particular importance to the Ismailis of medieval times. Theology, of course, remained the central concern of Ismaili thought; it played a key role in the teachings of the Ismailis not only as *kalam*, articulated by all Muslim communities, but also as a tradition influencing other intellectual activities of this community. This paper will deal briefly with Ismaili activities also in the fields of philosophy, law, historiography, as well as certain distinct traditions and institutions of learning.

The Imami Shi'i tradition, the common heritage of the Ismailis and the Twelvers or Ithna'asharis, was elaborated during the formative period of Shi'ism, lasting until the advent of the Abbasids in 750. This tradition culminated in the central Shi'i doctrine of the imamate, formulated by Imam Ja'far al-Sadiq and the coterie of his associates who included some of the foremost theologians of the time. Henceforth, the doctrine of the imamate served as the central theological teaching of the Imami Shi'is, including the Twelvers and the Ismailis.[1] The earliest Ismailis or Ismaili groups separated from the rest of the Imami Shi'is in 765, on the death of Imam al-Sadiq who had consolidated Imami Shi'ism. These splinter groups, centred in southern Iraq, now acknowledged the claims of al-Sadiq's eldest son Isma'il (hence the designation Isma'iliyya) or the latter's son Muhammad, to the imamate.[2] This is how the Ismailis appeared on the historical stage as an independent Shi'i movement with a particular theology.

In line with their doctrine of the imamate, the earliest Ismailis maintained that the Prophet Muhammad had appointed his cousin and son-in-law 'Ali b. Abi Talib as his successor, and that this designation or *nass* had been instituted by divine command. Like other Imami Shi'is, the early Ismailis held a particular conception of religious authority based on the assumption of the permanent need of mankind for a divinely-guided imam or spiritual leader, an authoritative teacher with a particular kind of knowledge (*'ilm*) not available to ordinary human beings. They maintained that this particular religious authority had been vested in 'Ali and certain of his descendants, the persons recognized by them as imams, all belonging to the Prophet's family or the *ahl al-bayt*. After the Prophet, only 'Ali and the succeeding imams possessed the required *'ilm* and religious authority, which enabled them to act as the sole authoritative channels for elucidating and interpreting the Islamic revelation. These imams were also believed to be divinely guided and immune from error and sin (*ma'sum*) and as such, they were infallible in both their knowledge and teachings after the Prophet.

The earliest Ismailis further held that after 'Ali (d. 661), the imamate was to be transmitted by the rule of *nass* among the

Fatimid 'Alids, the descendants of 'Ali and Fatima, the Prophet's daughter, and after al-Husayn b. 'Ali (d. 680) the imamate would continue in the Husaynid branch of the 'Alids until the end of time. Thus, there would always be in existence a single legitimate imam, designated by the *nass* of the previous imam, whether or not he was actually ruling as caliph. Indeed, the world could not exist for a moment without an imam, who was the proof of God (*hujjat Allah*) on earth. As in the case of *nass*, each imam's special *'ilm*, divinely inspired, was traced back to 'Ali and the Prophet Muhammad. It was on the basis of this *'ilm* that each imam was recognized as the authorized source of religious guidance and interpreter of the true meaning of the Qur'an as well as the commandments and prohibitions of Islam. From early on, Ismaili theology was also closely connected to soteriology; salvation would be reserved on the Day of Judgement only for those with faith in and devotion to the *ahl al-bayt*, and more particularly to 'Ali and the rightful imams after him.[3]

By the middle of the 9th century, a secret and rapidly expanding Ismaili religio-political movement, with revolutionary objectives, had been organized by a line of central leaders, who were in due course acknowledged as 'Alid imams from the progeny of the Shi'i Imam al-Sadiq. This movement, designated by its members simply as *al-da'wa* or *al-da'wa al-hadiya* (the rightly guiding mission), aimed at uprooting the Abbasids (who, like the Umayyads before them, were accused of having usurped the legitimate rights of 'Alids) and installing the Ismaili imam to the leadership of the Muslim *umma*. The revolutionary message of the Ismaili *da'wa* was propagated by a network of *da'is* or missionaries operating secretly in many regions of the Islamic world, from Central Asia to Persia, Iraq, Arabia, Yaman and North Africa. During the early, pre-Fatimid phase of their history, the Ismailis evidently produced only a few doctrinal works, preferring to disseminate their teachings by word of mouth. It is nevertheless possible, on the basis of a variety of pre-Fatimid and later Ismaili texts, as well as certain non-Ismaili writings, to convey the main doctrines of the early Ismailis, who laid the foundations of Ismaili theology and certain other intellectual traditions of their community.[4]

By the 890s, in elaborating their distinctive religious system, the Ismailis emphasized a fundamental distinction between the exoteric (*zahir*) and the esoteric (*batin*) dimensions of the sacred scriptures and the religious commandments and prohibitions. Accordingly, they held that the revealed scriptures, including especially the Qur'an, and the laws laid down in them had their apparent or literal meaning, the *zahir*, which had to be distinguished from their inner meaning or true spiritual reality (*haqiqa*) hidden in the *batin*. They further held that the *zahir*, or the religious laws enunciated by the messenger-prophets, underwent periodic change while the *batin*, containing the spiritual truths (*haqa'iq*), remained immutable and eternal. The hidden truths could be made apparent through *ta'wil*, esoteric exegesis, the process of educing the *batin* from the *zahir*. Similar processes of exegeses or hermeneutics existed in earlier Judaeo-Christian as well as various gnostic traditions, but the immediate antecedents of Ismaili *ta'wil*, also known as *batini ta'wil*, may be traced to the Shi'i milieus of the 8th century in southern Iraq, the cradle of early Shi'ism. The Ismaili *ta'wil* was distinguished from *tanzil*, the actual revelation of scriptures through angelic intermediaries, and from *tafsir*, explanation of the apparent or philological meaning of the sacred texts. In the era of Islam, the Prophet Muhammad had been charged with delivering the Islamic revelation, *tanzil*, while 'Ali was responsible for its *ta'wil*. 'Ali, designated as the *sahib al-ta'wil* or 'master of *ta'wil*,' was thus the repository of the Prophet's undivulged knowledge and the original possessor of Islam's true interpretation after the Prophet, a function retained by the 'Alid imams after 'Ali himself.

The passage from *zahir* to *batin*, from *tanzil* to *ta'wil*, or from *shari'a* to *haqiqa*, thus entailed the passage from the world of appearances to spiritual reality; and the initiation into this world of true reality, guided by 'Ali and his successors to the imamate, was paramount to spiritual rebirth for the Ismailis. Indeed, the Ismailis taught that in every age, the exoteric world of spiritual reality could be accessible only to the elite (*khawass*) of mankind, as distinct from the common people (*'awamm*) who were merely capable of understanding the *zahir*, the apparent meaning of the revelations. In the era of Islam, the eternal truths of religion could be revealed only to those who had been properly initiated into the Ismaili *da'wa* and community and recognized the teaching authority of the Prophet Muhammad's *wasi* or legatee, 'Ali, and the imams who succeeded him in the Husaynid 'Alid line; they alone, collectively designated as the *ahl al-ta'wil* or 'people of *ta'wil*' represented the sources of knowledge and authoritative guidance in the era of Islam. For the Ismailis, these authorized guides were, in fact, the very same people referred to in the Qur'an (3:7) by the expression *al-rasikhun fi'l-'ilm* or 'those possessing firm knowledge'.[5] These teachings explain the special role of the imams after 'Ali and of the religious teaching hierarchy in the *da'wa* organization instituted by the Ismaili imams. They also explain why the bulk of the religious literature of the early Ismailis is comprised of the *ta'wil* genre of writing which seeks justification for Ismaili doctrines in Qur'anic verses. Initiation into Ismailism, known as *balagh*, took place after the adept took an oath of allegiance, known as *'ahd* or *mithaq*. The initiates were bound by this oath to keep secret the *batin* which was imparted to them by a hierarchy (*hudud*) of teachers authorized by the imam. The *batin* was thus both hidden and secret, and its knowledge had to be kept away from the uninitiated common people, the non-Ismaili *'awamm* who had no access to it because they did not acknowledge the rightful guides of their era.[6]

The Ismailis taught that the eternal truths, the *haqa'iq*, hidden in the *batin*, represented the message common to Judaism, Christianity and Islam. However, the truths of these Abrahamic religions had been veiled by different exoteric laws. The early Ismailis developed the implications of these truths in terms of a gnostic system of thought, representing a distinctly Ismaili world-view. The two main components of this system were a cyclical history of revelation and a cosmological doctrine.

By the final decades of the 9th century, the Ismailis had already developed a cyclical interpretation of time and the religious history of mankind in terms of eras of different prophets recognized in the Qur'an, which they applied to the Judaeo-Christian revelations as well as a variety of pre-Islamic religions such as Zoroastrianism and Manichaeism. This cyclical view of revelational history was further combined with their doctrine of the imamate.[7] Accordingly, the early Ismailis believed that the religious history of mankind proceeded through seven prophetic eras (*dawr*s) of various duration, each one inaugurated by a messenger-prophet (*natiq*), of a divinely revealed message, which in its exoteric (*zahir*) aspect contained a religious law (*shari‘a*). The *natiq*s of the first six eras were Adam, Nuh, Ibrahim, Musa, ‘Isa and Muhammad. They had announced the outer aspects of each revelation with its rituals, commandments and prohibitions, fully explaining its inner meaning only to a few close disciples. Each *natiq* was succeeded by a *wasi* or legatee, also called *samit*, ‘the silent one,’ and later *asas* or ‘foundation,’ who expounded only to the elite the esoteric truths (*haqa’iq*) contained in the *batin* dimension of that era’s message. The *wasi* in the era of Islam was ‘Ali b. Abi Talib. The early Ismailis held further that each *wasi* was, in turn, succeeded by seven imams who guarded the true meaning of the divine scriptures and laws in both their *zahir* and *batin* aspects. The seventh imam of every era would rise in rank to become the *natiq* of the following era, abrogating the *shari‘a* of the previous era and proclaiming a new one. This pattern would change in the seventh, final era.

In the sixth *dawr*, the era of Islam, the seventh imam was Muhammad b. Isma‘il b. Ja‘far al-Sadiq who had gone into concealment as the Mahdi, the expected restorer of true Islam and justice in the world. On his return, it was believed, he would not bring a new *shari‘a*; instead, he would initiate the final eschatological age, divulging to all mankind the hitherto concealed esoteric truths of all the preceding revelations. In the messianic age of the Mahdi, an age of pure spiritualism, there would no longer be any distinction between the *zahir* and the *batin*. On his advent, Muhammad b. Isma‘il would rule in justice before the physical world ended. All this also explains the great messianic appeal and popular success of the early Ismaili *da‘wa*. Subsequently, the Ismailis of the Fatimid period developed a different conception of the sixth era, recognizing continuity in the imamate rather than limiting it to a single heptad and removing the expectations connected with the coming of the Mahdi and the final millenarian age indefinitely into the future. On the other hand, the dissident Qarmatis, who separated from the loyal Fatimid Ismailis around the year 899, retained their original belief in the Mahdiship of Muhammad b. Isma‘il and his eschatological role as the seventh *natiq*.[8]

The early Ismailis also elaborated a cosmological doctrine as the second main component of their *haqa'iq* system. This doctrine, based upon a gnostic cosmogonic myth, represented an original gnostic tradition in which cosmology was closely connected to soteriology and a specific view of the sacred history of mankind. In this system, too, man's salvation ultimately depended on his knowledge of God, the creation and his own origins – a knowledge which had been periodically made accessible to man through special messenger-prophets (*natiqs*) whose teachings were guarded and further expounded by their rightful successors.[9]

It was on the basis of such doctrines, rooted in a gnostic and ecumenical world-view, that the Ismailis developed their system of thought; and this system proved appealing not only to Muslims belonging to a diversity of communities of interpretation and social strata, but also to a variety of non-Islamic religious communities.

The success of the early Ismaili *da'wa* was crowned by the establishment of the Fatimid state in 909 in North Africa. The Fatimid period is often depicted as the 'golden age' of Ismailism. The revolutionary movement of the early Ismailis had finally led to the foundation of a state or *dawla* headed by the Ismaili imam, which soon expanded into a flourishing empire which extended from North Africa and Egypt to Palestine, the Hijaz and Syria. This was indeed a great success for the entire Shi'a, who now witnessed for the first time the succession of an 'Alid from the *ahl al-bayt* to the leadership of an important Muslim state. With the Fatimid victory, the Ismaili imam presented his own Shi'i challenge to Abbasid hegemony and Sunni interpretations of Islam. Ismailism, too, now found its place among the state-sponsored communities of interpretation in Islam. Henceforth, the Fatimid caliph, who was at the same time the Ismaili imam, could act as the spiritual spokesman of Shi'i Islam in general, as the Abbasid caliph had been the mouthpiece of Sunni Islam. Under the circumstances, the Ismailis were now permitted, for the first time in their history, to practise their faith openly without fearing persecution within Fatimid dominions, while outside the boundaries of their state they continued to observe *taqiyya*, or precautionary dissimulation, as before.

In line with their universal claims, the Fatimid caliph-imams did not abandon their *da'wa* activities on assuming power. Aiming to extend their authority and rule over the entire Muslim *umma,* they retained their *da'wa* and network of *da'is,* operating both within and outside Fatimid dominions. Special institutions of learning and teaching were also set up for the training of *da'is* and instruction of ordinary Ismailis. Educated as theologians, the *da'is* of the Fatimid period were at the same time the scholars and authors of their community, and they produced the classical texts of Ismaili literature on a variety of exoteric and esoteric subjects, ranging from biographical and historical works to elaborate theological, legal and philosophical treatises, as well as major works on *ta'wil,* a hallmark of Ismailism.[10] Some of these *da'is* elaborated distinctive intellectual traditions, amalgamating different philosophical traditions with Ismaili theology. Indeed, it was during the Fatimid period that Ismaili thought and literature attained their peak and the Ismailis made their seminal contributions to Islamic theology and philosophy in general and to Shi'i thought in particular. Modern recovery of Ismaili literature clearly attests to the richness and diversity of the literary and intellectual heritage of the Ismailis of the Fatimid period. In Egypt, the Fatimids patronized intellectual activities in general. They created major libraries in Cairo, their new capital city founded in 969, which rapidly grew into a centre of Islamic scholarship, sciences, art and culture, in addition to playing a prominent role in international trade and commerce. All in all, the Fatimid period represents one of the greatest eras in Egyptian and Islamic histories, and a milestone in Islamic civilization.[11]

The Fatimid *da'is* produced numerous theological treatises in which the doctrine of the imamate retained its centrality. The *da'i*-authors also dealt with a host of theological issues which had preoccupied other Muslim theologians, ranging from expressing distinctive views on the divine attributes to human salvation and the question of free will versus predestination. Like other Muslim thinkers, some of these *da'is,* especially those operating in the Iranian lands, also elaborated metaphysical systems in which they included a variety of cosmological doctrines.

By the end of the 9th century, much of the intellectual heritage of antiquity had become accessible to Muslims. This had resulted from the great translation movement into Arabic of numerous texts of Greek wisdom. The Muslims now became closely acquainted not only with different branches of Greek sciences, but also with logic and metaphysics. In philosophy, together with the works of the great Greek masters such as Plato and Aristotle, the writings of some of the authors of the so-called Neoplatonic school were also translated into Arabic with commentaries. These Arabic Neoplatonic materials, rooted in the teachings of Plotinus and his disciples but often wrongly attributed to Aristotle, proved to have seminal influences on the development of Islamic philosophy in general and the Ismaili thought of the Fatimid period in particular.

Neoplatonic philosophy proved particularly attractive to the learned *da'i*s of the Iranian lands who, in the course of the 10th century, set about to harmonize Ismaili theology with Neoplatonic doctrines. This led to the development of a unique intellectual tradition of philosophical theology within Ismailism, also designated as philosophical Ismailism. The *da'i*s of the Iranian lands, starting with Muhammad al-Nasafi (d. 943) and Abu Hatim al-Razi (d. 934), wrote for the ruling elite and the educated classes of society, aiming to attract them intellectually to the *da'wa*. This explains why they chose to express their theology in terms of the then most modern and intellectually fashionable philosophical themes, without compromising the essence of their religious message which, as before, revolved around the Shi'i doctrine of the imamate.

The Iranian *da'i*s elaborated complex metaphysical systems of thought with a distinct Neoplatonized emanational cosmology, representing the earliest tradition of philosophical theology in Shi'ism. It should be added that these *da'i*s also became involved in a long-drawn debate on various theological and metaphysical issues. At any rate, the success of the Iranian *da'i*s is attested by the fact that a number of rulers in Central Asia, Khurasan and northern Persia, including a Samanid *amir*, converted to Ismailism.

The early evidence of the tradition of philosophical theology in Ismailism is mainly preserved in the works of Abu Ya'qub al-Sijistani,[12] the *da'i* of eastern Persia and Transoxania who was executed as a 'heretic' on the order of the Saffarid ruler of Sistan, Khalaf b. Ahmad (963–1003). In the Neoplatonized Ismaili cosmology, God is conceived as absolutely transcendent, beyond human comprehension, beyond any name or attribute, beyond being and non-being, and hence essentially unknowable. This conception of God, reminiscent of the ineffable One of Greek Neoplatonism, was in close agreement with the fundamental Islamic principle of *tawhid*, the affirmation of the absolute unity of God. Through a dialectic of double negation, al-Sijistani refuted both *tashbih*, anthropomorphism, and *ta'til*, rejection of any particular divine attribute. Al-Sijistani and other Iranian *da'i*s also identified certain basic concepts of their emanational cosmology with Qur'anic terms. Thus, universal intellect (*'aql*) and universal soul (*nafs*), the first and second originated beings in the spiritual world, were identified with the Qur'anic notions of the 'pen' (*qalam*) and the 'tablet' (*lawh*), respectively.

The Ismaili theologian-philosophers of the Iranian world also propounded a doctrine of salvation as part of their cosmology. In their soteriological vision of the cosmos, man generally appears as a microcosm with individual human souls as parts of the universal soul. In the case of al-Sijistani, for instance, his doctrine of salvation, elaborated in purely spiritual terms, is closely related to his doctrine of soul and the Ismaili cyclical view of religious history of mankind. Here, the ultimate goal of human salvation is the soul's progression out of a purely physical existence towards its creator, in quest of a spiritual reward in an eternal afterlife. This ascending quest along a ladder of salvation, or *sullam al-najat* (chosen as the title of one of al-Sijistani's books), involves purification of man's soul, which depends on guidance provided by the terrestrial hierarchy of teachers; only the authorized members of this hierarchy are in a position to reveal the 'right path' along which the true believers are guided and whose resurrected souls will be rewarded spiritually on the Day of Judgement. In every era of human history, the terrestrial hierarchy consists of the law-announcing speaker-prophet (*natiq*) of that era and his rightful successors. In the current era of Islam, the guidance needed for knowing the truth and attaining salvation is provided by the Prophet Muhammad, his *wasi* 'Ali, and the Ismaili imams in 'Ali's progeny. In other words, man's salvation depends on his acquisition of a particular type of knowledge from a unique source or wellspring of wisdom. The required knowledge can be imparted only through the teachings of these divinely authorized guides, the sole possessors of the true meaning of the revelation who can provide its authoritative interpretation through *ta'wil*.

It is, thus, important to bear in mind that the proponents of philosophical Ismailism used philosophy (*falsafa*) in a subservient manner to their theology (*kalam*), resorting to sophisticated philosophical themes primarily to enhance the intellectual appeal of their message. Classical Ismaili theology, indeed, remained on the whole revelational rather than rational, despite the efforts of the Iranian *da'is* to amalgamate Islamic revelation and its Ismaili interpretation with reason and free enquiry. In sum, these *da'is* remained devout theologians propagating the doctrine of the imamate. The Neoplatonized Ismaili cosmology, developed in the Iranian lands, was endorsed by the central headquarters of the Ismaili *da'wa* in North Africa in the time of the Fatimid caliph-imam al-Mu'izz (953–975), replacing the earlier mythological cosmology of the Ismailis. As a result, the new cosmology was advocated by Fatimid *da'i*-authors at least until the time of Nasir Khusraw (d. after 1072), the last major proponent of philosophical Ismailism and the only Fatimid *da'i* to have written all his works in Persian.

Hamid al-Din al-Kirmani, perhaps the most learned theologian-philosopher of the Fatimid period and the chief *da'i* of Iraq and western Persia, developed his own metaphysics in the *Rahat al-'aql*, his major philosophical treatise completed in 1020.[13] Al-Kirmani's cosmology was partially based on al-Farabi's Aristotelian system of ten separate intellects. His system, too, representing a unique tradition within the Iranian school of philosophical Ismailism, culminates in a soteriological doctrine centred around the salvation of man's soul through the attainment of spiritual knowledge provided by the authoritative guidance of prophets and their legitimate successors. As in the case of his predecessors, in al-Kirmani's metaphysics there also exists numerous correspondences between the celestial and terrestrial hierarchies. For unknown reasons, however, al-Kirmani's cosmology did not prevail in the Fatimid *da'wa*, but it later provided the basis for the cosmological doctrine expounded by the Musta'li Tayyibi *da'wa* in Yaman. It may also be noted that al-Kirmani acted as an arbiter in the debate that had taken place among the *da'is* al-Nasafi, al-Razi and al-Sijistani; he reviewed this debate from the perspective of the Fatimid *da'wa* and sided with al-Razi against certain antinomian views expressed by al-Nasafi.[14] All this once again attests to the diversity of traditions espoused by the *da'i*s and the relative freedom they enjoyed in their intellectual enquiries within the compass of Ismaili Shi'ism.

Despite his central role as the representative of the Ismaili *da'wa*, very little seems to have been written by Ismaili authors on the subject of the *da'i*, who often acted as both a missionary and a teacher. The *da'i*s, appointed only by the imam's permission, enjoyed a high degree of autonomy in the regions under their jurisdiction. As a result, only persons of high educational qualifications combined with the required intellectual and moral attributes, and organizational abilities, could aspire to that position. The *da'i*s had to have sufficient knowledge of both the *zahir* and the *batin*, or the *shari'a* and its esoteric interpretation. Outside of Fatimid dominions, the *da'i*s often also acted as judges for the Ismailis of their community, and as such they were trained in jurisprudence, in addition to being knowledgeable in *hadith* and other religious sciences, as well as the languages and cultures of the regions in which they operated. As a result, the Fatimids paid much attention to the training of the *da'i*s and founded a variety of institutions for that purpose.

The high esteem of the Ismailis for learning resulted in a number of distinctive traditions and institutions in the Fatimid period. The Ismaili *da'wa* was concerned from early on with educating the converts and teaching them the *hikma* or 'wisdom', referring to Ismaili esoteric doctrines. Consequently, a variety of lectures or 'teaching sessions,' generally designated as *majalis* were organized. These sessions, which gradually became more formalized and specialized, served different pedagogical purposes and were addressed to different audiences, especially in the Fatimid capital. However, there were basically two types of teaching sessions, namely, public lectures for large audiences on Ismaili law and other exoteric subjects, and private lectures on Ismaili esoteric doctrines known as the *majalis al-hikma* or 'sessions of wisdom', reserved exclusively for the benefit of the Ismaili initiates.[15] To control admission to the *majalis al-hikma*, they were held at the Fatimid palace. The lectures, delivered by the *da'i al-du'at*, the chief *da'i* acting as the administrative head of the *da'wa* organization, were normally approved beforehand by the Ismaili imam. Only the imam was the source of *hikma*, with the *da'i* acting merely as his representative through whom the initiates received their instruction in Ismaili esoteric doctrines. Some of these lectures, culminating in the *majalis* of al-Mu'ayyad fi'l-Din al-Shirazi who held the office of *da'i al-du'at* for twenty years until shortly before his death in 1078, were in due course collected in writing.[16] The *majalis* gradually developed into an elaborate programme of instruction for different audiences, including women. Another of the major institutions of learning founded by the Fatimids was the Dar al-'Ilm, the House of Knowledge, sometimes also called the Dar al-Hikma. Established in 1005 by the Fatimid caliph-imam al-Hakim (996–1021) in a section of the Fatimid palace in Cairo, a multitude of religious and non-religious sciences were taught at the Dar al-'Ilm which was also equipped with a major library. Many Fatimid *da'is* received at least part of their training at this institution which variously served the Ismaili *da'wa*.[17] Religious scholars, jurists, scientists and librarians worked at the Dar al-'Ilm, drawing salaries from the Fatimid treasury or that institution's endowment set up by al-Hakim himself.

The Sunni polemicists, supported by the Abbasids, intensified their anti-Ismaili campaign after the establishment of the Fatimid state. Amongst various defamations, they claimed that the Ismailis did not observe the *shari'a* because they had found access to its hidden meaning in the *batin*; hence they also referred to the Isma'iliyya, often pejoratively, as the Batiniyya or 'esotericists' in addition to *malahida* or 'heretics'. It is a fact that the Fatimids from early on concerned themselves with legalistic matters, and Ismaili literature of the Fatimid period persistently underlines the inseparability of the *zahir* and the *batin*, of observing the *shari'a* as well as understanding its inner, spiritual significance. At the time of the advent of the Fatimids, there did not yet exist a distinctly Ismaili school of jurisprudence. Until then, the Ismailis belonged to a secret revolutionary movement and observed the law of the land wherever they lived. It was on the establishment of the Fatimid state that the need arose for codifying Ismaili law; and the process started by putting into practice the precepts of Shi'i law.

The promulgation of an Ismaili *madhhab* or school of jurisprudence resulted mainly from the efforts of al-Qadi Abu Hanifa al-Nu'man b. Muhammad (d. 974), the most learned jurist of the entire Fatimid period. He codified Ismaili law by systematically collecting the firmly established *hadith*s transmitted from the *ahl al-bayt*, drawing on al-Kulayni and other earlier Shi'i as well as Sunni authorities.[18] After producing several legal compendia, his efforts culminated in the compilation of the *Da'a'im al-Islam* (The Pillars of Islam), which served as the official legal code of the Fatimid state. The Ismailis, too, had now come to possess a system of law and jurisprudence, also delineating an Ismaili paradigm of governance. As developed by al-Qadi al-Nu'man, under the close scrutiny of the Fatimid caliph-imam al-Mu'izz, Ismaili law accorded central importance to the doctrine of the imamate, which also provided Islamic legitimation for an 'Alid state ruled by the *ahl al-bayt*. The authority of the 'Alid imam and his teachings became the third principal source of Ismaili law, after the Qur'an and the *sunna* of the Prophet which are accepted as the first two sources by all Muslim communities. Al-Qadi al-Nu'man was also the founder of a distinguished family of chief judges (*qadi al-qudat*) in the Fatimid state. It may be noted that the *Da'a'im al-Islam* has continued to be used by Musta'li Tayyibi Ismailis as their principal authority in legal matters.

The legal doctrines of the Ismaili *madhhab* were applied by the judiciary throughout the Fatimid dominions. However, the Ismaili legal code was new and its precepts had to be explained to Ismailis as well as other Muslim subjects of the Fatimid state. This was accomplished in regular public sessions, originally held by al-Qadi al-Nu'man himself, on Fridays after the midday prayers. In Cairo, public sessions on Ismaili law were held at the great mosques of al-Azhar, 'Amr and al-Hakim. The credit for using al-Azhar, founded as a mosque by al-Mu'izz, as a teaching centre on law from 988 onwards, belongs to Ibn Killis (d. 991), the first official vizier of the Fatimids who was also an accomplished jurist and patron of the arts and sciences.

The Ismailis were often persecuted outside the territories of their states, which necessitated the strict observance of *taqiyya* or precautionary dissimulation. Furthermore, the Ismaili *da'i*-authors, as noted, were for the most part trained as theologians who frequently served the *da'wa* in hostile milieus. Owing to their training as well as the necessity of observing secrecy in their activities, the *da'i*-authors were not particularly interested in compiling annalistic or other types of historical accounts. The general lack of Ismaili interest in historiography is attested to by the fact that only a few historical works have come to light in the modern recovery of a large number of Ismaili texts. These include al-Qadi al-Nu'man's *Iftitah al-da'wa* (Commencement of the Mission), the earliest known historical work in Ismaili literature which covers the background to the establishment of the Fatimid caliphate. In later medieval times, only one general history of Ismailism was produced by an Ismaili author, namely, the *'Uyun al-akhbar* (Choice Stories) of Idris 'Imad al-Din (d. 1468), the nineteenth Musta'li Tayyibi *da'i* in Yaman. Aside from strictly historical writings, the Ismailis of the Fatimid period also produced a few biographical works of the *sira* genre with important historical details.

There were, however, two periods in Ismaili history during which Ismaili leaders concerned themselves with historiography, and they encouraged or commissioned works which may be regarded as official chronicles. On the two occasions when the Ismailis possessed their own states and dynasties of rulers, the Fatimid caliphate and the Nizari state, they needed reliable chroniclers to record the events and political achievements of their states.[19] In Fatimid times, especially after the transference of the seat of the Fatimid state from Ifriqiya to Egypt in 973, numerous histories of the Fatimid state and dynasty were compiled by contemporary historians, both Ismaili and non-Ismaili. With the exception of a few fragments, however, the Fatimid chronicles have not survived. When the Ayyubids succeeded the Fatimids in Egypt in 1171, they destroyed the renowned Fatimid libraries. All types of Ismaili literature as well as the Fatimid chronicles perished as a result of Ayyubid persecutions of the Ismailis.

By 1094, the unified Ismaili *da'wa* and community of the Fatimid times were split into rival Musta'li and Nizari branches. The schism resulted from the dispute over the succession to the Fatimid caliph-imam al-Mustansir (1036–1094). The Musta'li Ismailis, who became further subdivided into a number of groups, eventually found their stronghold in Yaman. The Tayyibis, representing the only surviving Musta'li community, have been led by hereditary lines of *da'is*, who retained a number of Fatimid traditions of learning. The Tayyibis of Yaman and India, where they are known as Bohras, have also preserved a good share of the

Ismaili literature of the Fatimid period.

The Nizari Ismailis have had a different destiny. By 1094, the Ismailis of Persia were already under the leadership of Hasan Sabbah (d. 1124), who in the Nizari–Musta'li dispute upheld the rights of Nizar (d. 1095), al-Mustansir's original heir-designate who had been deprived of his succession rights. Hasan Sabbah, in fact, founded the independent Nizari state and *da'wa* centred at the mountain fortress of Alamut in northern Persia.[20] In due course, the Nizaris also established a subsidiary state in Syria. Hasan launched an open revolt from a network of mountain fortresses against the Saljuq Turks, whose alien rule was detested in Persia. The Nizaris remained preoccupied with their revolutionary campaign and survival in a hostile environment during the reigns of Hasan's successors at Alamut. As a result, the Persian Nizari community did not produce many learned scholars concerned with complex theological issues or metaphysics comparable to those living in Fatimid times. Instead, they possessed capable commanders suited to the nature of the Nizari struggle against the superior military power of the Saljuqs and other enemies. Furthermore, Hasan Sabbah, as an expression of his Persian sentiments, adopted Persian rather than Arabic as the religious language of the Persian Nizaris. Consequently, the Nizaris of Persia were in a sense cut off from the Ismaili literature of the Fatimid period, although some of these earlier works were accessible to the Nizaris of Syria who used Arabic. Nevertheless, the Nizaris did maintain a literary tradition and certain theological issues continued to provide the focus of the Nizari thought of the Alamut period.

Hasan Sabbah himself was a learned theologian grounded in philosophical thought; he is also credited with establishing an impressive library at Alamut soon after he set up his headquarters in that stronghold in 1090. Later, other major Nizari fortresses in Persia and Syria were equipped with significant collections of books, documents and scientific instruments. In the doctrinal field, the Nizaris from early on reaffirmed as their central teaching the doctrine of the imamate, or the necessity of authoritative teaching by the rightful imam of the time. Under the circumstances, the outsiders acquired the impression that the Nizari Ismailis had initiated a 'new preaching' (*al-da'wa al-jadida*) in contrast to the 'old preaching' (*al-da'wa al-qadima*) of the Fatimid times. The 'new preaching' did not actually represent any new doctrine however; it was essentially a reformulation of the old Shi'i doctrine of the imamate. It now became commonly known as the doctrine of *ta'lim* or authoritative teaching by the imam.

Hasan Sabbah restated the doctrine of *ta'lim* in a more rigorous form in a theological treatise which has not survived, but it has been quoted or fragmentarily preserved in other sources.[21] In a series of four propositions, Hasan restated the inadequacy of reason in knowing God and understanding the religious truths, arguing for the necessity of an authoritative teacher (*mu'allim-i sadiq*) for the spiritual guidance of mankind, and he concluded that this trustworthy teacher is none other than the Ismaili imam of the time. The doctrine of *ta'lim* served as the central teaching of the Nizaris, who henceforth were designated by outsiders as the Ta'limiyya. The intellectual challenge posed to the Sunni establishment by this doctrine, which also refuted the legitimacy of the Abbasid caliph as the spiritual spokesman of Muslims, called forth a new polemical campaign against the Ismailis. Many Sunni theologians, led by al-Ghazali (d. 1111), attacked the Ismailis and their doctrine of *ta'lim*; a detailed reply to al-Ghazali's anti-Ismaili polemics was later provided by the fifth Tayyibi *da'i* in Yaman.[22] The doctrine of *ta'lim*, emphasizing the autonomous teaching authority of each imam in his time, provided the theological foundation for all the subsequent Nizari teachings.[23]

The intellectual life of the Nizaris of the Alamut period culminated in the declaration of the *qiyama* or resurrection in 1164 by the fourth lord of Alamut, Hasan, whose name was always mentioned by the Nizaris with the expression *'ala dhikrihi'l-salam* or 'on his mention be peace,' and with whom the line of Nizari Ismaili imams emerged openly. However, relying on *ta'wil* and earlier Ismaili traditions, the *qiyama* or the long-awaited Last Day when mankind would be judged and committed eternally to either Paradise or Hell, was interpreted symbolically and spiritually for the Nizaris. The *qiyama* now meant nothing more than the manifestation of unveiled truth or *haqiqa* in the person of the Nizari imam. In other words, this was a spiritual resurrection reserved exclusively for those who acknowledged the rightful imam of the time and as such were capable of understanding the esoteric truths of religion. In this sense, Paradise was actualized in the corporeal world for the Nizaris. The Nizaris were now to rise to a spiritual level of existence, moving along a spiritual path from *zahir* to *batin*, from *shari'a* to *haqiqa*, or from the literal interpretation of the law to an understanding of its inner essence. On the other hand, those who did not recognize the Nizari imam and were thus incapable of apprehending the truth were rendered spiritually non-existent. Now the imam initiating the *qiyama* would be the *qa'im al-qiyama* or 'lord of the resurrection', a rank higher than that of an ordinary imam. The declaration of the *qiyama*, which was later elaborated in terms of a theological doctrine, represents the most controversial episode in the entire Nizari history; and modern scholars disagree among themselves on aspects of this event and its implications for the contemporary Nizari community. Be that as it may, the *qiyama* initiated a new spiritual and esoteric era in the life of the Nizari community. In a sense, this was the culmination of the Ismaili interpretation of Islam and the sacred history of mankind.[24]

The Nizaris also extended their patronage of learning to outside scholars, including Sunnis, Twelver Shi'is and even non-Muslims. A large number of such scholars found refuge in Nizari strongholds, especially in the wake of the Mongol invasions of Central Asia in the 1220s. These scholars availed themselves of the Nizari libraries and patronage of learning. The intellectual life of the Nizari community received a special impetus from the continuing influx of outside scholars during the final decades of the Alamut period. Foremost among such scholars was Nasir al-Din al-Tusi (d. 1274), who spent some three decades in the Nizari fortress communities of Persia until the Mongol destruction of the Persian Nizari state in 1256. A renowned theologian, philosopher and astronomer, al-Tusi made important contributions to the Nizari thought of the late Alamut period. Whilst in the Nizari fortresses, al-Tusi wrote his great works on ethics, notably the *Akhlaq-i Nasiri* (The Nasirean Ethics) dedicated to his original Ismaili patron Nasir al-Din 'Abd al-Rahim (d. 1257), and numerous other treatises on a multitude of subjects. The *Rawdat al-taslim* (Meadow of Submission), his major Ismaili work, as well as the *Sayr wa suluk*, his spiritual autobiography in which al-Tusi explains how he came to acknowledge the teaching authority of the Nizari imam, also date to that prolific period in his life. It is, indeed, primarily through al-Tusi's extant Ismaili works that Marshall G.S. Hodgson (1922–1968) and other modern scholars have studied the Nizari Ismaili thought as it developed during the *qiyama* and later Alamut period.[25]

The Nizari Ismailis of the Alamut period (1090–1256), too, developed a historiographical tradition and compiled chronicles recording the events of the Persian Nizari state according to the reigns of the successive rulers of Alamut. This tradition commenced with a work entitled *Sargudhasht-i Sayyidna* (Biography of our Master), covering the career of the founder of the Nizari state, Hasan Sabbah, and the major events of his reign (1090–1124). All these official chronicles, preserved at Alamut and other Nizari strongholds in Persia, perished in the Mongol invasions of 1256 or soon afterwards. But the Nizari chronicles and other writings were seen and used extensively by a group of Persian historians of the Ilkhanid period, notably Juwayni (d. 1283), Rashid al-Din Fadl Allah (d. 1318) and Abu'l-Qasim Kashani (d. ca. 1335), who remain our main sources for the history of the Nizari Ismaili state in Persia.

In the aftermath of the destruction of their state and fortresses by the Mongols in 1256, the disorganized Persian Nizaris survived clandestinely in scattered communities. The Nizaris now began to practise *taqiyya* for extended periods, adopting different Sunni, Sufi and Twelver guises to safeguard themselves against persecution. However, the Nizaris' total disintegration or complete assimilation into the religiously dominant communities of their surroundings was largely prevented by their religious traditions and identity revolving around the Nizari imamate. By the middle of the 15th century, when the Nizari imams emerged in Anjudan, in central Persia, initiating a revival in Nizari *da'wa* and literary activities, a type of coalescence had occurred in Persia and adjacent regions between Nizari Ismailism and Sufism, two independent esoteric traditions in Islam which share close affinities and common doctrinal grounds. During the Anjudan revival, lasting some two centuries until the end of the 17th century, the Nizari *da'wa* met with particular success in Central Asia and India. In Sind, Gujarat and other parts of the Indian subcontinent, the Hindu converts to Ismailism were generally designated as Khojas, while the specific form of Ismailism that developed in India became known as Satpanth or True Path.

In the post-Alamut period, different Nizari communities developed, more or less, independently of one another. However, four different literary traditions may be traced to the Anjudan period, when Nizari intellectual activities were somewhat revived and doctrinal works were once again composed by a few authors.[26] In the writings of authors such as Abu Ishaq Quhistani (fl. in the 15th century) and Khayrkhwah-i Harati (d. after 1553), we have examples of the Persian Nizari tradition permeated with Sufi ideas and terminologies such as *pir* and *murid*, terms referring to a Sufi master and his disciple. Nizari Quhistani (d. 1320), a poet who hailed from Quhistan in eastern Persia, may have been the first post-Alamut author to have chosen the poetic and Sufi forms of expression, partly as a form of *taqiyya* for concealing Ismaili ideas. The Nizari tradition that developed in Central Asia, particularly in Badakhshan, bore close affinity to the Persian tradition in using the Persian language as well as Sufi ideas. However, in the Central Asian tradition, the authentic and spurious works of Nasir Khusraw occupy a prominent role. Nasir Khusraw is indeed highly revered as the founder of their communities by the Nizaris of Badakhshan (now divided by the Oxus between Tajikistan and Afghanistan) and adjacent regions in Hunza and other areas of northern Pakistan. Central Asian Nizaris have also preserved the bulk of the extant Persian Nizari literature produced during the Alamut and later times. The Syrian Nizaris elaborated yet another literary tradition, based on Arabic, in which certain popular local Shi'i ideas as well as aspects of Fatimid Ismaili thought find expression.

The Nizari Khojas of the Indian subcontinent developed their own distinctive tradition, the Satpanth, as expressed in their indigenous religious literature, the *ginans*.[27] Composed in a number of South Asian languages, the hymn-like *ginans* were transmitted orally for several centuries before they were recorded mainly in the Khojki script developed in Sind by the Khoja community. Modern scholars of Satpanth have generally attributed the Muslim-Hindu interfacing of this Ismaili tradition to the preaching strategy of the *da'is*, generally known in India as *pirs*, who evidently designed Hindu-oriented conversion policies to maximize the appeal of their message. Consequently, they integrated their

Ismaili teachings with myths, images and symbols familiar to Hindu audiences. The doctrine of the imamate, too, found expression in a Hindu mythological framework.

The Ismailis emerged as an Imami Shi'i community, with the doctrine of the imamate as their central teaching. And this doctrine has constituted the foundation of the various intellectual and literary traditions elaborated by the Ismailis throughout their turbulent history in medieval times. Indeed, the Ismaili identity has continued to revolve around the devotion to the rightful imam of the time, the present or *hazir* imam of the Ismailis. It is their unwavering devotion to the institution of the imamate, as well as the rich intellectual, spiritual and cultural heritage of the Ismailis, that has enabled them to survive in many countries of Africa, Asia, the Middle East and the West as a united and cohesive religious community in spite of the vicissitudes of their history.

NOTES

1. See Abu Ja'far Muhammad b. Ya'qub al-Kulayni, *al-Usul min al-kafi*, ed. 'A.A. al-Ghaffari (Tehran, 1388/1968), vol. 1, pp. 168–548; al-Qadi al-Nu'man, *Da'a'im al-Islam*, ed. A.A.A. Fyzee (Cairo, 1951–61), vol. 1, pp. 1–98; partial English trans., *The Book of Faith*, tr. A.A.A. Fyzee (Bombay, 1974), pp. 1–111.

2. Al-Hasan b. Musa al-Nawbakhti, *Kitab firaq al-Shi'a*, ed. H. Ritter (Istanbul, 1931), pp. 57–8, 60–4; Sa'd b. 'Abd Allah al-Qummi, *Kitab al-maqalat wa'l-firaq*, ed. M.J. Mashkur (Tehran, 1963), pp. 80–1, 83–6, and F. Daftary, 'The Earliest Isma'ilis,' *Arabica*, 38 (1991), pp. 214–45.

3. See, for instance, al-Qadi al-Nu'man, *Sharh al-akhbar*, ed. S.M. al-Husayni al-Jalali (Qumm, 1409–12/1988–92), vol. 1, pp. 87–250.

4. For further details on early Ismaili *da'wa*, see W. Madelung, 'Das Imamat in der frühen ismailitischen Lehre,' *Der Islam*, 37 (1961), especially pp. 43–86, and F. Daftary, *The Isma'ilis: Their History and Doctrines* (Cambridge, 1990), pp. 91–143.

5. See al-Mu'ayyad fi'l-Din al-Shirazi, *al-Majalis al-Mu'ayyadiyya*, ed. M. Ghalib (Beirut, 1974–84), vol. 1, pp. 347–51.

6. Valuable details on this process of gradual initiation are related in the *Kitab al-'alim wa'l-ghulam*, in M. Ghalib, ed., *Arba' kutub haqqaniyya* (Beirut, 1983), pp. 13–75. See also H. Corbin, 'Un Ro-

man initiatique Ismaélien,' *Cahiers de Civilisation Médiévale*, 15 (1972), pp. 1–25, 121–42, and his 'L'Initiation Ismaélienne ou l'ésotérisme et le Verbe,' *Eranos Jahrbuch*, 39 (1970), pp. 41–142, reprinted in his *L'Homme et son ange* (Paris, 1983), pp. 81–205.

7. Ibn Hawshab Mansur al-Yaman, *Kitab al-rushd wa'l-hidaya*, ed. M. Kamil Husayn, in W. Ivanow, ed., *Collectanea* (Leiden, 1948), pp. 185–213; Ja'far b. Mansur al-Yaman, *Kitab al-kashf*, ed. R. Strothmann (London, etc., 1952), pp. 14ff., 50, 97, 104, 109–10, 113–14, 132–33, 138, 143, 169–70; Abu Ya'qub al-Sijistani, *Ithbat al-nubuwwa*, ed. 'A. Tamir (Beirut, 1968), pp. 181–93; al-Qadi al-Nu'man, *Asas al-ta'wil*, ed. 'A. Tamir (Beirut, 1960), pp. 315–67. See also H. Corbin, *Cyclical Time and Ismaili Gnosis*, tr. R. Manheim and J.W. Morris (London, 1983), pp. 1–58; P.E. Walker, 'Eternal Cosmos and the Womb of History: Time in Early Ismaili Thought,' *International Journal of Middle East Studies*, 9 (1978), pp. 355–66, and Daftary, 'Dawr,' *Encyclopaedia Iranica*, vol. 7, pp. 151–3.

8. On the Ismaili–Qarmati schism, see W. Madelung, 'The Fatimids and the Qarmatis of Bahrayn,' in F. Daftary, ed., *Mediaeval Isma'ili History and Thought* (Cambridge, 1996), pp. 21–73, and F. Daftary, 'A Major Schism in the Early Isma'ili Movement,' *Studia Islamica*, 77 (1993), pp. 123–39.

9. See S.M. Stern, 'The Earliest Cosmological Doctrines of Isma'ilism,' in his *Studies in Early Isma'ilism* (Jerusalem and Leiden, 1983), pp. 3–29; H. Halm, *Kosmologie und Heilslehre der frühen Isma'iliya* (Wiesbaden, 1978), pp. 18–127, and his 'The Cosmology of the Pre-Fatimid Isma'iliyya,' in Daftary, ed., *Mediaeval Isma'ili History*, pp. 75–83.

10. See I.K. Poonawala, *Biobibliography of Isma'ili Literature* (Malibu, Calif., 1977), especially pp. 31–132.

11. See Daftary, *The Isma'ilis*, pp. 144–255, 615–54, where full references are given; H. Halm, *The Empire of the Mahdi: The Rise of the Fatimids*, tr. M. Bonner (Leiden, 1996), pp. 121–274, and A. Fu'ad Sayyid, *al-Dawla al-Fatimiyya fi Misr* (Cairo, 1992).

12. In particular, see his *Kitab al-yanabi'*, ed. and French tr. H. Corbin, in his *Trilogie Ismaélienne* (Tehran and Paris, 1961), text pp. 1–97, translation pp. 5–127; English trans. in P.E. Walker's *The Wellsprings of Wisdom: A Study of Abu Ya'qub al-Sijistani's Kitab al-Yanabi'* (Salt Lake City, 1994), pp. 37–111. See also P.E. Walker, *Early Philosophical Shiism: The Ismaili Neoplatonism of Abu Ya'qub al-Sijistani* (Cambridge, 1993), pp. 67–142; his *Abu Ya'qub al-Sijistani: Intellectual*

Missionary (London, 1996), pp. 26–103, and W. Madelung, 'Aspects of Isma'ili Theology: The Prophetic Chain and the God Beyond Being,' in S.H. Nasr, ed., *Isma'ili Contributions to Islamic Culture* (Tehran, 1977), pp. 53–65, reprinted in his *Religious Schools and Sects in Medieval Islam* (London, 1985), article XVII.

13. Hamid al-Din al-Kirmani, *Rahat al-'aql*, ed. M. Kamil Husayn and M. Mustafa Hilmi (Cairo, 1953); ed. M. Ghalib (Beirut, 1967). See also D. de Smet, *La Quiétude d'intellect: Néoplatonisme et gnose Ismaélienne dans l'oeuvre de Ḥamîd ad-Dîn al-Kirmânî (Xe/XIe s.)* (Louvain, 1995), and P.E. Walker, *Hamid al-Din al-Kirmani: Ismaili Thought in the Age of al-Hakim* (London, 1999).

14. See al-Kirmani, *Kitab al-riyad*, ed. 'Arif Tamir (Beirut, 1960), and Madelung, 'Das Imamat,' pp. 101–14.

15. Taqi al-Din Ahmad al-Maqrizi, *Kitab al-mawa'iz wa'l-i'tibar fi dhikr al-khitat wa'l-athar*, ed. A. Fu'ad Sayyid (London, 1995), pp. 91–4; H. Halm, 'The Isma'ili Oath of Allegiance (*'ahd*) and the 'Sessions of Wisdom' (*majalis al-hikma*) in Fatimid Times,' in Daftary, ed., *Mediaeval Isma'ili History*, pp. 91–115, and his *The Fatimids and their Traditions of Learning* (London, 1997), especially pp. 23–9, 41–55.

16. See, for instance, al-Qadi al-Nu'man, *Ta'wil al-da'a'im*, ed. M.H. al-A'zami (Cairo, 1967–72), which is the *batini* companion to his *zahiri* legal compendium, the *Da'a'im al-Islam*; Abu'l-Qasim b. Wahb al-Maliji, *al-Majalis al-Mustansiriyya*, ed. M. Kamil Husayn (Cairo, 1947), and al-Mu'ayyad fi'l-Din al-Shirazi, *al-Majalis al-Mu'ayyadiyya*, vols 1 and 3; the remaining *majalis* contained in vols. 4–8 are still in manuscript form.

17. Al-Maqrizi, *al-Khitat*, pp. 300–4, and Halm, *The Fatimids*, pp. 71–7.

18. W. Madelung, 'The Sources of Isma'ili Law,' *Journal of Near Eastern Studies*, 35 (1976), pp. 29–40, reprinted in his *Religious Schools*, article XVIII, and I.K. Poonawala, 'Al-Qadi al-Nu'man and Isma'ili Jurisprudence,' in Daftary, ed., *Mediaeval Isma'ili History*, pp. 117–43.

19. See C.H. Becker, *Beiträge zur Geschichte Ägyptens unter dem Islam* (Strassburg, 1902–3), vol. 1, pp. 1–31; C. Cahen, 'Quelques chroniques anciennes relatives aux derniers Fatimides,' *Bulletin de l'Institut Français d'Archéologie Orientale*, 37 (1937–38), pp. 1–27; M. Kamil Husayn, *Fi adab Misr al-Fatimiyya* (Cairo, 1950), pp. 108ff.; A. Fu'ad Sayyid, 'Lumières nouvelles sur quelques sources de l'histoire Fatimide en Égypte,' *Annales Islamologiques*, 13 (1977), pp. 1–41, and F. Daftary, 'Persian Historiography of the Early Nizari Isma'ilis,' *Iran*,

Journal of the British Institute of Persian Studies, 30 (1992), pp. 91–7.

20. F. Daftary, 'Hasan-i Sabbah and the Origins of the Nizari Isma'ili Movement,' in his *Mediaeval Isma'ili History*, pp. 181–204.

21. See, for instance, 'Ata-Malik Juwayni, *Ta'rikh-i jahan-gusha*, ed., M. Qazwini (Leiden and London, 1912–37), vol. 3, pp. 195–9; English trans., *The History of the World-Conqueror*, tr. J. A. Boyle (Manchester, 1958), vol. 2, pp. 671–73, and Abu'l-Fath Muhammad b. 'Abd al-Karim al-Shahrastani, *Kitab al-milal wa'l-nihal*, ed. W. Cureton (London, 1842–46), pp. 150–2; partial English trans., *Muslim Sects and Divisions*, tr. A.K. Kazi and J.G. Flynn (London, 1984), pp. 167–70.

22. See Abu Hamid Muhammad al-Ghazali, *Fada'ih al-Batiniyya*, ed. 'A. Badawi (Cairo, 1964), and the Ismaili reply of 'Ali b. Muhammad b. al-Walid, *Damigh al-batil*, ed. M. Ghalib (Beirut, 1982), 2 vols. See also H. Corbin, 'The Isma'ili Response to the Polemic of Ghazali,' in Nasr, ed., *Isma'ili Contributions*, pp. 69–98.

23. For the history and doctrines of the Nizaris of the Alamut period, see Marshall G.S. Hodgson, *The Order of Assassins* (The Hague, 1955), especially pp. 41–61, 121–39, 160–246, and Daftary, *The Isma'ilis*, pp. 324–434.

24. On the doctrine of the *qiyama*, see *Haft bab-i Baba Sayyidna*, ed. W. Ivanow, in his *Two Early Ismaili Treatises* (Bombay, 1933), pp. 4–44; English trans. in Hodgson, *Order of Assassins*, pp. 279–324. See also Juwayni, *Ta'rikh*, vol. 3, pp. 222–39, tr. Boyle, vol. 2, pp. 686–97; Hodgson, *Order of Assassins*, pp. 146–59; Daftary, *The Isma'ilis*, pp. 385–91, and Ch. Jambet, *La Grande résurrection d'Alamût* (Lagrasse, 1990).

25. Nasir al-Din al-Tusi, *Rawdat al-taslim*, ed. and tr. W. Ivanow (Leiden, 1950); French trans., *La Convocation d'Alamût*, tr. Ch. Jambet (Lagrasse, 1996), and al-Tusi's *Sayr wa suluk*, ed. and tr. S.J. Badakhchani as *Contemplation and Action* (London, 1998). See also H. Dabashi, 'The Philosopher/Vizier: Khwaja Nasir al-Din al-Tusi and the Isma'ilis,' in Daftary, ed., *Mediaeval Isma'ili History*, pp. 231–45.

26. Poonawala, *Biobibliography*, pp. 263–80.

27. See A. Nanji, *The Nizari Isma'ili Tradition in the Indo-Pakistan Subcontinent* (Delmar, N.Y., 1978), pp. 50–96; W. Ivanow, 'Satpanth,' in Ivanow, ed., *Collectanea*, pp. 1–54; Ali S. Asani, 'The Ismaili *Ginans* as Devotional Literature,' in R.S. McGregor, ed., *Devotional Literature in South Asia* (Cambridge, 1992), pp. 101–12; his 'The Isma'ili *Ginans*: Reflections on Authority and Authorship,' in Daftary, ed., *Mediaeval*

Isma'ili History, pp. 265–80, and C. Shackle and Z. Moir, *Ismaili Hymns from South Asia: An Introduction to the Ginans* (London, 1992), especially pp. 3–54.

7

Nasir Khusraw: Fatimid Intellectual

Alice C. Hunsberger

In thinking about the Fatimid intellectual tradition, a number of the essays in this book have taken a 'big picture' approach, giving an overview of the larger cultural and historical issues. I should like to move away from this approach and focus on one compelling individual, Nasir Khusraw, who lived primarily in Khurasan during the 11th century. In keeping with the theme of the book, I shall concentrate on a few of his ideas. From them, perhaps, one can start to see what makes him such a noteworthy character.

In New York City, a group of scholars are currently busy making an encyclopaedia which will fill in the gaps of Iranian history and culture not adequately covered in other encyclopaedias, such as *The Encyclopaedia of Islam*. This new encyclopedia, *Encyclopaedia Iranica*, contains many articles one would expect: cities of Iran, historical personages of Iran, and so on. But it also contains articles on more unusual topics. Under the letter 'E', for example, there is an article on 'Eagles'. Now, this may make sense were there some unique species of eagle in the Iranian world. Indeed, the article does mention the actual birds found in Iran. But the article is also about Nasir Khusraw, because of a famous poem he wrote about an eagle.[1] It begins with these lines:

Ruzi zi sar-i sang 'uqabi bi hava khwast
Bahr-i talab-i tu'mih, par o bal biyarast.[2]

The poem tells the tale of how, one day, an eagle rose up from
its rocky perch, luxuriously extended its wings and feathers, and
flew off to look for food. While soaring at great heights, the eagle
marvelled at his superior talents, on eyesight so keen he could
even discern a tiny hair at the bottom of the sea, or a gnat moving
on a twig. He boasted, 'Who is a better creature than I, anywhere
on earth or sky?' But suddenly, in the midst of this reverie of self-
satisfaction, he is struck by a terrible pain and falls, hurtling to
the ground below. In shock, he looks around to see the cause of
his disaster and spies an arrow lodged deep within him. But his
disbelief continues. He cannot fathom how something made of
wood and metal, two heavy and earth-bound elements, could fell
a creature of the air, a creature with powers superior even to those
of man. It is only when his eye catches sight of the feathers attached to the end of the arrow, the feathers of an eagle, that he
understands the source of the arrow's power. The implications of
this sink deep within his soul, and he exclaims:

Zi tir nigah kard o par-i khwish baru did,
Gufta: zi ki nalam? Ki az mast ki bar mast!

He realizes that it is the feathers that have brought his doom,
the very feathers which carried him to the skies have brought him
down. The climactic words '*az mast ki bar mast*' still signify today
that we, too, have within ourselves the very thing which will take
us up as well as down. The poet's point is to be careful of its power.
Nasir Khusraw ends the poem with straightforward advice:

Khusraw! Cast out your ego and your selfishness.
Look at this eagle full of selfish pride.
It was his selfishness, excessive sense of self,
That brought him down.

So who is Nasir Khusraw, whose moralizing poem merits an

encyclopaedia entry for a bird? This is a man who woke up one day and decided to turn his life around and devote it to the attainment of true, spiritual wealth instead of just the wealth of this world. He has left us both a poem and a piece of prose detailing this change of heart. This is a man who left all family and all possessions behind and set off from Khurasan for a journey to Jerusalem, Mecca and Egypt which would eventually last for seven years before he saw his homeland again. This is a man who became such a successful preacher of the Ismaili faith, much of it spread in today's Tajikistan and Afghanistan, that those of other Islamic schools turned viciously against him so that he had to flee for his life. He spent his last 15 or 20 years in exile in Yumgan, a remote mountain town in the Pamir mountains of Badakhshan under the protection of a local Ismaili prince.[3]

But besides the drama of his life, which is dramatic indeed, I think what makes Nasir Khusraw a most beguiling character – so much so that people still memorize his poems today – is that while his vision remains steadfastly fixed on some faraway perfection to which he calls us all to aspire, his feet remain firmly planted on the ground of this world. Nasir Khusraw is no Sufi longing for *fana*, annihilation in God, the Beloved. He is no ascetic totally repudiating the pleasures of this world. Rather, he urges us to be fully in this world and to actively use it for achieving our own perfection. He exhorts his readers to become the best human beings they can.

Abu'l-Mu'in Nasir ibn Khusraw al-Qubadiyani al-Marwazi (1004– ca.1077), better known as Nasir Khusraw, is a beloved figure in Persian literature. Zabih Allah Safa (1911–1999) ranked him as one of the greatest and most talented poets and writers of the Persian language.[4] Nasir Khusraw further distinguishes himself in his unique capacity as the only eminent philosophical writer of his era to have composed all his works in the Persian language. Besides his acclaimed virtuosity with words, Nasir displayed his linguistic virtuosity by leaving us three different genres of writing: a prose memoir of his travels, the *Safar-nama*, his poetry gathered in his *Diwan*, and a number of philosophical works in which he lays out the doctrines of Ismailism. Of these philosophical books, so far six have been edited and published: *Gushayish wa rahayish*, *Jami' al-hikmatayn*, *Khwan al-ikhwan*, *Shish fasl*, which is another name for his prose *Rawshana'i-nama*, *Wajh-i din*, and *Zad al-musafirin*,[5] but many more treatises still remain in manuscript form in libraries in cities like St. Petersburg and Dushanbe.[6]

But Nasir Khusraw earned his title 'Hakim', which may, per-haps, be best translated as 'sage,' for more than just his skill with language. He earned it through his broad training in philosophy and other sciences, including finance and mathematics. All his writings betray a wide knowledge encompassing Greek philoso-phy and science, ancient Iranian religions and culture, and all the fields of Islamic literature, philosophy and theology. Beyond his empirical knowledge, however, he exhibits a certain honesty and directness which, I suggest, is what has drawn people to him for over 900 years. He tells of the everyday things of life, of his pain, his hopes, and his gratitude for God's creations, in a very candid style. His *Safar-nama* is admired particularly as an example of beautiful Persian prose, not because it performs linguistic ac-robatics (a style which seriously came into vogue a bit later), but because it is plain and unadorned. In fact, sometimes his writing is so terse, one wishes for more elaboration. For example, the first line, 'I was a clerk by profession and one of those in charge of the sultan's revenue service,'[7] is one such simple sentence, with no play on words, no allegorical meaning to discover. One only wishes for more detail.

Around his fortieth birthday, Nasir Khusraw underwent a spir-itual awakening so profound that he set aside his privileged life in the royal Saljuq court and set out on his journey. While it seems we cannot know all the steps that led to this turning point, we can examine each of his writings carefully, since most of them date from the period after his conversion, looking for clues as to how he understood the event and how it echoed in his later life. We can also compare these texts to see how each one mirrors differ-ent aspects of his personality.

In the *Safar-nama* we encounter a man very conscious of the way cities are fortified and how they are administered. Nasir makes a point of telling how many gates each city has, how thick are its walls and where its water comes from.[8] He actually paces out the length and breadth of cities.[9] He also goes into markets and records how much certain items cost, and then gives comparisons for the people back home in Khurasan.[10] While we may be grateful for these details, we are often not sure whether he is just writing in his administrative style, recording numbers as in a ledger, or if there is some sociological or historical reason for him to mention them. The answer always seems to be the former – that he is interested in the details of everyday life and he wants to share them with others. However, when he does offer some of the historical background to his narrative, it is often too cryptic to be very satisfying. In the story of his visit to the city of Lahsa (al-Ahsa), then still the capital of the Qarmati state of Bahrayn, he speaks about the time some people of Lahsa attacked Islam's sacred mosque in Mecca, stole the Black Stone out of the Ka'ba, and carried it off to Lahsa.[11] Nasir Khusraw uses the anecdote as an opportunity to make a preacherly point. He criticizes the people of Lahsa for foolishly thinking that the stone itself was some kind of 'human magnet' which draws people to Mecca, and for not understanding that it was in fact the excellence of the Prophet Muhammad and his message which attracted people to Mecca as a place of pilgrimage, and not the stone. After this brief criticism, which takes only two lines or so, Nasir lists the animals they eat in Lahsa. The reader is left wishing for more analysis and explanation from this traveller who is so sensitive and astute an observer, as well as opinionated.

Besides his record of the facts of what he observed in his physical environment, Nasir allows a few glimpses of himself. There was the joke he shared with his brother who travelled with him about the shopkeeper from Kharzavil who had nothing they asked for.[12] Thereafter on the journey, whenever someone did not have the thing they were looking for, the two brothers would look at each other and say, 'This is just like the grocer from Kharzavil!' Then there was the other comment Nasir made after spending a day with a teacher in Simnan.[13] The teacher had grouped his students close to the pillars of the courtyard. At one pillar a group was studying medicine, at another mathematics. The teacher kept remarking in earshot of the visitor that he had heard this or that from Ibn Sina. But in a direct conversation with Nasir Khusraw, this teacher, who had hundreds of students around him, confessed, 'I do not know anything about mathematics.' Nasir Khusraw went away wondering how the fellow could possibly teach anything if he did not even know the subject.

These little remarks show us a tiny piece of his personality; but they account for a small portion of the travelogue, which is otherwise filled with descriptive details. We may fault Nasir for being too terse, but we can at the same time rest assured that when he does tell us something, it is based on the fact of his own experience. When the locals outside Jerusalem tell him about the nearby valley of Gehenna (i.e. Hell) and explain that it has that name because when you lean over the edge you can hear the cries of the people in Hell, Nasir tries it out. He writes that he went over there but did not hear anything.[14] The picture that arises of the author of this travelogue is of a man who is very observant, who takes the responsibility of recording and presenting facts truthfully for others, and who wants to help others learn from his experience, as in the story of the baths at Basra.[15]

On the homeward leg of the journey, having taken months to get across the deserts of the Arabian peninsula, Nasir and his brother arrive in Basra in a condition of extreme poverty and dishevelment. They are thirty dinars in debt just for the rent of their camel and have nothing left to sell. They look so terrible that even the bathkeeper chases them away from the public baths. Nasir writes, 'I retired to a corner to contemplate the changes in the world.' He quickly came upon a solution. Nasir composed a beautiful letter to the ruler of the city, introducing himself and showing, in content and style, that he was a man of great learning and court experience. His strategy worked. Two sets of fine clothing were soon delivered and the travellers were admitted to court, where they spent some time. Before they left Basra, however, the two returned to the baths dressed in all their finery and accompanied by servants. They were admitted with great apologies. But for Nasir the story does not end there. The victory of being allowed in and of showing the bathkeeper that things are not always what they appear to be on the outside may indeed have given Nasir personal pleasure. But he finds a serious lesson here. He writes that he included this incident in his travelogue so that his readers would not despair in times of adversity, but would know that sometimes God's mercy does come through. 'For He is most merciful indeed,' he adds. With this, we see even more clearly that Nasir Khusraw is writing his *Safar-nama* as a gift to others. He uses it to proclaim that what is here in this world matters and that having hope for the future matters ultimately. The same attitude can be seen even more clearly in his two other types of writing, poetry and philosophy.

Well-schooled in the intellectual traditions of his day, Nasir Khusraw brought his learning to the cause of defending and proclaiming the Ismaili faith. From his philosophical books, we can see that he was familiar with the full scope of religious enquiry, from metaphysics to ethics. In them, he addresses a broad range of questions: How did the world come to be? What is meant by space, time and matter? What is the relationship of matter to spirit? What is soul and what is intellect? What are the central ethical issues a believer should be concerned with? After his conversion, Nasir used all his knowledge and intellectual curiosity in the service of the Ismaili cause, specifically to lead others to its truth and to defend it against its enemies.

Let us take, for example, the concept of creation. The creation story, that is the narration of how things came to be as they are now, is of fundamental importance in all religions because it provides the rationale for rules and regulations now and, in addition, it explains the human relationship with God, including requirements for salvation. If we can determine how this world came to be, then we can figure out why and how we should seek salvation. In the Qur'an, as in the Judaic and Christian scriptures, the creation takes place when God says 'Be!' ('*kun*'). For many people, this raises a number of questions because, when God gives the creative command, where does the world actually come from? Does it come from God? From His essence? For, if so, then how could it not have existed before, for there cannot be a new part of God's essence that suddenly came into being. But, even if we acknowledged some new essence in God, where would that essence have come from? If it had already existed somewhere else, the creation could not have been in God's essence from the beginning. And if it was in God's essence eternally, how can we call it a creation? And if we try to say that it was an idea of God, one of His thoughts, then we get into a similar problem, in that any idea God had, He must have had from eternity since He could not have changed His essence to produce the idea.

One of the streams of philosophical thought which Muslim philosophers and theologians adapted for their own use (as did intellectuals in the Jewish and Christian religions) was Neoplatonism which offered a conceptual framework of creation that found a way around some of these questions. Nasir Khusraw and other Ismaili thinkers, especially those in the Iranian lands, used the tools of Neoplatonism to explain rationally the creation of the physical world from a bodiless, non-physical God.[16]

Nasir Khusraw writes in his *Shish fasl* that the human soul can only attain eternal bliss (*baqa*) through knowledge of *tawhid*, which he defines as a knowledge of God that is equally free of *tashbih*, anthropomorphism, and of *ta'til*, which divests Him of any attributes.[17] God totally transcends all creation, that is, He is so far beyond all that exists and so far beyond human comprehension that He also transcends all language, thought and being. However, as Nasir Khusraw says, we know that the first action coming from God was His word (*sukhan*) 'only to make it easier for everyone to understand'.[18] This word was perfect (*tamam*) and caused universal intellect ('*aql-i kull*) to come into existence.

Intellect thus has the closest relationship with the Neoplatonic One. In its closeness with the One, intellect overflows into another hypostasis called universal soul (*nafs-i kull*). When soul 'looks back' (or refers back) and sees that intellect is between it and God, it generates nature which contains within it the material world (*hayula*). We now have a spiritual hierarchy descending from God to intellect, soul and nature. The four principal elements of the material world are earth, air, fire and water, and from them everything else is constituted.

The hierarchy of creation now starts to ascend. At the lowest level, the four elements combine to make, first, the minerals (which occupy space but cannot move by themselves nor reproduce), then the plants (which cannot move but can reproduce), and then the animals (which can move as well as reproduce). Of the animals, the highest ranked are the humans (which can not only move and reproduce but can also think). Thus, a clear path from humans to God has been established. Once we clarify the relation of the human soul to the universal soul, as well as to the human intellect and universal intellect, we will have the necessary grid onto which religion can spread its ethics.

Notice that, for Nasir Khusraw, it is the universal soul that desires perfection. Universal intellect already has perfection. This is certainly not the gnostic idea of the soul descending to the earth and being imprisoned by desire for it. For Nasir Khusraw, the soul's desiring of perfection leads to the creation. This then provides the groundwork for an appreciation of the physical world. We can see the root, then, of some lessons in Nasir Khusraw's writings – in order to achieve the higher world, one must be in this world, and this world is a vital part of the whole scheme.

More than the specifics of his particular view though, what is inherently interesting about all this in the Islamic tradition is that there was another version of the cosmogonic explanation of how the world was created, how we got from absolute spirit to the physical world. The other version involved ten intellects and had been well articulated by Abu Nasr al-Farabi (d. 950).[19] So, instead of a scheme of God, intellect, soul, nature, here one has God and the first intellect, the second intellect, and so on down to the tenth, which is identified with the Prophetic intellect, or Gabriel. This then constitutes the connection, the ladder for human souls' ascent up the hierarchy of the ten intellects toward God. Al-Farabi's cosmogonic system was adopted by some among the Ismailis, such as Hamid al-Din al-Kirmani (d. ca. 1021).[20] We see then these two cosmogonic traditions at work in Ismaili thought of the Fatimid period – the God-intellect-soul-nature model and the ten-intellect model. Why would al-Farabi's system of ten descending intellects move in on the territory of the earlier system so that some Ismaili thinkers adopted it and abandoned the earlier version?

I suggest that it supported the philosophers' claim that people do not have to give up their intellect in order to have faith. The philosophers preferred this system in which man's intellect connects to the hierarchy of intellects, and through that connection gets him to God. Their concern was how to make the ontological connection between humans and a God who is so totally different, totally other. But what the proponents of the ten intellects left out, and what Nasir Khusraw did not, is the creative energy of the soul. As he points out, the soul creates the physical world and is in charge of running it. For Nasir Khusraw, the universal soul is not just that which creates and animates, though it surely is that; it is all of these at once, as well as the very thing that will be saved, that is, the human soul. We never hear of the intellect being saved.

We see that the soul has the creative power to save itself. The soul (*nafs*), according to Nasir Khusraw, is therefore conscious of its current state and a better future; it is active and creative, and always trying to drive itself to perfection.

Besides the travelogue and the philosophical works, we also have Nasir Khusraw's corpus of poetry, and as we saw with the poem on the self-centred eagle, the poet employs this genre to teach and give moral advice. He also puts poetry to use in the service of his philosophical theology, hiding profound doctrine in verse. But the poetry also makes it possible to see the poet's personality more fully. Here, I would like to look for a moment at one of these emotions, sadness, and then at one theme which comes up in his poetry, that of reason or intellect.

A good portion of Nasir's poetry – which dates from his period of exile – grapples directly with his sadness and the bitterness of losing much that was dear to him. Sometimes he is sad at the loss of everything that ever mattered to him; often he is very bitter at the ignorant fools who reject all the knowledge and wisdom he wishes to bring. At such a moment, he describes his pain as sharper than anyone has ever known:

> The scorpion of exile did sting me so,
> As if heaven invented suffering just for me.[21]

In another verse, he bitterly declares:

> Though sinless, I have become the enemy
>   of the Turk, the Arab, the Iraqi and the Khurasani.
> Always searching for a fault and finding none, they still
>   call me 'heretic' and an enemy of the Companions![22]

Nonetheless, at some point in each of his poems, Nasir Khusraw changes from anger or sadness to a reaffirmation of his life's work. He reminds himself of his commitment to the Fatimid caliph-imam and the truth of the Ismaili faith. He consoles himself that the rule of this fickle world means that not only can good turn to bad but, since change is inevitable, bad will also necessarily change, some day, to good.

With one prominent theme in his poetry, that of reason or

intellect ('aql), Nasir shows clearly how he despises ignorance. He finds most people so stupid he can barely tolerate it, and compares them to all sorts of animals, like donkeys and asses of course, but also like silent fishes and noisy little birds. He takes seriously the famous *hadith* of the Prophet Muhammad: 'Seek knowledge even unto China.' On an exoteric (*zahir*) level, the travels he recounts in the *Safar-nama* may certainly be seen as a way of seeking wisdom, but only on an exoteric level. When he speaks in his poetry of another China, this one called 'Ma Chin', we realize it is an esoteric Orient that calls for an inner journey, and we realize he is taking us to a deeper level. According to Nasir Khusraw, this esoteric China is to be found in the family of the Prophet, who are the gateway to the hidden truths of religion.

What we see in Nasir's *Diwan* of poetry is a man struggling with conflicting emotions, between warning others against the physical world which entraps and ultimately betrays a spiritual person, and asserting at the same time that the physical world is essential in the effort of following the spiritual path. While it may be easy to see the puritanical tenor of this message of the seductive dangers of the physical world, it requires more thought to understand the positive value of the physical world that Nasir holds for the spiritual person. For a spiritual person, one who holds the other world more important than this world, the greater challenge is to actively and productively engage in the physical world than to reject it. The physical world is essential to a life of faith because it holds the tools for learning true wisdom, namely reason (or intellect) and knowledge, that is, '*aql* and '*ilm*. In his *Wajh-i din*, Nasir explains that animals act without knowledge, while angels know without acting. But humans must combine both knowledge and action, just as they represent a combination of animal bodies and angelic knowledge.[23] While among the Sufis, reason ('*aql*) was a boundary to be overcome, an obstacle in the path of achieving union in the wellspring of love, for Nasir Khusraw reason is not something to be surpassed or suppressed but to be used for increasing knowledge and strengthening faith. In another poem, here translated in Victorian style by Edward G. Browne (1862–1926), Nasir says:

Reason was ever my leader, leading me on by the hand

Till it made me famed for wisdom through the length and breadth
   of the land.
Reason it was which gave me the crown of faith, I say, and faith
   hath given me virtue, and strength to endure and obey.[24]

For Nasir Khusraw, then, reason is not opposed to faith, nor
does it represent an alternative way of life. Rather, it is integral to
both, leading a believer to proper faith and then strengthening
that conviction.

On the other hand, for Nasir Khusraw, knowledge without
proper action is hollow. It is not sufficient to know what is true;
and it is not enough to know the imam of the time. To him that
would be 'like a string of pearls in which you have placed a common stone in the centre.' One must also act in accordance with
this knowledge. He preaches the usual ethics, but he always
grounds them in practicality; he explains that good deeds are not
advocated simply because they are good, but because they bring
you good either in this world or the next. He says that the scor-
pion that causes you pain will one day also suffer equal pain, so
there is no need to fear suffering because you will get your reward
later. Nasir Khusraw's popularity may indeed spring from this
practical sense; he has his feet very much on the ground and gives
this world its proper due, no matter how dangerously attractive it
may appear. Since a part of Nasir's virtuous behaviour is to guide
others, his ethics call for a dual path of using the intellect: to
learn for oneself and to teach others. It is not enough to acquire
knowledge; one must also point out the path to others. For example, in the dream that turned him around to a spiritual life of
preaching, the voice proclaimed: 'He cannot be called wise who
leads men to senselessness; rather, one should seek out that which
increases reason and wisdom.'[25]

Let us look at his teachings on the *shari'a*, the religious law of
Islam. Once we have made the distinction between the exoteric
and the esoteric, the *zahir* and the *batin*, and once we have shown
that in many ways *ta'wil* or the esoteric understanding of the *shari'a*
is more important than its external manifestation, it would not be
a great leap to conclude that one could forego or eliminate its
strictures altogether. Indeed, the Ismailis were often charged by
their opponents with the offence of not taking seriously the

prescriptions of the *shari'a*. Nasir Khusraw, for his part, vigorously attacked the critics, both within his community and without, by maintaining that a believer must certainly follow the *shari'a*, and that he cannot be excused from its requirements simply because he has attained inner knowledge. In the *Khwan al-ikhwan*, he asks rhetorically: 'If the observance of the *shari'a* is so critical to the proper expression of faith, why would its strictures be lifted when the Lord of the Resurrection (*khudawand-i qiyamat*) comes?'[26] He responds to his own question by affirming that the *shari'a* is partly rational ('*aqli*) and partly specified (*wad'i*).

The *shari'a* is rational, he argues, in its prohibitions against murder, fornication and stealing in that if these prohibitions were eliminated, the social order of the world would collapse. These rules are vital for a functioning society, an *umma*. The part of the *shari'a* which is specified, he continues, involves items like ablution, prayer, almsgiving, pilgrimage, and so on, which have been prescribed. They may not seem to be as serious as stealing and murder, but these rules are also there because of what lies beneath them. Nasir gives a number of arguments to support this position. First, he likens the *zahir* of the *shari'a* with the physical world around us, in that just as the physical world is comprised of a whole variety of different things, so too are religious practices, and each duty has many layers. For example, prayer involves different physical requirements such as speaking, listening, standing and bowing. Fasting involves not only keeping away from food but also drinking, along with other abstentions. Similarly, making the pilgrimage to Mecca involves a variety of activities. In this way, he shows that the multiplicity of the physical world is mirrored in the multiplicity of the *shari'a*.

Nasir notes, further, that besides this parallel multiplicity, physical and religious things share a parallel internality as well, in that each can be shown to derive from four things. That is, just as all physical things can be shown to derive from the four elements, in the same way all religious things are derived from four spiritual elements, that is, the Qur'an, the *shari'a*, *ta'wil* and *tawhid*. Furthermore, not only is everything, therefore, based on four things in both the physical and the spiritual worlds, but the four are also connected to each other. For example, air and water join together to make moisture, and fire and water join together to make

warmth. The world's existence thus depends on the connection
of the elements. From these pairings has come good. Nasir writes
that the good things join each other in the same way in the spiritual world. Each prophet brought a *shari'a* which is dependent
on its parts, and if these are all taken apart, then disaster would
result in the spiritual world. He also compares the observance of
the *shari'a* with taking medicine when we are sick. We may not
want to do it, he says, and we may not like it when we do it, but we
do it because the one who has prescribed this action is a physician
who can heal the physical body. The one who brings medicine for
souls is the Prophet Muhammad and the medicine he brings to
heal our souls is the *shari'a.* Thus, by means of this parallel external and internal multiplicity, parallel derivations from four things,
and the interconnectedness of the four elements, Nasir Khusraw
lays out his arguments to prove that the believer must carry out
the requirements of the *shari'a* properly so as to attain the highest
level of knowledge. It is through the observance of the *shari'a* and
its physical actions that believers can bring about the arrival of
the imam into the heart.

Since the *shari'a* is grounded in physical requirements for the
body, and also because the search for knowledge itself requires
that the mind be housed in a physical body, with eyes and ears,
with access to books, pens and papers, Nasir Khusraw, like many
religious thinkers, must reserve a place of honour for the body
within his spirituality. Thus, what develops almost surprisingly
within this traditional Neoplatonic hierarchy, in which matter
occupies the lowest level, is the critical importance Nasir attaches
to the role of the individual human being and, by extension, to
matter itself, in the process of purification and perfection of one's
soul. Since the physical world is a product of the universal soul's
desire to achieve the ontological perfection of the universal intellect, the physical world cannot be approached by Nasir Khusraw
with the same repugnance given to it by Plotinus and other
Neoplatonists.

True pleasure for mankind, then, lies in seeking perfection,
that is, in repeating the pattern by which the whole cosmos began
and returns to its source. Nasir Khusraw makes this spirituality of
pleasure and desire a critical feature of his philosophy. He
connects pleasure and desire with the human will, the process of

self-realization, and the relationship between the universal soul and the individual soul. While the superiority of the spiritual or intelligible world over the material or physical world can be sustained in pure metaphysics, we encounter a difficulty when we try to translate this superiority into the actual functioning of physical bodies in space and time. That is why religion has to deal both with theory and codes of conduct. Nasir Khusraw's detailed analysis of human salvation reveals the limit of the Neoplatonic dualism of body and soul.

Moreover, as a conscientious and responsible thinker, Nasir Khusraw lets the consequences of the theory lead him to its logical conclusion, one in which the body is not just the lowest form of the Neoplatonic realm, but is raised to an instrument of spiritual perfection. For it is through the body that the soul can be perfected by carrying out the *shari'a*. In this way, by modifying the Neoplatonic system, Nasir took what could have been its metaphysical limit and transformed it into an enriched dynamic between the power of the soul and its use of a bodily instrument for human perfection. Since man is responsible for his actions, the effects of his actions are transferred to his soul. This transference will lead to the purification or perfection of man's soul, which can only occur by observing the *shari'a*. What Nasir Khusraw achieves in his theology is to make the body an intermediary agent in the purification of the soul – the soul is purified by acts of the body. While he allowed Ismaili philosophical theology to remain Neoplatonic in its metaphysics up to this level with its emanations and hierarchies, and in conformity with the Ismaili polarity of *zahir* and *batin*, he created a critical synthesis by making the ethical scheme clearly Islamic. In this way, Nasir Khusraw reveals the centrality of the body and the material world in not only the day-to-day intellectual and ethical processes of our lives, but also in the ultimate perfection of the soul.

NOTES

1. William L. Hanaway, Jr., 'Eagles: ii. The Eagle in Persian Literature,' *Encyclopaedia Iranica*, vol. 7, pp. 625–6.

2. Nasir Khusraw, *Diwan*, ed. N. Taqavi et al. (Tehran, 1304–7/

1925–28), pp. 615–16. A shorter, four-couplet version is contained in Nasir Khusraw's *Diwan*, ed. by M. Minuvi and M. Mohaghegh (Tehran, 1353/1974), p. 523.

3. Biographical information on Nasir Khusraw may be found in his own works, such as his *Safar-nama*, ed. M. Dabir Siyaqi (Tehran, 1356/1977); English trans., *Naser-e Khosraw's Book of Travels (Safarnama)*, tr. W. Thackston Jr. (Albany, N.Y., 1986). For studies of his life and thought, see W. Ivanow, *Nasir-i Khusraw and Ismailism* (Bombay, 1948); his *Problems in Nasir-i Khusraw's Biography* (Bombay, 1956); A.E. Bertel's *Nasir-i Khosrov i ismailizm* (Moscow, 1959); Persian trans., *Nasir-i Khusraw wa Isma'iliyan*, tr. Y. Ariyanpur (Tehran, 1346/1967); E.G. Browne, *A Literary History of Persia* (Cambridge, 1928), vol. 2, pp. 218–46; J. Rypka, *History of Iranian Literature*, ed. K. Jahn (Dordrecht, 1968), pp. 185–9; H. Corbin, 'Nasir-i Khusrau and Iranian Isma'ilism,' in *The Cambridge History of Iran*: Volume 4, *The Period from the Arab Invasion to the Saljuqs*, ed. R.N. Frye (Cambridge, 1975), pp. 520–42; F. Daftary, *The Isma'ilis: Their History and Doctrines* (Cambridge, 1990), pp. 215–20, 639–42, and Alice C. Hunsberger, *Nasir Khusraw: The Ruby of Badakhshan* (London, 2000).

4. Zabih Allah Safa, *Ta'rikh-i adabiyyat dar Iran* (4th ed., Tehran, 1342–/1963–), vol. 2, pp. 165–6, 443–56, 893–8.

5. The following editions and translations of Nasir Khusraw's works may be noted here: *Gushayish wa Rahayish* ed. S. Nafisi (Leiden, 1950); ed. and tr. F.M. Hunzai under the title *Knowledge and Liberation* (London, 1998); *Jami' al-hikmatayn*, ed. H. Corbin and M. Mu'in (Tehran and Paris, 1953); French trans., *Le Livre réunissant les deux sagesses*, tr. I. de Gastines (Paris, 1990); *Khwan al-ikhwan*, ed. Y. al-Khashshab (Cairo, 1940); *Shish fasl*, ed. and tr. W. Ivanow (Leiden, 1949); *Wajh-i din*, ed. G.R. A'vani (Tehran, 1977); *Zad al-musafirin*, ed. M. Badhl al-Rahman (Berlin, 1341/1923).

6. See I.K. Poonawala, *Biobibliography of Isma'ili Literature* (Malibu, Calif., 1977), pp. 111–24.

7. Nasir Khusraw, *Safar-nama*, tr. Thackston, p. 1.

8. Ibid., p. 7, representing as one such example his description of the city of Mayyafariqin: 'The place has an enormous fortification made of white stone, each slab of which weighs five hundred maunds, and every fifty ells is a huge tower of this same white stone. The top of the rampart is all crenellated and looks as though the master builder had just finished working on it. The city has one gate on the west side set in a large gateway with a masonry arch and an iron door with no

wood in it.'

9. For instance, in his entry on Acre, *Safar-nama*, tr. Thackston, p. 16, Nasir writes that he measured the city, and determined its length to be 2000 cubits and its breadth 500. In Ramla, he paced out the courtyard of the Friday mosque at 200 by 300 paces.

10. See Nasir's shopping excursions for barley and bread in Quha on the road to Qazwin; grapes in Arzan; food, fruit and paper in Tripoli; olives in Jerusalem; and especially the bazaars in Cairo, as described in *Safar-nama*, tr. Thackston, pp. 3, 7, 13, 21, 53–6.

11. Ibid., pp. 86–9.

12. Ibid., pp. 3–4.

13. See ibid., pp. 2–3, where Nasir names this teacher as 'Master 'Ali Nasa'i ... a young man who spoke Persian with a Daylamite accent and wore his hair uncovered.'

14. Ibid., p. 22.

15. Ibid., pp. 90–4.

16. For information on the introduction and development of Neoplatonic thought in Islam, see P. Kraus, 'Plotin chez les Arabes,' *Bulletin de l'Institut d'Égypte*, 23 (1940–41), pp. 263–95, reprinted in his *Alchemie, Ketzerei, Apokryphen im frühen Islam*, ed. R. Brague (Hildesheim, 1994), pp. 313–45; S. Pines, 'La Longue récension de la Théologie d'Aristote dans ses rapports avec la doctrine Ismaélienne,' *Revue des Études Islamiques*, 22 (1954), pp. 7–20, and R. Walzer, *Greek into Arabic* (Oxford, 1962).

17. Nasir Khusraw, *Shish fasl*, p. 33. This brief schema is derived also from this text.

18. Ibid., p. 41.

19. For more on al-Farabi, see I.R. Netton, *Al-Farabi and his School*, (London and New York, 1992), and H.A. Davidson, *Alfarabi, Avicenna, and Averroes on Intellect* (Oxford, 1992).

20. See Daniel de Smet, *La Quiétude de l'intellect: Néoplatonisme et gnose Ismaélienne dans l'oeuvre de Ḥamîd ad-Dîn al-Kîrmânî (Xe/XIes)* (Louvain, 1995), and Paul E. Walker, *Hamid al-Din al-Kirmani: Ismaili Thought in the Age of al-Hakim* (London, 1999).

21. Nasir Khusraw, *Diwan*, ed. Taqavi, p. 6.

22. Ibid., p. 429. Here, the word *yaran* refers to the Companions of the Prophet, those who were closest to him from the very beginning of his prophethood.

23. Nasir Khusraw, *Wajh-i din*, pp. 60–1.

24. Browne, *Literary History*, vol. 2, p. 241.

25. *Safar-nama*, tr. Thackston, p. 1.

26. Nasir Khusraw, *Khwan al-ikhwan*, p. 282. I have discussed this in more depth in my dissertation, 'Nasir-i Khusraw's Doctrine of the Soul: From the Universal Intellect to the Physical World in Isma'ili Philosophy' (Ph.D. thesis, Columbia University, 1992), pp. 204–13, and in *Nasir Khusraw: The Ruby of Badakhshan* (London, 2000).

8

Reason and Mystical Experience in Sufism

Annemarie Schimmel

When I received the invitation to contribute to this collection and saw the proposed title, I decided to pen just one sentence, a verse by Mawlana Rumi who writes in his *Diwan*:

> Every morning, out of love for you, this intellect becomes crazy, climbs upon the roof of the brain and plays the lute.[1]

Of course, we cannot sum up the whole question of reason and love or, as we may say, *nomos*-oriented religion and *eros*-oriented religion, in this one verse; but I think that it gives us a good idea of how some of the great Sufis – and Mawlana Rumi (d. 1273) is certainly the most eloquent spokesman of them, saw the problem. Mawlana Rumi also has a fine way of pointing to the difference between intellect and love:

> Those with intellect run away from a dead ant out of caution; love tramples carelessly on dragons.[2]

It is love, this great intuitive force that goes through all creation, which inspired him to these verses. And they were taken up 700 years later by Muhammad Iqbal (1877–1938) who owes so much to Rumi's ideas, even though he may have criticized the so-called Sufis in very harsh terms. Iqbal takes a Qur'anic example to show this difference between love and intellect:

> Love leaps without hesitation into Nimrod's fire;
> intellect is still busy with looking from the rooftop.[3]

That is, intellect has first to ponder things, whereas love tries to jump into the heart of the matter without thinking of the consequences, and that is how it is saved.

Intellect is, of course, nothing bad in itself, even though Rumi and other Sufis sometimes poke fun at it; rather, intellect is absolutely necessary. It is, as the Muslim mystics and many other Muslims would say, a guide, an indispensable guide, which leads the believer on the broad path of the *shari'a* towards the goal. Intellect is sober and useful as a *qadi*,[4] and it is, in the parlance of the Sufis, a male power, while the *nafs*, the lower soul, is considered to be female. Throughout the history of classical Sufism you find stories about the contrast between love and intellect – Mawlana Rumi again being the most eloquent spokesman of the debates that go on between the two spiritual powers in the human being. In the *Mathnawi* he has a lovely scene of a family argument, intellect being the father and *nafs*, the lower soul, the mother. The mother wants to spoil the child, the human being, by keeping it at home, close to her bosom, in order to avoid all kinds of hardship in life; but intellect, the father, teaches her to send the boy to school in order to prepare him for a decent life.[5] This scene is typical of the way most Sufis would talk about the relationship between intellect and *nafs*, the lower natural faculties.

Intellect has a very important role in human development, even though it has no right to enter the bridal chamber of love, as Rumi says. In the mystical tradition it is connected with Gabriel, the archangel, and as always, the Sufis take their cue from the experience of the Prophet Muhammad. It is told that when the Prophet was taken on his *mi'raj* into the immediate presence of God, the angel Gabriel had to remain at the *sidrat-i muntaha*, 'the lotus tree of the farthest distance,' because he can reach only the

borders of the created universe, while the loving heart can enter
the presence of God.[6] So in Sufi tradition and particularly under
the influence of Rumi, Gabriel is equated with the leading intellect which can bring the Prophet Muhammad and everyone who
follows him to the borders of this universe, but only love can take
the seeker further. Rumi explains that in another verse:

> Intellect says, 'This world, this universe, has six borders which you
> cannot transgress.'
> Love says, 'There is a way, and I have gone over it very frequently.'[7]

It is a question of approach and, therefore, intellect appears
often as a somewhat pedestrian person, a guardian of man's decent behaviour, but a guardian who may fall asleep once in a while;
then love comes stealthily, like a thief, to carry away the person
whom intellect is supposed to guard.[8]

Intellect can be a *qadi* who loses his turban under the influence of love.[9] He can be intoxicated by a small piece of love's
meal, and although he will first retreat into a corner when love
comes with *kabab* and *sharab*, with roast and wine,[10] after all, the
slightest morsel of this will intoxicate him, so that he will forget
his duties.[11] Intellect may be a Plato in his own right,[12] but again
according to Rumi, when love comes, it hits him with a mace over
the head.[13] This may sound strange and anti-intellectual, but it is
a problem which has been faced by mystics and mystically-minded
– I might even say religiously-minded – people throughout the
world and has been expressed in a *hadith* ascribed to the Prophet.
When he was asked how to behave in a certain case, he replied:
'Ask your heart for a *fatwa*,' because it is the heart that gives the
true answer to the problems which beset human intellects.

In this respect, in claiming that the heart and its experiences
are deeper than the experiences of intellect, we need only to look
at the beautiful work of Evelyn Underhill, *Mysticism* (London,
1942), where she writes:

> Love is a life movement of the self, more direct in its methods,
> more valid in its results. Even in the hands of the least lettered of
> its adepts, it is more valid than the most piercing vision of the
> greatest philosophical mind.

Intellect, so the Sufis and again their spokesman Rumi say, is clever. His dainties, his *nuql*, are tradition, *naql*, and analogy. Love comes as a kind of vision from the sun of *kun fa-yakun*, from the sun of divine creation.[14] Intellect is necessary to give us *khabar*, information, but what the heart craves is *nazar*, direct vision. Already in early times of Islamic history, this problem was discussed time and again by the mystical thinkers, and it has found its most beautiful and profound expression in a parable which all of us know. It is the parable of the moth and the candle. Al-Hallaj (d. 922), the outstanding representative of living mystical experience, has written in his *Kitab al-tawasin*,[15] a small book in Arabic, the story of the moth that approaches the candle and first sees its light, then feels its warmth, and finally casts itself into the flames because it does not want only sight or feeling; it wants to become the flame itself and to be led to a new, higher life by burning itself in the candle. This parable, as everyone knows, especially those who have read Persian, Turkish or Urdu poetry, has permeated the literatures of the Islamic world, particularly in its eastern part, and it has been taken over through a German translation of the poetry of Hafiz by Goethe (d. 1832),[16] who formed it into one of the finest poems in his great *West-Östlicher Divan*, published in 1819, where he speaks of the blessed longing, *Selige Sehnsucht*, in which the 'dying and becoming' by death in the candle's flame forms the central issue – a topic which was, of course, very close to the hearts of the Sufis who would repeat the words *mutu qabla an tamutu*, 'die before you die', for every death is a step upward on the ladder of ascent. *Nazar*, the true experience is, as I said, what the Sufis wanted, and that is why they have always stressed the extreme importance of love.

Iqbal, who depends so much upon Mawlana Rumi's poetry and imagery, has written in a little Persian verse in his *Payam-i Mashriq*,[17] a book which he wrote actually as an answer to Goethe's *West-Östlicher Divan*. I hope no one who is a philosopher takes issue with this verse:

The bookworm who was living in the manuscript folios of al-Farabi and Avicenna, asked: What is the meaning of life?
But the moth, half burned in the candle, told him: Become like me and you will know it!

It is exactly the difference between the reading from learned manuscripts and the living experience that is important for the true mystics – and I agree with Professor M. Arkoun that the word *tasawwuf*, mysticism, ought to be defined more carefully because it is almost ridiculous to see that now so many Europeans and Americans call themselves 'Sufi' without knowing that from the 17th/18th centuries onwards, this term was used in a pejorative sense, and that the great mystical thinkers of Persia and Muslim India refused to be called Sufis.[18] They were the people of '*irfan*, or just the Muhammadis, the ones who followed the path of the Prophet completely.

Again, we can juxtapose in our analysis of love and intellect the two modes of perception, *dhikr* and *fikr*. Thought, *fikr*, is necessary to analyse the human world, to analyse everything that is created and can be understood with our intellectual faculties; and *fikr*, or *tafakkur*, thinking, pondering, is an important duty of the believer – unless he wants to ponder and figure out the essence of God, and that is prohibited. But *fikr*, as an intellectual activity, is almost as important as *dhikr*, the thinking about God, the constant remembrance of God which is supposed to polish the human heart until it becomes like a clear mirror. The Qur'an (13:28) has emphasized the importance of *dhikr*, particularly in the beautiful *aya* where it is said *a-la bi-dhikr Allahi tatma'innu'l-qulub*, 'Verily, by remembering God the hearts become peaceful (or quiet).' These two modes of thinking, the intellectual, *fikr* and *tafakkur*, and the love-intoxicated and loving *dhikr*, are always used together; they form the warp and weft of our human life.

It is what Iqbal calls '*ilm* and '*ishq*, and here again, when we use the word '*ilm*, in the sense used by Iqbal and by many other modernists, it is the activity of discursive reason or of 'science' in our modern sense. '*Ilm* is, indeed, the knowledge which is given to the Muslim by the revelation and the way he or she can hope to reach a happy life here on earth and a happy future in the other world. '*Ilm* is the true guide – that is the traditional way to explain it and this is the way of the '*ulama*. After all, they are the ones who are responsible for leading the community along the *shari'a*, the broad path, by using their intelligence, their '*aql*. So all these things belong together and we should never lose sight of the fact that here the basis of orthodox and orthopractic Islam is found. For those intoxicated by love, it is perhaps not a very inspiring way, but it is a safe way – never forget that the word *shari'a* means a broad path or road, which leads you in the desert to the well, because if you do not follow this broad path along with the caravan you will lose your way and perish as do so many. This is why the concepts of *shari'a*, *'ilm* and *'aql* belong together.

When Iqbal speaks of the dichotomy of *'ilm* and *'ishq*, of knowledge and love, then he uses *'ilm* in the modern sense of 'science'. Those who have read Iqbal's *Payam-i Mashriq*, his Persian poetical collection of 1923, know that in a famous poem he has juxtaposed these two values and, without condemning one or the other, he makes love say to science:

> We are two tunes of one melody, we belong together, we were
> born together; let us get together again,
> let us not work against each other, but rather together turn the
> world into a paradise,[19]

because if you, *'ilm*, science, are separated from '*ishq* – something we may translate as love or intuition or the innermost experience – then you become satanic, you become dangerous, you become destructive; and one cannot repeat these words often enough. Certainly this kind of *'ilm*, namely 'science' as Iqbal understands it, is also necessary because it grasps reality in pieces, it gives us a detailed analysis of everything, while '*ishq*, love or intuition, grasps it in its wholeness, in its entirety, and thus enables us to see the details on which *'ilm* concentrates in a different light. But, as he says correctly, if this analytical *fikr*, intellectual endeavour, is separated from synthetic thought, then it becomes dangerous. It is interesting to note that a hundred years before Iqbal, Goethe had expressed the same idea that purely analytical knowledge is dangerous; we need the synthesis and the way of 'seeing the whole,' that is, seeing it not only with one's intellect but also with one's heart.

The idea that intellect can be dangerous and is not necessary for human beings is expressed by many Muslim thinkers, or rather poets, in contrasting the philosophical approach with love. Whosoever has read Persian, Turkish or Urdu medieval poetry knows that the *failasufak*, the 'little shabby philosopher,' is one of the great laughing stocks of the poets. And strangely enough, it is particularly Avicenna, with a strong mystical element to his thought, who is generally blamed for being a terrible intellectualist and out of touch with true religion. It is a case of the *imaginaire* developments referred to by Professor Arkoun. Interestingly, this whole distrust of Avicenna is very much located in the Sufi tradition of Majd al-Din Baghdadi who in his dream saw the Prophet throwing Avicenna into hell; this whole 'dream' concept has coloured much of later mystical poetry, while the true works of Avicenna, as they have been explained by Henry Corbin (1903–1978), have barely been studied by the circles which perpetuated this aversion to him.[20] It is to the disadvantage of philosophy, so it seems not only with Sufis but even more with the so-called orthodox circles, that it has coloured a large part of Islamic intellectual history. The struggle between the philosophical approach to the basic truth of Islam and the orthodox criticism on the one hand, and the mystical on the other hand, gives the entire medieval history of Islamic thought a very interesting colour.

But let us return once more to Iqbal's idea of science as separated from love and intuition, as being something demonic, something Iblisian, dangerous as it were. He has again taken up here an idea from Rumi which he quotes in the *Payam-i Mashriq*, in his dialogue between Rumi and Goethe, in which both agree that cunning intellect, *ziragi*, is from Satan, while love is the particular part of Adam.[21] That is a verse found in Rumi's *Mathnawi*.[22] Iqbal has also stressed the feeling which was very much in existence in previous centuries that intellect is something that 'creates new idols' every moment. It basically leads human beings to associate something with God, because as long as intellect draws you to, and dwells upon, the various aspects of our earthly life, it is certainly dangerous because it makes us forget that there is only one Creator upon whom the world and what is in it depend; so, one could even say that intellect is responsible for associating other things with the one and unique Creator. Again Iqbal expresses this in a traditional way using an image known to all of us from Persian poetry, when he reminds us of Sultan Mahmud of Ghazna who invaded India seventeen times between the years 1000 and 1026:

Everything in the world bows to love.
Love is the Mahmud who conquers the Somnath of intellect.[23]

Note that Somnath was the great Hindu temple, which has served in Persian poetry for the last nine centuries as an allusion to the idols which were found there. When Iqbal says that intellect belongs to Somnath, he means it is something in which things other than the one and unique God are worshipped and venerated, but when love comes, these idols are all destroyed, just as Abraham destroyed the idols of his father. One can, of course, use this kind of imagery everywhere.

But what happens when the Sufis – and I use this term in its broadest possible sense – attempt to write down their experiences? Rumi says at the beginning of the *Mathnawi*, as hundreds have said before and after him, that when the pen comes to write the word 'love,' it breaks into pieces.[24] It is impossible to describe this experience of the overwhelming presence of the One whom one loves, the presence of the Divine who is always the beloved of the soul. The soul, as Rumi says or at least implies, like so many Persian, Turkish, Urdu and Arabic verses and commentaries of the Qur'an, is like the loving Zulaykha and the eternal beauty of God is reflected in Yusuf whom the soul can reach only after terrible sufferings.[25] The pen breaks when it writes about love, but – very strange! – the same pen also has written an enormous quantity of books and poetry about this very love. It is one of the paradoxes in literature that the mystics, who always emphasized the fact that one cannot express the experience of love, were the ones who wrote the most verbose books. When you look at the *Futuhat al-Makkiyya* of Ibn al-'Arabi,[26] or the numerous books written from North Africa to the Indian subcontinent on questions of mystical love, I would say they are not much more inspired or inspiring than many of the long, dry juridical or grammatical commentaries which non-Sufis wrote at the same time. It is, therefore, a question of whether the pen really breaks or not. Besides, if one looks at the poetry of the great masters of Sufism, particularly Ibn al-Farid (d. 1235), one gets the impression of dealing with a work chiselled like the finest jewellery. As Reynold A. Nicholson (1868–1945) once put it: 'It is a work where every word seems to be crafted by a master jeweller to reach the most perfect impression,'

and yet, we have to believe that this poetry was written under inspiration, without intellectual effort.

Even today, we have examples of the so-called *waridat*, 'things
that come' to the mystic. The *dogush* in Turkey, poems that are
'born' without any preparation are produced even by illiterate
people, and when we ask the reason for all this the poets answer:
'These are things that are given to us from the *'ilm laduni* [which
is mentioned in the *Sura al-Kahf*, verse 65]; it is a higher inspiration to which we are only the vessels.' For us, many of these works
look as if they have been written by highly sophisticated masters
of the word in Arabic, Persian or Turkish. Ibn al-'Arabi's *al-Futuhat*
and Khwaja Mir Dard's works in 18th-century Delhi are prime
examples of this experience. How do we account for the fact that
both of them claim that they had never written these things by
using their intellect? They did not even think of it, and yet the
books sound perfect. It is their feeling that by intense love of their
subject, they were able to grasp eternal meanings which were impossible to understand for others. The recent books by Michel
Chodkiewicz on Ibn al-'Arabi give us an excellent introduction to
this non-intellectual working of Ibn al-'Arabi in his vast writings,[27]
which – at least to a person from a later generation who does not
belong to Ibn al-'Arabi's spiritual chain – looks as if they were
crafted with much intellectual effort.

Thus, in the works of the Sufis we have a strange interplay of a
supra-intellectual knowledge and its expression, which appears
in such a way that everyone can or should be able to interpret it in
an intellectual way. This is one of the paradoxes in mystical writing – and there are no end of paradoxes. For that reason the Sufis
always objected to the interpretation of their works by non-spe-
cialists. Professor Arkoun is critical of the tendency to read only
what is written in historical texts; but this tendency is even more
important when it comes to Sufi texts which have been misinter-
preted time and again. It is very interesting that an Orientalist
who certainly had great reservations about Islam, namely W.H.T.
Gairdner, writes in his introduction to his translation of al-Ghazali's
Mishkat al-anwar[28] – or rather asks the question – about Sufi writings: 'Do we not take their language too seriously? This language
parades as scientifical, but is in reality poetical.' I think his question is absolutely correctly put, because our tendency is exactly

this. We cannot do otherwise than interpret texts according to what we know words and concepts meant at the time they were written; and yet, we also know that something escapes us which we cannot pin down with our 20th-century attitude and knowledge.

It is precisely this great danger inherent in our interpreting mystical texts that Seyyed Hossein Nasr once mentioned in an article on 'The Islamic Book,' where he says that it is not enough to read the texts as they stand, we have to read 'the white between the lines', that is, we have to understand the meaning of the texts by being introduced to them by someone who has the true experience. It is not only the letters that matter; the white between the lines is as important as the facts that are stated in black letters on the white paper. This is, I believe, one thing we all have to consider when we deal with religious texts – not only in Islam but in any religious tradition. It is certainly due to our tendency to read only the black letters that we find in a book on Islamic libraries a sentence like: 'Many books and manuscripts were lost because the Sufis washed them off.' Now, there are a few stories in which it is mentioned that a great Sufi leader, Abu Hafs 'Umar al-Suhrawardi, for example, told his student to wash all his knowledge from his heart, and perhaps some people really did wash a few manuscripts – as did a disciple of Najm al-Din Kubra (d. 1221), as Jami (d. 1492) relates in his *Nafahat al-uns*. But to presume that every Sufi just took his library, put the books in water and washed the texts is, of course, perfect nonsense, but it is a typical way of misunderstanding allegorical interpretations or anecdotes which should not be taken at face value.

One thing, of course, is certain: the Sufis had an aversion to bookishness and to bookish scholarship, not only in the field of philosophy, but also in the field of *kalam*, theology, and particularly in *fiqh* or jurisprudence. It is very revealing to see that all over the Islamic world, many great Sufic leaders, such as Yunus Emre shortly after 1300 in Anatolia, or Shah Abdul Latif in Sind in the 18th century, and many, many more, are regarded as *ummi*, illiterate. They knew only, as the sources say, the letter *alif*, the first and essential letter of the alphabet which, by its numerical value of 'one', points to the one and unique God, Allah. Such stories are told about so many legendary and also well-known Sufis that one immediately understands that it is something *imaginaire*.

For many of the Sufis who were, in fact, well-read in Arabic, Persian and their own native languages, are known – in a broader sense – as *ummi*. They all think that the *alif* is enough – 'O mullah, don't beat me because I know only the *alif*,' as the Sindhi folksong says – and they all ridicule scholarly books like the *Kanz quduri kafiya*, that is, the great collection of *hadith*, the handbook of Hanafi *fiqh* and the often used poem on Arabic grammar. These are all unnecessary for one who has learnt the *alif*, in which 'the wisdom of the four revealed books is contained', as Yunus Emre sang.

When the Sufis claimed for themselves, or were called by, the honorific title *ummi*, we should not overlook their relationship with the Prophet, because the Prophet is called in the Qur'an *nabiyyun ummi*, which basically meant that he is the Prophet sent to a people who had not yet received a revelation. But the word was then interpreted, especially in mystical circles, as meaning 'unlettered'. All those who have read mystical and other poetry in any Islamic language know that this concept of the Prophet as *ummi* is central; he is the *ummi*, as Farid al-Din 'Attar says, 'whose knowledge destroyed a hundred thousand books'. Mawlana Rumi has explained in what way the Prophet was *ummi*, and when we look at this explanation we understand better the high value of the word 'unlettered'. He says in his prose work *Fihi ma fihi* that Muhammad was not called unlettered because he was unable to read and write.[29] No, 'a person who writes signs on the face of the moon' – an allusion to the Qur'an (54:1) on the *shaqq al-qamar* – cannot be called unlettered; it rather means that he had no need of the partial intellect for he was always connected with the source of all intellectual activity, with *al-'aql al-awwal*, the First Intellect. Given this definition of the word *ummi*, we can see that it is by no means a deprecating expression used to denote a person who has no intellectual ability; rather it means the one who has direct contact with the highest source of inspiration, one who possesses, as the Sufis would say, *'ilm laduni*, 'a knowledge from within us', that is directly inspired by God. Then we understand the connection of this ideal of leaving grammar and everything behind with the immediate experience of love, as it is expressed very beautifully in one of the verses of Qadi Qadan, a Sindhi poet who died in 1551, who said in a verse that has been repeated unceasingly in Pakistan, especially in Sind:

Leave grammar and syntax to the people,
I am contemplating the beloved!

There is, however, another question about the verbosity of the
Sufis and the intellectuals. Iqbal, once more critical of Sufism,
says in his last Urdu work:

In the Sufis' path, people are intoxicated by mystical states, in the
scholars' path, people are intoxicated by empty words.[30]

It is indeed, at least for late-born non-scholars like us, sometimes difficult to find our ways through the scholastic definitions
as they have developed in the course of the centuries in the Islamic world, and in which the living and active God of the Qur'an
is very often chained and fettered by dogmatic formulations – as
is, for instance, the case in the *'Aqida Sanusiyya* which was widely
used from the 15th century onwards, and which dwells upon the
possible, impossible and necessary qualities of God – so that we
really do not recognize any more the living God as the Qur'an has
shown Him. Therefore, the Sufis, and also the less dogmatic Muslims, would often revert to a verse which I frequently found in
Turkey, but which is certainly known all over the Muslim world:

Subhana man tahayyara fi sun'ihi'l-'uqul,
Subhana man bi qudratih ya'jizu al-fuhul.
Glory to Him whose work makes the intellects confused!
Glory to Him by whose power even the greatest heroes
    are incapacitated!

It is this feeling that God cannot be fettered in definitions which
accounts for the frequent references to the 'anti-intellectualism'
of Sufis and their kind.

It must have become clear throughout our discourse that we
have tried to juxtapose 'love' and 'intellect' or intellectual endeavour. But I personally would, rather than using this kind of
juxtaposition, think of another aspect of Islamic culture which
seems to me even more relevant to our understanding the different
approaches to the central truth. This is – I have mentioned it in
passing already once – the contrast between *nomos*-oriented

religion and *eros*-oriented religion. On the one hand, we find a religion which is bound by the law and where the law, the *shari'a* – and again we can bring in here the *'aql*, intellect – leads human beings on a strictly prescribed way in which salvation is guaranteed, God willing of course; and, on the other hand, the Sufi way of feeling, of experiencing the immediate presence of God already here and now. It is a contrast known in virtually all religions, but in Islam it becomes particularly clear because here the words of the loving intoxicated Sufis stand against the words of the scholars who intellectually explained the law and its minutest details. And if we think of this contrast we may be able to understand a little bit more of the dynamics inside Islam, because here – at least to me personally – is the real, if not battlefield, at least point of encounter, between the two major aspects of Islam. But it is also this kind of anti-intellectualism among the Sufis that was blamed so often as a cause for the decline of the Muslim world.

In European scholarship, particularly in Germany, there was in the 1920s and 1930s a certain tendency to ascribe the deteriorating conditions of Islamic civilization after 1300 not so much to the conquest of Baghdad by the Mongols and the whole Mongol onslaught between 1220 and 1260, but rather to the detrimental influence of Ibn al-'Arabi and his school which, with the concept of the 'unity of being', *wahdat al-wujud*, seemed to have stifled the whole intellectual approach to truth and inhibited further philosophical enquiry and scholarly thinking in Islam. Indeed, many of the modernists in contemporary Islamic countries, as well as Orientalists, have also claimed that Sufism, particularly as developed by Ibn al-'Arabi, has barred the Muslim world from intellectual development. Iqbal, again one of our main witnesses to this development, says that the theory of *fana*, annihilation, has been more dangerous for the Islamic peoples than the destruction of Baghdad by the Mongol hordes. He does not write such a verdict in his poetry, but mentions it in a letter, which is perhaps even more revealing. Two centuries before him, the great Delhi mystical leader Shah Wali Allah had already written that 'the books of the Sufis may be useful for the elite, but for untutored people they are more dangerous than poison.' This idea that mystical writings, when they fall into the hands of untutored people, are highly dangerous and are really poisoning the minds of the believers, is found already earlier: 'Talk to people accordingly to their understanding', is an old rule, and to tell the mysteries of love openly, is the major sin. That holds true for every truly religious experience.

If we take Sufism as a living force, it is not its expression in the *turuq* system which, as Professor Arkoun has argued in his books, has certainly done much to stop intellectual activity in the Muslim world. But one should not deny that there have always been great Sufi leaders who knew that intellectual activity was necessary. It is not the danger of this 'deadly poison' which we should take as the rule in history, for every good Muslim knows that one can, by one's intellectual activity, reach a deeper understanding of the world and of God. The saying, 'Think about the work of God and the qualities of God, but do not think of God's essence', is traditional wisdom. The Qur'an says also that *hikma*, wisdom, is something very good and important. Iqbal quotes this Qur'anic remark in a section in his *Javidnama* on 'The world of the Qur'an'.[31] After all, the Qur'an has invited people to seek His signs, *ayatihi, fi'l-afaq wa fi anfusihim,* 'in the horizons', that is, in the outer world, 'and in themselves' (41:53), that is, to find the traces of God, the traces of His work, everywhere in the world, by introspection and by scholarly discoveries. And this is certainly a sentence which could be taken as encouraging Muslim scholars, and in our day also Muslim scientists, to look deeper and deeper into the marvels of nature, as well as the marvels which the human being contains in himself, and to invent ever new ways for a profounder understanding of the world.

Al-Ghazali writes in a very important sentence in his *Ihya 'ulum al-din,* which seems to sum up almost what we have said, that one who looks at the world because it was created by God, because it gives the human being the possibility of worshipping God and seeing Him in His signs, is the real *muwahhid,* the real monotheist, because he finds everywhere the traces of God and is, by looking at the world and understanding it as God's work, led back to the source of everything, the origin of everything. This means that intellectual activities are not at all to be excluded from the way of the Sufi nor of the Muslim in general, provided he keeps in mind the signs of God in the world. It is certainly the way that may lead us a little bit farther in our understanding of the problems of this world. The Muslims have not yet found a way toward a brighter future in the modern context, but I think that the very idea of looking at the signs, pondering them and approaching them with a curious, intellectual, enquiring mind can be of great help; and this is certainly in tune with orthodoxy, with Sufism and with everything in Islam. And yet we should never forget that all intellectual activities, great and useful as they may be, are still only a little step towards the mystery, because I want to close as I began with a provocative verse by Rumi, and want you to ponder it. He says: 'When you make a house for your chicken, a camel does not fit into it.'[32] Intellect is a chicken and love is a camel – a great, proud and beautiful camel.

NOTES

1. Jalal al-Din Rumi, *Diwan-i kabir ya kulliyyat-i Shams*, ed. Badiʻ al-Zaman Furuzanfar (Tehran, 1957–75), no. 2601; numbers refer to the number of poems in this ten-volume edition, hereafter referred to as *Diwan*.

2. Rumi, *Diwan*, no. 182.

3. Muhammad Iqbal, *Zabur-i ʻajam* (Lahore, 1927), part 2, no. 38.

4. Rumi, *Diwan*, no. 2233.

5. Rumi, *The Mathnawi*, ed. and tr. Reynold A. Nicholson (Leiden and London, 1925–40), vol. 6, lines 1433 ff.

6. See the beautiful poems in Farid al-Din ʻAttar's *Ilahiname*, ed. H. Ritter (Istanbul, 1940), p. 16.

7. Rumi, *Diwan*, no. 132.

8. Ibid., no. 2807.

9. Ibid., no. 1288.

10. Ibid., no. 507.

11. Ibid., no. 2170.

12. Ibid., no. 2231.

13. Ibid., no. 1276.

14. Ibid., no. 1940.

15. Al-Husayn b. Mansur al-Hallaj, *Kitab al-tawasin*, ed. L. Massignon (Paris, 1913), pp. 16ff.

16. *Der Diwan* (Stuttgart, 1812–13).

17. Muhammad Iqbal, *Payam-i Mashriq* (Lahore, 1923), p. 119.

18. See, for instance, A. Schimmel, *Mystical Dimensions of Islam* (Chapel Hill, 1975).

19. Iqbal, *Payam-i Mashriq*, p. 111.

20. See H. Corbin, *Avicenne et le récit visionnaire* (Tehran, 1952–54); English trans., *Avicenna and the Visionary Recital*, tr. W.R. Trask (New York, 1960).

21. Iqbal, *Payam-i Mashriq*, p. 247. For other remarks about Goethe's importance in Iqbal's thought, see. A. Schimmel, *Gabriel's Wing: A Study into the Religious Ideas of Sir Muhammad Iqbal* (Leiden, 1963), pp. 330–1.

22. Rumi, *Mathnawi*, vol. 4, line 1402.

23. Muhammad Iqbal, *Asrar-i khudi* (Lahore, 1915), line 135.

24. Rumi, *Mathnawi*, vol. 1, line 114.

25. Ibid., vol. 6, lines 4021 ff.

26. Ibn al-'Arabi, *Kitab al-futuhat al-Makkiyya* (Cairo, 1329/1911), 4 vols.

27. M. Chodkiewicz, *Seal of the Saints: Prophethood and Sainthood in the Doctrine of Ibn 'Arabi*, tr. L. Sherrard (Cambridge, 1993).

28. Abu Hamid Muhammad al-Ghazali, *Mishkat al-Anwar*, tr. W.H.T. Gairdner (London, 1924), pp. 1–73.

29. Jalal al-Din Rumi, *Fihi ma fihi*, ed. B. Furuzanfar (Tehran, 1338/1959); English trans., *Discourses of Rumi*, tr. A.J. Arberry (Richmond, U.K., 1961).

30. Muhammad Iqbal, *Zarb-i kalim* (Lahore, 1937), p. 35.

31. Muhammad Iqbal, *Javidnama* (Lahore, 1932); English trans., *Javid-Nama*, tr. A.J. Arberry (London, 1966).

32. Rumi, *Diwan*, no. 2937.

9

Some Observations on the Religious Intellectual Milieu of Safawid Persia

John Cooper

The Safawid dynasty in Persia, whose origins lay in militant Turkish Sufism, spanned more than two centuries, from 1502 to 1736. There were twelve shahs of the dynasty, although the last three were rulers in name only. In the time of Shah 'Abbas I (1588–1629), under the banner of Twelver Shi'ism, they effectively united Persia, although that term is to be understood as comprising a larger area than it does today, approaching the extent of the old Persian Sasanid empire. These features, the re-emergence of an Iranian empire and the religious underpinning of that empire, were the two major novelties, and they have left their mark down to the present day. It is unnecessary to enter into all the details of the way in which the Safawids forged the new Persia, but the establishment of Twelver Shi'ism and the subsequent fate of mystico-religious life need to be examined because of their bearing on the intellectual life of that and later periods.

Shah Isma'il's announcement of the Twelver Shi'i kingdom in Tabriz in 1502 heralded the fairly swift conversion of the major part of the settled population, and sealed the twin destiny of the country as both Persian and Shiʻi. But the Shiʻi credentials of the Safawid dynasty needed first to be established themselves. The eponymous ancestor of the Safawids and founder of the Safawiyya Sufi order was Shaykh Safi al-Din Ardabili (d. 1334). Works written during the Safawid period trace his lineage back to the seventh Twelver Imam Musa al-Kazim (d. 799), but in pre-Safawid biographical literature no mention seems to be made of either his descent or his Shiʻism. The Safawids liked to use the *Safwat al-safa* of Ibn Bazzaz, a work which was chiefly concerned with Shaykh Safi al-Din's life.[1] It was written around 1358 and later edited by Mir Abu'l-Fath Husayni on the order of Shah Tahmasp I (1524–1576), and had what remained of its Sunni clothing removed. Its introduction and *hadith* and expressions of a Sunni nature were removed. The title 'Sayyid' was prefixed to the ancestors' names, miracles attributed to Shah Ismaʻil, and at the end a section on the descendants of the Shaykh was added. Apparently the first Safawid to add the title 'sayyid' to his name was the son of Shah Ismaʻil, Shaykh Haydar, and thereafter it became the practice. But the origins of the family of Shaykh Safi al-Din go back not to the Hijaz but to Kurdistan, from where, seven generations before him, Firuz Shah Zarin-kulah had migrated to Adharbayjan.

Shaykh Safi al-Din's father had moved from Adharbayjan to Shiraz, where Shaykh Safi al-Din came under the guidance of a Sufi *shaykh*, Zahir al-Din b. Najib al-Din Bazghash-i Shirazi. This latter instructed him to repair to Gilan in order to benefit from service to Shaykh Zahid Gilani, a pupil of the famous Najm al-Din Kubra. When Shaykh Zahid died, Shaykh Safi al-Din went to Ardabil where he in turn became a Sufi *shaykh*, followed by his descendants Shaykh Sadr al-Din Musa, Sultan Junayd and Sultan Haydar. Sultan Haydar's son, Ismaʻil, who had been in Lahijan, returned to Ardabil at the end of the 15th century with seven of his father's followers, and within two years he had conquered Shirwan, Armenia and Adharbayjan, and had defeated Alwand Beg Aq-Quyunlu at Nakhchawan (1501); ten years later he was master of the rest of Persia from Khurasan to Iraq.

Shaykh Safi al-Din had been known as a Shafiʻi, so what had made his descendants opt for Shiʻism? Firstly, theirs was a militant brand of Sufism – that is to say, Sufism and tribal leadership went hand in hand – of a kind in which the charismatic model was one of popular affection for the Prophet Muhammad's family (*ahl al-bayt*). Second, the ground had already been prepared to a certain extent by the Sarbadars of Sabzawar (1338–1381) and the Mar'ashi Sayyids of Mazandaran (1358–16th century)² for the political combination of Sufism and Shi'ism. Third, although the Iranians of the time were mostly Sunni by *madhhab*, the environment was strongly coloured by affection for the family of the Prophet, and formed what was effectively a Shi'itized Sunnism.

The Safawids at first retained the Turkish character of their rule. Persian had by this time become the political and literary language both of the Ottoman Empire and of India, but the Turkish language was retained by Shah Isma'il, whose followers were mostly Turkoman and Tartars. Although the Shi'i colouring of the early dynasty led the young Isma'il to lay claims even to being the Mahdi, it was still the Sufi dimension which determined the power and authority of the early Safawids. It was to Shi'ism that the Safawids looked to consolidate that power, but it was from other Sufi groups that they feared rivalry and in whom they saw alternative centres of authority which could potentially undermine their own. It was thus in terms of what might now be called 'ideology' that the Safawids turned increasingly to Twelver Shi'ism to consolidate their new empire, forming a fateful link between Shi'ism and *de facto* political identity which has characterized much of the subsequent history of Persia.

We can, therefore, briefly characterize the early Safawid period as one in which power lay with what had now become the most powerful and wealthy of many Sufi groups, a group moreover with a strong popular Shi'i flavour. In order to hold on to their wealth and power, which was being increasingly added to by conquests and alliances, the Safawids had to keep in check other Sufi groups who could wrest their as yet shaky authority from them. But they gradually perceived the importance of the Twelver Shi'ism of the scholars as a stabilizing factor. It could provide a unifying force which did not run the danger of the pluralistic tendency of the Sufism of the day, and by encouraging the Shi'i *'ulama* they were also discouraging rivals to earthly power; but this was a dimension of the *'ulama*'s authority which would have to wait several centuries before being realized or even formulated.

As Shi'i *'ulama* came to take up the religious posts that had formerly been held in the name of Sunnism, and the *madrasas* became centres of Shi'i learning, Shi'i *'ulama* were gradually attracted from other areas of the Muslim world, so that by the time of Shah 'Abbas there were both indigenous *'ulama* who had turned to Shi'ism and Shi'i *'ulama* who came from the Shi'i tradition itself and now found a powerful state willing to support them. There had also been a significant migration of indigenous scholars and literary persons away from Persia, most notably to the Indian subcontinent, where they could enjoy the patronage of the Moghul courts with their predilection for philosophy and the Persian language.

The Shi'i *'ulama*, as might be expected, showed themselves to be somewhat ambivalent towards Sufism which underpinned their Safawid patrons' authority. Strongly independent and legalistically minded *'ulama* such as Ahmad b. Muhammad al-Ardabili, better known as Muqaddas Ardabili (d. 1585),[3] saw Sufism as characterized by unacceptable belief in unification with the divine and the manifestation of the divine in human beings, something which the early Safawids were certainly guilty of encouraging in a crude and tribal fashion. But Muqaddas Ardabili directed his attack at the more scholarly manifestations of this tendency, which he obviously regarded as threatening the religious authority of the teachings of the Shi'i imams. He was thus prepared to condemn the Sufis as *kafirs* and *zindiqs*, unbelievers and heretics: 'Some of the recent unitarians [believers in *ittihad*], such as Ibn al-'Arabi, Shaykh 'Aziz Nasafi, and 'Abd al-Razzaq Kashani, have been the origins of *kufr* and heresy. They believe in *wahdat al-wujud* (unity of being) and say that every existent is God.' He believed that the source of their errors was the reading of philosophy, and that they had taken their wicked ideas from Plato and dressed them up in new clothes, so that when people asked them about their ideas they would say it was impossible to understand them without first seeking initiation under a *pir* and submitting to lengthy periods of asceticism.

Philosophy had, indeed, become a recognizable element in the religious milieu in Persia long before the coming of the Safawids. In the two centuries following the Mongol conquests of the 13th century and the death of Ibn al-'Arabi in 1240, there had been slowly evolving that particular brand of speculative thought which was to become so noticeable a feature of the Persian and Shi'i Islamic world. The Sufism of the 14th and 15th centuries had been thoroughly penetrated by the teachings of the *shaykh al-akbar*, Ibn al-'Arabi, with prominent figures of Persian literary Sufism, such as the poets Jami and Mahmud Shabistari, presenting a sophisticated theoretical teaching to back up the popular practices of Sufism. Peripatetic, Aristotelian philosophy was also widely studied, a notable pre-Safawid figure being the philosopher Jalal al-Din Dawwani (d. 1502), celebrated for his reworking of the ethical tradition bequeathed by Nasir al-Din al-Tusi (d. 1274). Dawwani was also a Sufi and a commentator on Shihab al-Din al-Suhrawardi, and thus foreshadowed the mixture of three traditions – Peripatetic, Akbarian (after the tradition of Ibn al-'Arabi) and Illuminationist (after al-Suhrawardi) – which would be the most remarkable feature of the philosophical environment of Safawid Persia.

It has been said that the leading scholars of philosophy in Safawid Persia were the indigenous scholars turned Shi'i, and while this may be an over-simplification, there seems to be a strong bias in this direction. The leading Safawid philosopher, Sadr al-Din Shirazi better known as Mulla Sadra (d. 1640), was indeed from such a family, and one of his major achievements was to have added to the mixture of Peripateticism, Akbarism and Illuminationism, the teachings of the Twelver imams. He was not the first to attempt a synthesis: Haydar Amuli (d. after 1385) had sought to present Imami Shi'ism, as represented by the teachings of the imams, as the ultimate perfection of the views of Ibn al-'Arabi, and other scholars like Qadi Nur Allah al-Shushtari (d. 1611),[4] who had been among those to migrate to India and was designated as the 'third *shahid*' by the Twelver Shi'is. The latter had expressed the view in his *Majalis al-mu'minin* that Ibn al-'Arabi was in fact a crypto-Imami. But it is to Mulla Sadra that we owe that systematic incorporation of Imami theology into the inherited philosophical framework, effectively producing a new school of Imami theology which would henceforth be virtually a branch of philosophy. This move had, of course, already been initiated by Nasir al-Din al-Tusi, but it had yet to become substantially more than the incorporation of philosophical ideas into an Imami theology which was beginning to shed its *kalam* dialectics in favour of a systematized philosophical discourse.

Mulla Sadra's *magnum opus*, the *Asfar al-arba'a* (The Four Journeys),[5] covering the fields of metaphysics, theology and the mystical path, was interestingly given a title and a division into four parts borrowed from the Sufi tradition. The four journeys into which it is divided parallel this particular representation of the Sufi journey as consisting of four stages. The first – the journey of creation or the creature (*khalq*) to the Creator of the Truth (*al-haqq*) – contains the philosophical germ of the work: in it Mulla Sadra lays out the basis of his existentialist metaphysics, mirroring the stage in the Sufi's path (*tariqa*) where he seeks to control his lower *nafs* under the supervision of his *shaykh* or master. The second journey – in the Truth with the Truth, the stage at which the Sufi begins to attract the divine manifestations – is where Mulla Sadra deals with the simple substances, the intelligences, the souls and their bodies, including therefore the natural sciences. In the third journey – from the Truth to creation with the Truth – the Sufi experiences annihilation in the godhead, and Mulla Sadra deals with theodicy; and in the fourth stage – the journey with the Truth in creation – where he gives a philosophical account of the development of the soul, its origin, becoming and end, is where the Sufi experiences persistence in annihilation, witnessing the beauty of oneness and the manifestations of multiplicity.

But Mulla Sadra's Sufism was discriminating, and other works by him help to fill in details of the way in which his mystical ideas were taking shape. Two works of his, in particular, deal with Sufism: one in Persian, the other in Arabic. The Persian work, the *Sih asl*, is in fact a polemic against the legalistic, anti-Sufi *'ulama*, a type we have already met in the person of Muqaddas Ardabili. Mulla Sadra condemns these *'ulama* for their seeking of worldly power while totally ignoring the spiritual and the next-worldly side of religion. Mulla Sadra, thus, identifies with the Sufis and expresses in his prose a concept which has a long tradition in Persian poetry of despising the *'ulama* for their exploitation of believers and their condemnation of sincere spiritual practices as innovation.[6] Another of Mulla Sadra's works, this time in Arabic, the *Kasr al-asnam al-jahiliyya*, is by contrast an anti-Sufi polemic, condemning the kind of popular Sufism which had brought the

Safawids themselves to power. He criticizes many Sufis for desert-
ing both knowledge and good actions, and for peddling
superstition and obedience to Satan as the unveilings of those
who have attained spiritual perfection. With their *shatti* (unfath-
omable, koan-like sayings), he says, they fool the people into
thinking they are witnessing miracles. This kind of criticism also
had a long tradition among the *hadith* scholars, particularly late
Hanbali scholars such as Ibn Taymiyya and Ibn al-Jawzi, and also
sounds very near to the views of the Imami legalists such as
Muqaddas Ardabili, and therefore bears witness to the intellectual disdain for the kind of extreme popular tendencies which
have been a feature of Sufism from the earliest times. It also bears
witness to the danger which traditionists, both Sunni and Shi'i,
have felt that Sufism presents within Islam to the authority of the
hadith and the person of the Prophet Muhammad (and in the
Shi'i case, of the imams from his family). Popular Sufism threat-
ens this authority by its tendency to substitute the wisdom of the
Sufi *shaykh* or *pir* for the teachings handed down by the scholars
of *hadith*. It substitutes the immediacy of miracle and inspiration
for the more remote scholarship of memorization and writing. It
is, therefore, significant that the anti-legalist *Sih asl* should have
been written in Persian, and thus addressed to those educated
persons who were able to look back to the pre-Safawid Iranian
and Persian-speaking scholarly tradition, while the anti-Sufi *Kasr
al-asnam al-jahiliyya* should have been written in Arabic, and thus
addressed to the more traditionist and legalistic scholars whose
lingua franca that was.

The prevalent tradition in Twelver Shi'ism, from the time of
Shaykh al-Mufid in the 10th century, when the *kalam* tradition
found widespread acceptance, has been for theologians to be at
the same time scholars of *hadith*. Mulla Sadra was no exception to
this. He produced an extensive commentary on the first parts of
the early collection of Shi'i *hadith* by al-Kulayni.[7] It is a commentary of a largely theo-philosophical character, but it also
demonstrates Mulla Sadra's knowledge of the science of *hadith*,
in particular of his knowledge of the science of the biographies of
the transmitters ('*ilm al-rijal*).

The Safawid period can be viewed as a period marked by the
tendency which in Shi'ism has been called Akhbari, or traditionist,

as opposed to the Usuli tendency with its foundation on *usul al-fiqh*, the methodology of law. The Akhbaris perceived the corpus of Shi'i Traditions as the sufficient guarantee of the continued charismatic presence of the imams in the Shi'i community, while the Usulis saw that presence as being confided in the *'ulama* with their learning and scholarly expertise. Akhbarism of the 16th century can also be understood as a break from the systematic, scholastic law of its predecessors to a more innovative, independent practice. A *sadr* of the Safawid court was quoted in the early 17th century as saying that not a single Shi'i *mujtahid* remained in his time in Persia or the Arab world. If the Akhbari tendency of the Safawid era was more strongly expressive of an anti-mystical, anti-Sufi, anti-philosophical trend, the Usulis can be understood as having at least more respect for the speculative, philosophical mysticism then coming into its own, because it was also a scholarly tradition which required intellectual training and expertise.

The Akhbaris and the Usulis should not be thought of as two camps, to one of which every religious figure owed his allegiance. It is rather more useful to think of an Akhbari-Usuli intellectual spectrum, a particular instance of the general tension between tradition and reason, between the *naqli* and the *'aqli*, which runs through virtually all the main schools of Islamic thought. Yet even with this proviso it is difficult to see exactly where Mulla Sadra might fit in this spectrum. He is not a legist, although he would undoubtedly have studied the legal sciences, and he shows deep commitment to the Shi'i Traditions, but he is first a philosopher and a rationalist (in the best sense of the word). It is an indication that he wished to step outside this spectrum and develop a more analytic perspective that he named his philosophical systems 'metaphilosophy' (*al-hikma al-muta'aliyya*), a term he incorporated into the full title of his *magnum opus*, *al-Hikma al-muta'aliyya fi'l-asfar al-'aqliyya al-arba'a* (The Transcendent Wisdom Concerning the Four Intellectual Journeys).

Another figure of the previous generation whose complex personality again brings out the contrasting facets of the Safawid period is Shaykh Baha al-Din al-'Amili (d. 1622), generally known as Shaykh Baha'i. When still a child, his father had moved from Lebanon to Persia to fulfil religious functions, and Shaykh Baha'i himself travelled extensively in Palestine and the rest of the Middle

East. In Persia he became the leading scholar of his day and the *shaykh al-Islam* of Isfahan. Outside Persian territory he seems to have presented himself as a Sufi, dressing in the appropriate clothing and perhaps disguising his Shi'ism under the more acceptable veneration for the *ahl al-bayt* which was common among the Sufis. His *Kashkul*, a kind of commonplace book in which he recorded numerous passages of poetry and prose in Arabic and Persian gives, through its examples, an intricate representation of his views on Sufism. He was a versatile scholar whose interests ranged from the legal to the rational sciences and included poetry; he was, among other accomplishments, an architect of *madrasas* and even a bathhouse which was allegedly fuelled by a single candle. Local hearsay attributes the disappearance of this sole means of heating to a team of French researchers, who apparently either destroyed it or removed it while subjecting this miracle of 'green development' to scientific scrutiny. Persian lore also attributes to him the invention of *nun-i sangak*, a type of bread which is baked on small hot pebbles.

An aspect of Shaykh Baha'i's attitude towards Sufism can be understood from a passage in which he defines it as a classical science:

> Sufism is a science in which are studied the essence of unity and God's names and attributes, in so far as they are connections for every manifestation of them to the divine essence. Its subject (*mawdu'*) is the unitary essence, its eternal blessings and everlasting attributes. Its objects of enquiry (*masa'il*) are: how multiplicity came forth from it and returns to it, the explanation of the manifestations of the divine names and lordly blessings, how the journey and striving should be accomplished, the methods of asceticism, and the explanation of all actions and remembrances in this world and the next in a sure way in reality. Its foundations (*usul*) are to know its definitions and its aims.

Such a systematic definition combines mysticism and the speculative sciences in a way which is reminiscent of Ibn Sina and Nasir al-Din al-Tusi, and is another indication that scholars of the Safawid period were rescuing Sufism from its associations with popular practice and reconfirming it as one among the religious sciences, a legitimate subject for investigation among the learned.

A number of anti-Sufi works were written in the period by those who were associated with the Akhbari position. Al-Hurr al-'Amili (d. 1693), the author of a large compendium of Shi'i legal *hadith* arranged according to the divisions of *fiqh*, wrote one such work, the *Fawa'id al-diniyya fi'l-radd 'ala'l-hukama wa'l-Sufiyya*, against both philosophers and Sufis. He was reputed not to have been on good terms with either Muhammad Baqir al-Majlisi, rather surprisingly, and Mulla Sadra's son-in-law and pupil Fayd Kashani (d. 1600).[8] Muhammad Baqir al-Majlisi (d. 1699) was the author of the largest compilation of Shi'i *hadith*, the *Bihar al-anwar*, stretching to some 110 volumes in the current edition. This work is interspersed with al-Majlisi's comments, but it is almost breathtaking in its size and indiscrimination, inevitably reinforcing the view of him that has become current that he too represents the Akhbari tendency. He also wrote one of the most widely used commentaries on al-Kulayni's *al-Kafi*. Al-Majlisi's father, Muhammad Taqi al-Majlisi (d. 1659), was also a noted scholar, frequently described as an Akhbari, but one who had a reputation for having a sincere interest in Sufism. This was a fame of which his son was keen to disabuse his contemporaries, and so he gave the following account of his father's behaviour:

> Concerning the fact that it is supposed that my father was a Sufi, or that he believed in their ways and doctrines, [I say that] he was remote from this path ... His path was asceticism (*zuhd wa wara*). He let himself become known at the beginning as a Sufi, so that a group of Sufis would gravitate towards him and not be frightened of him. He wanted them to leave the evil and innovative ways, and he guided many of them to the true path by kind debate. ... At the end of his life he condemned their invalid beliefs as *kufr*. I knew his ways better than anyone else, and his writings on this subject are with me.

The Safawids' relations with their own people were like those of *murshid* and *murid*, a Sufi master and his disciple, but their kind of Sufism might best be described by the contemporary sense of fundamentalist. So severe was their persecution of other Sufis, aided often quite unscrupulously by the legalistic *'ulama*, that this was yet another cause for the migration of mystics to India, where they were assured of a warmer welcome, and where Suhrawardis, Chishtis, Ni'mat Allahis, Qadiris and other Sufis flourished. Qadi Nur Allah al-Shushtari, who had migrated to take up important posts in India including that of *qadi al-qudat* in Lahore and ended his life by being executed in Agra, wrote many biographical notices of Sufis and *'arifs* in his *Majalis al-mu'minin,* which is where he expressed the view that Ibn al-'Arabi was a crypto-Shi'i; and it is also mentioned that he wrote a six-volume commentary on Rumi's *Mathnawi.*

Sufis and scholars who were unwilling to abandon allegiance to Sufism were, thus, prompted to move to the more congenial atmosphere outside the Safawid domain, away from persecution and possible death, where they did not need to dissimulate or revise their outward behaviour. Others, like Shaykh Baha'i, while acting in all good conscience as respected legal authorities inside Safawid territory, were also apparently in all good conscience, happy to be considered Sufis when abroad. Those who remained entirely within the Safawid empire, except perhaps for journeys on the *hajj*, struggled to redefine their mystical legacy. By incorporating it firmly within the speculative sciences, they preserved its teachings without too great a risk of retribution from the state or the *'ulama.* Mulla Sadra, it is true, spent a good ten years of his life in a kind of exile in the village of Kahak near Qumm, an exile which the strongly anti-clerical tone of the *Sih asl* seems to imply was due to persecution by the *'ulama.*[9] But he returned to Shiraz to enjoy royal patronage and had his own *madrasa* constructed.

To be a practising Sufi in the Safawid period must have been a hazardous vocation. But several *tadhkiras* (memoirs) of Iranian Sufi *silsilas* (particularly the Nurbakhshis) include figures such as Shaykh Baha'i and Mulla Muhsin Fayd Kashani as adherents of their orders. How should we understand this? Were these scholars secretly practising Sufism while presenting another face to the authorities? A possible solution suggests itself from al-Majlisi's account of his father's activities. Sufis would have been keen to cultivate association with Islamic scholars for the protection which this offered them, however minimal and risky that might have been. Sympathetic scholars might also have been willing to do what they could for those to whom they themselves attached no blame, and whom they considered to be also sincere travellers on the path; or perhaps there were scholars, as al-Majlisi claims his father was, who saw it as their religious duty to cultivate association with the Sufis in order to guide them 'on the straight path'. The *silsila*s would record these associations in future *tadhkira*s as formal affiliations, perhaps out of sincere conviction that these scholars were genuine mystics, or perhaps out of feelings of sympathy and gratitude.

At any rate, the results of this reorientation of mysticism had its lasting effects on Shi'i intellectual life. The power of the empire lay in the hands of Sufi shahs turned political shahs. Basing the structures of court loyalty on the legacy of militant Sufism, the Safawids brought the Sufi orders into the political sphere. What Sufi order one belonged to forced the consideration of his political stance. This marriage has continued to the present day, and the fortunes of Sufism have, from the 16th century onwards in Persia, often been linked to the court and to court patronage. Rarely has Sufism been allowed to flourish when it has been seen to threaten the political and religious authority of the day.

At the same time, by making it the political ideology of the state, the Safawids also ensured that the fortunes of Shi'ism were henceforth linked to the latter's civic authority. It was the 20th century Iranian religious critic, 'Ali Shari'ati (1933–1977), who drew the distinction between the Shi'ism of Imam 'Ali and the Shi'ism of the Safawids. Aspirations to worldly authority had been in abeyance for the Twelver Shi'a from the time of the fifth Imam, Muhammad al-Baqir (d. ca. 732), but in the 16th century it once again became an alternative to consider. This might not exactly be what Shari'ati had in mind, but if for him the revolutionary social role of Shi'ism had turned into an alliance with the state against the weak, it was surely in the Safawid period that such an alteration took place.

For the first time in its history, Twelver Shi'ism now had the backing of a state, and had thus become a kind of ideology. The *'ulama*, or at least the *fuqaha*, were evolving into a more structured body than had been present in the profligate days of the 15th century. Critics of this ideological approach had to be careful, for criticism of Shi'ism now, to some extent, meant criticism of the state. And so, in Shari'ati's view, Shi'ism no longer stood

for a free, somehow almost anarchic and liberated dimension to
the religious life, but instead had become an ossified, authoritar-
ian, state-allied monopoly.

The main crux of the religious controversies of the early Safawid
period was not just Shi'ism and its structure, but the Sufism which
came to prefer the title '*irfan* (gnosis). It was rescued from its
militancy and extremism to become intellectualized and thoroughly incorporated into Shi'i theology, which consequently came
to take on a much more interiorized form. Sufism in Persia would
be the victim, both of '*irfan* and of the Safawids, but the eventual
victor was Shi'ism in the new speculative direction which '*irfan*
was taking it. There would always be anti-philosophical '*ulama*,
but at least the place of philosophy within the religious sciences
had been secured for the next four centuries.

NOTES

1. See Erika Glassen, 'Ibn al-Bazzaz al-Ardabili,' *Encyclopaedia of
Islam*, new ed., Supplement, pp. 382–3.

2. They traced their genealogy back to the fourth Shi'i Imam, 'Ali
b. al-Husayn Zayn al-'Abidin (d. 714), and were related by marriage
to the Safawids.

3. He was responsible for the development of an independent,
systematic, rational approach to Islamic law which liberated itself from
the opinions of his predecessors.

4. He was a grandson of Diya al-Din Nur Allah al-Mar'ashi al-
Shushtari, who had moved from Mazandaran to Khuzistan in
south-western Persia and took an active part in spreading Shi'i ideas
in the territory of the Musha'sha', an independent Arab tribal movement based in Huwayza from around 1436 to the Safawid period, to
whose leadership they acceded after several military confrontations.
Their tribal power lasted until the beginnings of the 20th century.

5. Mulla Sadra Shirazi, *Asfar al-arba'a*, ed. R. Lutfi (Qumm, 1378–
89/1958–69), 9 vols.

6. Notable examples can be found in both Rumi and Hafiz.

7. Abu Ja'far Muhammad b. Ya'qub al-Kulayni, *al-Usul min al-kafi*,
ed. 'A.A. al-Ghaffari (Tehran, 1388/1968), 2 vols.

8. Perhaps a more understandable antipathy because of the latter's interest in philosophy and mysticism, although he too was a

prolific collector of *hadith*.

9. It should be noted that the attribution of the *Sih asl* to Mulla Sadra has been recently questioned.

10

Woman, Half-the-Man?
The Crisis of Male Epistemology
in Islamic Jurisprudence

Abdulaziz Sachedina

INTRODUCTION

Islamic sacred law, the *shari'a*, has been regarded by Muslims as a perfect, divinely ordained religious-ethical-legal system. The *shari'a* relates Muslims to God's purposes by providing comprehensive directives in the two spheres of human activity: those actions that relate humanity to God, and those that relate humans to fellow humans. The former actions are categorized as *'ibadat* (literally, 'acts of honouring God', technically, God-human relationships) and the latter are known as *mu'amalat* (literally, 'transactions', technically, inter-human relationships). Whereas the God-human relations have remained more or less immutable in the *shari'a*, the area of inter-human relationships has demanded rethinking and reinterpretation of the normative sources like the Qur'an and the *sunna* (Tradition) to deduce new directives under changed social conditions. There are, however, epistemological problems connected with the way normative sources are retrieved and interpreted by Muslim jurists which have hampered the necessary progress towards one particular area in the inter-human relationships, namely, the personal status of Muslim women. The juridical deliberations in the exclusively male-oriented traditional centres of Islamic learning, the *madrasa*, have disregarded female voices in the emerging discourse connected with women's issues and human rights. The redefinition of the status of a Muslim woman in modern society is one of the major issues that confronts Muslim jurists' claims to authority on legal-ethical sources of Islam. But such a redefinition, as I argue in this essay, is dependent upon Muslim women's participation in the legal-ethical deliberations concerning matters whose situational aspects can be determined only by women themselves. Without their participation in legal-ethical deliberations, women's rights will always depend on a 'representational discourse' conducted by male jurists who, in spite of their good intentions, treat the subject as 'absent' and, hence, lacking the necessary qualification to determine her rights in a patriarchal society.

MALE JURISTS AND FEMALE RELATED RULINGS

It was in the late 1960s when I began my studies in Islamic jurisprudence at the *madrasa* of the Ayatollah Milani in Mashhad, Iran. Studies in the *madrasa* were structured around texts, both initial expositions and commentaries on them. In general, classical Islamic juridical texts were organized to undertake 'first things first'. Hence, in Shi'i jurisprudence, with which I commenced my studies in Islamic law, immediately following theoretical discussion about the necessity of following one of the living *mujtahids* (theologian-cum-jurist), the teacher began with the rulings connected with ritual purification, *kitab al-tahara* (book of purification).

I always sensed some uneasiness in the teacher as well as all male fellow students when the rulings on *tahara* reached intimate matters connected with female ritual purification, the *taharat al-niswan*. At that point, as if sensing a need to justify the embarrassment, my teacher often told the story about the discomfort and inadequacy felt by the late Ayatollah Burujirdi (d. 1961) when he had to lecture on the *taharat al-niswan* to his largely male audience made up of senior members of the religious establishment of the Qumm *madrasa*. Such sessions were part of the advanced lectures given by Burujirdi on juristic principles that were applied to deduce these rulings. Since the traditional centres of Islamic learning neither allowed female participation nor public discussion on matters concerning women's specific physical condition, the lectures on the *taharat al-niswan* dealt only with closing judicial decisions, leaving the detailed explications of the method and reasoning behind them for individual perusal.

However, that does not seem to have been the case in the early days of Islam. The Prophet Muhammad himself was at various times asked questions regarding the rules of purification for women. Significantly, on many such occasions the women of the Prophet's household were the interlocutors and even the interpreters of the religious guidance that affected women's ritual purity. 'A'isha, according to the Muslim traditionist al-Bukhari, was present when a woman in Medina came to ask the Prophet about the rules of cleanliness after finishing menses.

> He replied 'Take a piece of cloth perfumed with musk and clean the private parts with it thrice.' The Prophet felt shy and turned his face. So I ['A'isha] pulled her to me and told her what the Prophet meant.[1]

In the same section another Tradition reports that when the Prophet replied that she should purify herself with a piece of cloth scented with musk, the woman asked, 'How shall I purify myself with it?' He said, 'Glory be to God, purify yourself!' At that point 'A'isha came to the rescue of the Prophet and pulled her to herself and taught her the method of cleansing herself.[2]

The Traditions clearly show that in the early days of Islam in issues dealing with women's ritual purification, leading Muslim women were provided with necessary instruction. The Prophet could not and did not exclude women in dealing with their own particular situation in the performance of their religious duties. Moreover, as one can sense in some of these Traditions, the Prophet himself sensed discomfort in going beyond expressing simply the rulings dealing with women's ritual purification. This feeling of inadequacy in dealing with peculiarly female concerns

in Islamic rituals continues in the way later jurists treated juridical decisions affecting women. Certainly, the difference was that
while the Prophet's wives and daughters were full participants in
the legal deliberations affecting Muslim women, we have no record
to suggest that the womenfolk of the jurist had similar opportunity to intervene in female ritual concerns.

Anecdotes about the male legal scholar dealing with intimate
female issues and the problems he faces in conveying innermost
contents of female ritual purification constitute legitimate enter-
tainment among the 'puritanical' members of the Muslim religious
class. The subtle language of the Muslim 'seminarians' speaking
about the 'unspeakable' deserves a separate study. But the contents of these anecdotes that lead modern researchers to the
contextualization of the rulings about menses and sexual inter-
course also point to the way in which a powerfully gender-oriented
Muslim culture treats matters connected with the 'other gender,'
by excluding them in the interpretive process.

In the male-dominated religious discourse of the *madrasa*, information about women's experience is mediated through the
'intertext' of the oral transmission of the anecdotes about women.[3]
The above cited anecdote about the senior male legal scholar
embarrassed by female ritual purification provides a symbolic link
in contextualizing the experience of something absent: the
elicitation of the condition of being a woman by a man in a legal
investigation.

While intelligible re-enactment of the subjective experience of
the 'other' through the formation of a figurally represented relation is not entirely impossible, its cognitive content is not free of
suspicion. For instance, in the context of a legal ruling pertaining
to a woman's situation in a society, the legal language constitutes
the meaning of utterance about the female 'other' mediated
through male representation of interpersonal relations, the
mu'amalat. The legal utterance, in such circumstances, without
taking full account of the concerns and conditions peculiar to
female life, is promulgated and interpreted by a male jurist to
apply to all women in a society. Hence, what we have in the text is
figural rather than the actual representation of woman's situational
and objective condition.

To overcome this cognitive impediment, one needs to

undertake the analysis of the symbolic network of Islamic legal discourse. In other words, contextualization of the rulings about sexual segregation, for instance, that still stand unvitiated among religious-minded Muslims today, cannot be explained by merely referring to the textual and cultural validation of the practice in Muslim societies. One needs to understand the intertextual network of symbols expressed by means of the narratives developed through interlocutory devices in which women are represented as actors, as questioners, even occasionally as disputants. To be sure, these narratives extend beyond the legal rulings about male-female segregation. They, in fact, contribute to the formation of a symbolic configuration of Islamic cultural values.

Let me elaborate on this particular issue of segregation. In general, rulings about female segregation are based on the concept of '*awra*, meaning 'indecent to expose'.[4] On the basis of this concept, jurists regard a woman's body, including her face, as '*awra*. However, there are controversial texts ascribed to the Prophet and some of his Companions that regard even her voice as '*awra* and hence, 'proper for veiling and covering' at all times.[5] Through such an extension of the '*awra* to include the voice, Islamic law seems to advocate the position in which a woman is legally silenced, morally separated and religiously veiled.

Going beyond the text and the context of these rulings, as I want to demonstrate in this essay, could lead us to such an analysis of the intertextual dimension of the cases that form an entire genre in Islamic juridical texts. It could, furthermore, direct us to pose a fundamental question in the Muslim juridical studies: Can the male-dominated religious epistemology provide an authentic voice in the interpretive process connected with the female 'other'? How can male jurists undertake to map the subjective experience of the silent 'other' of a Muslim society?

At this juncture I need to point out my reservations about lending wholehearted support to the feminist jurisprudence that regards male-dominated legal decisions as being conditioned by ideological interpretation of law and the male bias as the source of violation of women's human rights. The reason is that even in the male-dominated Islamic culture, at the level of figural representation, male jurists have been able to transmit female existence and experience, however imperfectly, by eliciting that segment of their ideological utterances that regard both genders to be part of humanity. Without such an acknowledgement of essential humaneness of men and women, it would have been impossible for them to transmit those values in the culture that saw woman and man in relational terms as parents, sister and brother, daughter and father, mother and son, and husband and wife. Islamic legal discourse has not always conceived of male-female relations in terms of gender power struggle.

The argument to be developed in this paper is that a major part of the present epistemological crisis in Muslim jurisprudence over women's issues is due to the blatant absence of female voice in Islamic legal discourse. It is remarkable that even when women transmitters of *hadith* were admitted in the *'ilm al-rijal* (science dealing with the scrutiny of the reporters),[6] dealing with source criticism to authenticate *hadith*-reports in the *sunna*, and even when their narratives were recognized as valid documentation for deducing various rulings, they were not participants in the intellectual process that produced the prejudicial rulings encroaching upon the personal status of women. More importantly, the revelational text, regardless of its being extracted from the Qur'an or the *sunna*, was casuistically extrapolated in order to disprove a woman's intellectual and emotional capacities to formulate independent decisions that would be more sensitive and more accurate in estimating her radically different life experience. The demand today for new and expanded methodology of *usul al-fiqh* among the Muslim fundamentalist leaders, clearly shows the crisis that faces the male-dominated epistemology in coming to terms with the demands about the recognition of the women's personal status and the substantive-cognitive role of their reason in reversing prejudicial decisions that deny her dignity as a full person.[7]

In order to demonstrate the serious nature of this crisis in Muslim legal studies, let me begin by setting forth some preliminary observations about Muslim religious epistemology. There are four basic components that constitute legal studies:

1. The *usul:* fundamental sources that provide paradigm cases and the general principles that are behind them.
2. The *furu':* present instances for which legal decisions are being sought in the light of paradigm cases provided in the

fundamental sources.

3. The *mawdu'at:* 'objects' or 'situations' that determine the status of present instances and the ordinances that could be based on them to decide whether it is an obligatory act, a recommended act, or an act permitted at discretion, and so on.

4. The *ahkam:* ordinances that specify the religious practice.

Whereas Muslim scholars are in agreement that acquisition of knowledge regarding the *usul* (fundamental sources) is incumbent individually on the community members who should undertake to investigate these sources themselves, in matters of *ahkam* (religious ordinances) they must follow the judicial rulings of a qualified jurisprudent or *mujtahid*. However, the practice of the community throughout history has been to follow the juridical authority in acquiring knowledge regarding both fundamental sources and the rulings derived from them. This method of acquisition of religious knowledge on the authority of a learned member of the community is identified as *taqlid* (following the authority of a leading legist), which is theoretically permissible only in matters related to religious practice. What is the status of *mawdu'at* (objects in a case)? Is *taqlid* permissible in acquiring knowledge about 'objects' and 'situations'?

Mawdu' (singular of *mawdu'at*) signifies the actual state of a thing before a ruling can be deduced. For instance, before a jurist issues a ruling regarding the shortening of the daily worship for those who travel between two neighbouring cities, such as Berkeley and Palo Alto in California, he needs to define the legal extent of a large city. Such an explanation of the size of a city for legal purposes is known as *mawdu'*, that is, substantive information about factors that characterize a city. Or, in order to rule about ritual impurity of the blood that stains a shirt, a jurist needs to ascertain that it is definitely human and not insect blood, because the status of human blood is different in determining ritual impurity of the shirt.

Muslim scholars acknowledge that in investigating the *mawdu'at* one need not be an expert. In fact, an ordinary believer is in some instances even more proficient than a scholar in determining the factual state of an object or a situation. What matters is the practical knowledge about an issue under investigation. As such, one need not follow another person's knowledge in *mawdu'* if he or she is certain about its actual state. Moreover, juridical principle states that knowledge about *mawdu'* does not fall under the category of *taqlid*, that is, one need not follow the juridical authority in order to determine objects and situations of a case; rather, one should undertake its investigation individually. The presumption is that determination of the state or contextual situation of the case is a rational process open to all who possess sound reasoning. One should not let someone else determine the object on which a judicial decision would be based. However, there is a stipulation in Islamic law that in the case of a legally incompetent person or a minor, determining the *mawdu'* could be assumed by a legal guardian (*wali*), including a jurist.

To recapitulate, of the four fundamental components of Islamic legal system it is only *ahkam* (ordinances) that require following a jurist's research and conclusions based on the main sources of Islamic legal formulations. The other three parts are open to individual research and their ultimate acknowledgement or rejection. More importantly, it is in the area of *mawdu'at*, as they affect the religious praxis, that there exists the space in which interpersonal negotiations between different groups and individuals are possible. The *usul* that should be based on firm rational enquiry have their place in the hearts and minds of the believers. Unlike the *mawdu'at*, the *usul* (the paradigm cases in the Qur'an and the *sunna*) have only an indirect influence on the final outcome of a juridical ruling.

This male-dominated religious epistemology has given rise to several fundamental questions related to the determination of the situational aspects of cases in connection with women. First of all, are women any different from men in understanding the process of identifying objects and their contexts as required prior to issuing the legal decision? How about their role in ascertaining the particular substantive state of woman's situation related to sexuality and reproduction, marriage and divorce? Is there any principle in the juridical theory that would suggest a form of thinking that distinguishes between the concerns of men and those of women?

If one follows the prerequisite individual rational enquiry in the *mawdu'at*, it would be correct to conclude that the Islamic belief system dictates that women need to represent their own concerns in all matters of family and maternity care. Implicit in this proposition is the recognition of women's right to assess their particular social situations and determine the legal applications in accordance with their sense of priorities. Furthermore, since the Islamic belief system does not speak about justice in terms of equality of sexes, and treats the underlying difference of sex as natural and not the creation of society, defining a particular *mawdu'* has to be undertaken by the party concerned.

From the juridical literature examined in its historical context, it is evident that, relatively speaking, Muslim jurists succeeded in pursuing the Qur'anic impulse towards family relationships and asserting individual rights on the basis of God-centred equality. And although man retained wide authority over his wife, laws were enacted to give women unprecedented respect and protection in the patriarchal context.

In family law, the rights of women, children and other dependants were protected against the male head of the family who, on the average, was stronger than a woman and more independent, since he is free of pregnancy and immediate care of children. Islamic marital rules encouraged individual responsibility by strengthening the nuclear family. Islamic law protected male prerogative on the grounds that men were required to support the household, whereas women were protected primarily by their family. All legal schools gave a husband one-sided divorce privileges because for a woman to divorce a man would mean to unsettle her husband's economic investment. Under these rules, a husband could divorce his wife almost at will, but a wife who wished to leave her husband had to show good reason. The main legal check upon the man in divorce was essentially financial and a matter of contract between equal parties that included a provision about bridal gift. Part of the gift (*sidaq* or *mahr*), which might be substantial, was paid at the time of marriage; if he divorced her without special reason, he had to pay her the rest.

The equality of women in the law carried with it an important financial independence. Muslim women could own property which could not be touched by any male relative, including her husband who was required to support her from his own resources. Moreover, women had a personal status which might allow them to start their own business. However, this potential female independence was curbed primarily by cultural means, keeping marriages within the extended family, so that family property would not leave the family through women marrying out.

Hence, although wives and daughters were given a stronger position than they had in the pre-Islamic Arab culture, in one area the Qur'an left the status of a woman to become the *mawdu'* for laws that permitted, though mitigated, an inequality of status between men and women, reducing a woman to 'half-the-man'. Her distinctive contribution in determining her own social context was thoroughly excluded by eliminating her as the interpreter of her own objects and situations. Patriarchal structures of Arab culture, in the form of loosely camouflaged Traditions ascribed to the Prophet, left her intellectually crippled, while the male jurists prepared the text of the laws for her insidious domination by the male members of society.

It is relevant that it is mainly in the sphere of interpersonal relationships, the *mu'amalat* section of jurisprudence, that woman's input in clarification of her *mawdu'* (her substantive social context) was kept in check. In the sphere of the God-human relationship, the *'ibadat* (worship) section of law, her equality with man before God was never questioned. Nevertheless, the manner in which her input in the *mu'amalat* was circumscribed had implications for her performance of the *'ibadat*, the requirements of the God-human relationship. Thus, for instance, the prohibition for a woman to travel on her own without a male relative has directly affected her religious freedom to undertake the performance of the obligatory *hajj* (annual pilgrimage) in Mecca. This prohibition, it must be pointed out, was based on the juristic principle that 'averting causes of corruption has precedence over bringing about that which has benefit' (*dar'u al-mafasid muqaddam 'ala jalb al-masalih*). This and other similar juristic principles have been regularly invoked to curb not only women's rights but also the rights of minorities to function as full citizens in some Muslim societies.

PARADIGM CASES IN RULINGS ABOUT WOMAN'S STATUS

The paradigm cases in dealing with the status of women are derived directly from an investigation of the sources of law. The sources are treated hierarchically, reflecting the religious evaluation of the epistemes contained in the Qur'an and the *sunna*. Thus, in formulating judicial decisions (*fatawa*) a jurist goes first to the Qur'an, then to the exegetical works in conjunction with the *sunna* and, finally, to the juridical corpus, in that order, to follow the process of extrapolating fresh decisions from paradigmatic cases. I follow this approach with the methodological concern that any study of this kind requires a normative interpretation of the religious underpinnings presented in the Qur'an. It is foundational to my study to raise the question: Should 'Islam' as a belief system be defined and judged by its practitioners, or should its practitioners be defined and judged by a normative standard provided by the revelational sources on which the religious belief system is constructed? I believe I need an interpretive standpoint from which I can judge that some affirmations regarding women are peripheral or incidental to the tradition and that others are central and essential, that some are privileged and can serve as a guide for the interpretation of others. With this in mind, I begin to respond to my question: 'Woman, half-the-man?' by looking at the Qur'an and its exegesis as the source of religious affirmations that altered, in decisive ways, the objects and situations within which legal-moral judgements were made regarding women in the Muslim society.

The estimation of a woman's position in jurisprudence is contextualized in the following pertinent reference in the Qur'an (2:282), which relates to contracting a debt:

> O believers, when you contract a debt one upon another for a stated term, write it down, and let a scribe write it down between you justly, and let not any scribe refuse to write it down, as God has taught him; so let him write, and let the debtor dictate, and let him fear God his Lord and not diminish anything of it. ... *And call in to witness two witnesses, men; or if the two be not men, then one man and two women, such witnesses as you approve of, that if one of the two errs the other will remind her;* and let the witnesses not refuse,

whenever they are summoned. ... And fear God; God teaches you, and God has knowledge of everything.[8]

This passage is regarded as the scriptural basis for the law of evidence (*shahadat*) in jurisprudence. Moreover, it has also been evoked to communicate the inferiority of a woman's evidence as compared to a man. Exegetical literature discusses variations in the reading of the phrase: 'if one of the two errs (*an tadilla ihdahuma*),' and considers whether the clause is conditional and if it connotes the superiority of male memory power.[9] In fact, al-Tabarsi cites a specified opinion which he rejects and which maintained that the Qur'an made this provision of 'reminding' in women's evidence because 'forgetfulness overcomes women (inherently) more than it does men'.[10]

None of the commentaries in the classical age go beyond lexical and grammatical exposition of the statement to establish that women are in need of being reminded in order to render their evidence equal to that of a man who enjoys impeccable memory. To be sure, al-Baydawi maintains that the Shafi'i jurists implemented the terms of this verse only in the case of business and financial transactions (*amwal*), whereas the Hanafis extended the requirement of two women equal to one man to criminology and law of retribution.[11]

Yet, the grammatical conclusion that the Qur'anic statement 'if one of the two errs ...' is a conditional clause had enormous implications in explicating the nature of divine commandment in jurisprudence. This grammatical specification had been acknowledged despite the fact that it was only one among the early transmitters of the Qur'anic text who had insisted in reading the clause as conditional with *in*, if. For the jurists looking at the denotation of the statement the question is: Is the conditional commandment given for the specific situation in the Medinese society to be interpreted as an unconditional commandment, evincing the probable conclusion that regardless of whether a woman errs or not, her evidence is to be reduced to half of a man's evidence?

In fact, some later exegetes, like the Shi'i Mulla Fath Allah Kashani, maintained that the statement is unconditional because woman is inherently weaker in her rational judgement than man who is intellectually stronger, and forgetfulness is far from his nature.[12] Furthermore, he asserts that, according to Sufyan b. 'Uyayna, the verse's requirement of two women brings together the evidence of two women and raises it to be equivalent to that of one man.[13] However, both the explicit denotation and the implied context of the verse in the exegetical literature strictly allowed a conditional commandment to be surmised. It denied the unconditional purport with its implications for the inherent inferiority of a woman that was asserted in the legal decisions, including those maintained by the Shafi'is in the limited area of financial transactions.

In legal texts, the object and social situation of a Muslim woman, as extracted from the conditional commandment of the Qur'an, was defined in terms of her position in the regional culture. The cultural evaluation of a woman was transmitted in some of the *hadith* reports that were used to overcome the conditional denotation of the Qur'anic law of evidence. These were used as evidentiary documentation to extrapolate unqualified stipulations that a woman's evidence equals half of that of a man, regardless of the situational factors.

When we examine the *hadith* literature to determine how far the above verse of the Qur'an had reinforced the cultural estimation of a woman's intelligence in providing evidence, we discover that al-Bukhari has preserved an interesting rubric in one of the odd places towards the end of his compilation dealing with the evidentiary nature of a 'single' narrative (*khabar al-wahid*).[14] Al-Bukhari's rubrics actually serve as his judicial decisions (*fatawa*) for which he produces *hadith* reports that follow as documentation. Thus, under the rubric of *khabar al-mar'at al-wahida* (narrative reported by a 'single' woman), he cites the following Tradition:

['Abd Allah] ibn 'Umar said: Some Companions of the Prophet, including Sa'd, were going to eat meat. But one of the wives of the Prophet called them, saying, 'It is the meat of a certain reptile (*dabb*)!' The people then stopped eating it. On that the Prophet said, 'Carry on eating, for it is lawful.' Or, he said, 'There is no harm in eating it, but it is not from my meals.'[15]

An important dietary matter is the object of the narrative, on the basis of which a legal ruling permitting a particular kind of meat is being deduced. However, this permission is stated on the authority of the Prophet, who reportedly reverses an opinion prohibiting its consumption expressed by one of his wives. The implications of this *hadith* for the admissibility of a woman's evidence in specifying the object of a ruling cannot be sufficiently emphasized. The *hadith* indicates that a narrative related by a 'single' woman transmitter, even if she happens to be one of the Prophet's wives, cannot be permitted as evidence for a prohibitive legal ruling. On the contrary, as reported in another Tradition in the same section, a *hadith* reported by a 'single' truthful male transmitter is admissible as documentation for all kinds of ordinances.[16]

The purpose of al-Bukhari's compilation is not to provide additional documentation by citing the above verse as proof for his implied conclusion that a 'single' female narrator's credibility is vitiated by the absence of another female. However, the law of evidence in the Qur'an (2:282) is the unmistakable context of this tradition.

This and other similar *hadith*s raise serious questions not only about the authenticity of these narratives that ignored the intertextuality of the daily details of the lives of women entrapped in male jurists' subjectivity and skewed vision of her social role; it also puts in doubt the claim by the pious for the validity and applicability of these legal rulings in all ages and at all times. Moreover, in the absence of a re-evaluation of the relevant authoritative texts within their historical and cultural contexts, Islamic jurisprudence has been impaired by irrelevant hair-splitting exercises, reflecting an acute formalistic rather than a substantive approach to religious knowledge. Hence, instead of squarely confronting the question of *mawdu'at* dealing with women's situation in Muslim societies under variable historical circumstances, the jurists have vacillated between the prestige of the written tradition and non-essential conceptual and terminological devices developed in the Islamic legal theory to interpret it. Both the methods of enquiry and the forms of argument indicate inadequacies in the juridical tradition to furnish solutions to the concrete problems faced by Muslim women.

The nature of religious discourse employed in the *madrasa*

setting makes it epistemically impossible to speak about specific objects and situations peculiar to Muslim woman's personal status without referring to the revelational knowledge preserved in the prestigious texts. It is ultimately the written tradition, and not human reason, that can negotiate the intertextuality of the judicial decisions made by a male jurist. Application of human reasoning, in any of its forms, has been permanently crippled by the *madrasa* attitude, articulated in various works of Islamic thought that human reason on its own is not capable of extracting practical knowledge regarding an ideal Islamic order.

The legal rulings regarding the inferiority of woman's evidence were extrapolated mainly on the basis of the Qur'an (2:282), fortified by some Traditions that accepted the inherent inferiority of women in matters of religion and intelligence. These rulings reveal even more serious problems in defining the object and situational context (*mawdu'at*) particular to women's social and personal condition. Undoubtedly, it was in the area of evidence that al-Bukhari's implicit conclusion regarding a single woman's testimony was inferred as half of a man's. Yet the conditional commandment of the Qur'anic verse (2:282) could not be interpreted so explicitly in view of the contextual restriction imposed by the kind of transaction. To resolve this apparent contradiction between the restrictive and conditional terms of the verse, and the unqualified terms related in some *hadith*s, jurists had to define the objects and situations in which female evidence and attending conditions could become operative.

Investigation in the specific text and context of the Qur'an and the *hadith* led jurists to recognize substantially different situations in Muslim interpersonal relations where women functioned as witnesses, providing objective testimony for ultimate judicial rulings. The Qur'anic law of evidence treated only one instance of the social situation in which her evidence in the matter of contract involving financial obligation was, for practical reasons, rendered to be half that of a man. Muslim jurists were cognizant of other situations in which this conditional and situational enactment of the Qur'anic law could not be generalized. Consequently, they promulgated three situations in the process of validating a woman's testimony on any interpersonal situation, including contractual agreements:

1. A non-permissible situation in which women's testimony is not admissible at all;
2. A permissible situation in which women testified with men; and, therefore, their testimony is admissible;
3. A permissible situation in which women's testimony is admissible, even if there were no men testifying with them.

It is worth noting that in none of these cases is a woman admitted as the only witness. In all instances she is mentioned in the plural, not necessarily in the formula of two women equal to one man, as implied in the Qur'anic verse 2:282. In most of the examples cited for each situation, it is not difficult to find the underlying concern of the Muslim culture in which a woman's role was defined by the powerful male functioning as her manager.[17] More pertinently, while her testimony was admitted in instances of marriage and debts or in areas of her expertise such as determining cases of rape and pregnancy, her evidence was excluded from cases of divorce and murder. When it came to cases of adultery, Islamic law admitted two women's testimony if accompanied by that of three men. However, if there was only one male witness and six or more female witnesses, their collective testimony could not be regarded as valid. On the other hand, a single woman's claim that she is virgin when accused of adultery by four male witnesses, stands unvitiated provided a midwife establishes the validity of her claim.

CONCLUDING REMARKS

Rulings about woman's testimony have filled the sections of the *kitab al-qada* (book on administration of justice) where the jurists have identified minutely where and when women can function as qualified witnesses. It is not difficult to discern underlying concern for justice when one takes into account the stringent requirements to establish evidence for accusation against anyone in Muslim society. However, there is no doubt that the tone of the rulings is set by the powerful male jurist who, in most cases, ignores the female evaluation of her own social situation, for instance in divorce, that furnishes the object of the ruling. There is almost an *a fortiori* argument derived from the Qur'an (2:282) to support the implied inherent inequality of sexes which then makes men take charge of a woman's affairs as determined by the competent legal authority. The religious epistemology that was constructed on revelational knowledge in juridical studies has served the Muslim jurists' endeavours in extracting unconditional commandments from the conditional and culturally conditioned references, both in the Qur'an and *hadith*, dealing with the historical Muslim social universe.

The treatment of women in Islamic legal tradition is a classic example of the 'epistemological crisis' faced by *madrasa*-educated scholars of Islamic law. Honest and critical evaluation of this crisis is dependent upon the appraisal of the historical development of theoretical and conceptual structures of the Islamic religious sciences, including jurisprudence. In order to provide an authentic intertextuality to the text and the context of legal rulings that reduce women, in a mathematical fashion sometimes, to half a man, Muslim male jurists have to include women in communicating the *mawdu'at* about women. Without such participation in the interpretive process of the text to communicate its context and intertext that has been the source of her cultural subjugation, Muslim women stand little chance to overcome being reduced to the legally silent, morally segregated and religiously veiled half-the-man.

NOTES

1. *Sahih al-Bukhari, Bab ghusl al-mahid, hadith* no. 312.

2. Ibid., *hadith* no. 311.

3. In the context of juridical studies in Islam, it is necessary to develop an interpretive process that could take into consideration materials that are not usually part of the normative texts. Women's issues in Muslim culture need to go beyond the traditional interpretive assumptions based on official corpus to include oral transmissions that reflect the social negotiations between gender within a particular context. Although he does not use the term 'intertext,' the idea is suggested by J. Derrida in his *Margins of Philosophy*, tr. A. Bass (Chicago, 1982). See also Vincent B. Leitch, *Deconstructive Criticism: An*

Advanced Introduction (New York, 1983), pp. 87–163 for Derrida and 'intertext'.

4. The term *'awra* is defined as 'the pudendum, or pudenda, of a human being, of a man and of a woman, so called because it is abominable to uncover, and to look at, what is thus termed (E.W. Lane, *An Arabic-English Lexicon*, Beirut, 1968, vol. 5, p. 2194). In the *shari'a*, for man the *'awra* (indecent to expose) is between the navel and the knee; for woman, it refers to all the person, except the face and the hands as far as the wrists. The term also applies to times of the day, as in the Qur'an (24:57), when it is improper for a grown-up child to appear in his/her parent's private chamber.

5. Whether *'awra* includes a woman's voice has been a matter of dispute among Muslim jurists. Some interesting comments on this matter are to be found in Muhammad al-Ghazali, *Qadaya'l-mar'a bayna'l-taqalid al-rakida wa' l-wafida* (Cairo, 1992), pp. 164–65. The author represents the modernist trends among some of the traditional Muslim scholars and, hence, rejects the view that a woman's voice is also part of the *'awra*.

6. The term *rijal*, meaning 'men of prominence' lexically excludes women. It should be pointed out, however, that these biographical dictionaries did include women reporters of *hadith*. In fact, without these women reporters there are numerous issues dealing with the religious practice in Islam which would have never reached the early doctors of law.

7. See, for instance, Hasan al-Turabi, *Tajdid usul al-fiqh al-Islami* (*Revitalization of the Islamic Legal Theory*) (*Jeddah*, 1984), published during the early years of the Iranian Revolution, which speaks about the expansive application of rational juristic devices like *qiyas* (analogical deduction), *istishab* (principle of continuity) and *istislah* (principle of public interest) formulated in the classical juristic theory to deduce new rulings.

8. For the translation of the Qur'an, I have used A.J. Arberry, *The Koran Interpreted* (London, 1955), with some minor revision to conform with the original Arabic text.

9. Muhammad b. Jarir al-Tabari, *Jami' al-bayan fi tafsir al-Qur'an* (Beirut, 1972), vol. 3, pp. 82–3, and Abu 'Ali al-Fadl b. al-Hasan al-Tabarsi, *Majma' al-bayan fi tafsir al-Qur'an* (Beirut, 1959), vol. 1, pp. 398–9.

10. Al-Tabarsi, *Majma'*, vol. 1, p. 398.

11. 'Abd Allah b. 'Umar al-Baydawi, *Anwar al-tanzil wa-asrar al-ta'wil*

(Cairo, 1939), vol. 1, p. 64

12. Fath Allah Kashani, *Minhaj al-sadiqin fi ilzam al-mukhalifin* (Tehran, 1969), vol. 2, pp. 155–56. This is contrary to the classical Shi'i authorities on Qur'anic exegesis, like Muhammad b. al-Hasan al-Tusi, *al-Tibyan fi tafsir al-Qur'an* (Najaf, 1957), vol. 2, pp. 373–4, and al-Tabarsi, *Majma'*, vol. 1, p. 398.

13. Kashani, *Minhaj*, vol. 2, p. 157, where he cites al-Zamakhshari for Sufyan b. 'Uyayna's opinion.

14. A narrative or *hadith* that was reported by a single transmitter was not easily accredited because of the doubt about its reliability. Hence, its use as a documentation for formulating a judicial opinion was questionable. Nonetheless, jurists had a number of criteria that were used to approbate a 'single' narrative for its evidentiary use in a legal case.

15. *Sahih al-Bukhari, Bab khabar al-mar'at al-wahida, hadith* no. 372.

16. Ibid., introduction to *hadith* no. 352.

17. The dominant role of man has been traditionally extrapolated from the following verse of the Qur'an (4:39): 'Men are the managers to the affairs of women for that God has preferred in bounty one of them over another, and for that they [men] have expended of their property.'

11

Present-Day Islam Between its Tradition and Globalization

Mohammed Arkoun

'The devil hides in the details'

The title of this essay announces three major fields of enquiry
and critical analysis: *present-day Islam;* the *living tradition* dating
back to the emergence of the *Islamic fact* between 610–632 and
661; and *globalization.* My objective in including under the same
critical scrutiny themes as complex as these is to set apart, in every
possible manner, the *implicits* that are lived but unthought in each
of these three areas of individual existence and historical action,
from the *explicits* that are problematized, thought for the first time
or rethought, in the perspectives opened up by the new phenomenon of globalization.

For methodological and epistemological reasons which will
become apparent in the course of the exposé, I will begin by defining the new context created by the forces of globalization and
then tackle the questions of present-day Islam and Islamic
tradition.

1. WHAT IS GLOBALIZATION?

Until the years 1960–70, human thought had known a particular idea of the world, or worlds in the plural. This idea itself nourished a large number of representations whose spiritual, artistic and scientific productivity varied according to their cultural environments and historical conjunctures. It is thus that with Copernicus, Galileo and Kepler, one passed '*from the closed world to an infinite universe*'. What has long been called international relations by no means covers the concept of globalization, the active forces and the realities of which all individuals and societies are discovering or experiencing at the present time.

Globalization upsets all the known cultural, religious, philosophical and politico-juridical traditions; even modernity that issued from the reason of the Enlightenment does not escape from it. That is why, since the 1980s, various analysts, thinkers and researchers, particularly in the United States, speak of *post-modernity*. I prefer to avoid this term, which refers to a concept badly and little elaborated and which keeps us in the linear historical trajectory inaugurated in Western Europe during the 17th and 18th centuries. Globalization forces the Europeans themselves to speak of the limits and perverse effects of the reason of the Enlightenment which has allowed, among other things, the construction of the secular, democratic and liberal nation-state, the progress of scientific research, and the transition from the solidarities of clan, blood and confession to the contractual solidarities regulated by the state of law. With the resolute march towards European Union, one crosses a new historical stage in the organization and widening of the spaces of citizenship, which is at the same time the basis and object of democratic life. The nation-state is in the process of accomplishing its mission in Europe by putting in place civil societies, sufficiently emancipated juridically, to act as effective and necessary partners of the states of law. However, crossing this historical stage proves as difficult and uncertain as that which led absolute monarchies of divine law to become constitutional monarchies and democratic republics. The problems arise, in effect, from diverse European cultures and visions of the world linked to the slow and difficult ascent of nation-states, which reveal their provincial limits, their exclusion of other cultures of the world, their xenophobia and their latent violence, always ready to be exercised against the foreigner, however near geographically (as was the case in the Franco–German wars).

The economic, monetary and technological forces of globalization have achieved a primacy and priority in the process of history, while snatching from abstract idealism the spiritual, philosophical, ethical, political and juridical values, whose bases or concrete material components are increasingly better explicated. However, political idealism continues to seek refuge in nationalist discourse, as can be noted in the resistance to the progress of the European Union which began as no more than a simple community formed to regulate the production of coal and steel. The claims of national specificity, authenticity and exception curb the advances towards the revision of national historiographies, intellectual frames of interpretation and re-appropriation of values. The example thus given by the 'old' nations to their former colonies, which became 'emerging nations' without transition, provides dangerous 'arguments' to the *party-nation-states* which assumed power in these countries during the years 1950–70 in conditions that are known to us, and which are leading programmes of 'national construction' in the new context created by globalization. This remark must be retained for a better evaluation of the role of Islam and its tradition in the mounting tensions between these party-nation-states and societies whose democratic structure and legitimate aspirations towards democratization are not really taken into consideration.

Since the dissolution of the Soviet Union as a geopolitical power, the United States exercises a hegemonical control of all the forces of globalization. The Europeans, including Russia and its former satellites, rather than nourish rivalries, seek alliances, contracts and collaboration with the United States. Thus, the burden of this hegemony makes itself felt more upon peoples and nations in the process of emancipation and unification. 'The right of peoples to self-determination', which nourished so many illusions about national emancipation in the context of the Cold War, has become an ideological insanity in the face of intolerable civil wars which tear apart so many societies long-seized in the grip of totalitarian nationalisms and projected suddenly into the savage liberalism of *McWorld* (which I discuss in the next section). The latter invented a new concept, 'humanitarian aid for peoples in danger of genocide', which is as vague and illusory as its predecessor. But the economic and monetary forces of globalization do not today concern themselves with humanitarian aid any more than the bourgeois capitalist conquerors of the 19th century worried about the emancipation of their own womenfolk, the working classes, or *a fortiori* the colonized peoples. Humanitarian aid, the rights of peoples, human rights and democratic sermons form part of the panoply of political slogans, adapted to every geo-political conjuncture by those who contrive to their advantage the operations of globalization. It is thus that the nationalist 'elites' – who believed that they were giving real content to these slogans by engaging, in the years 1960–70, with the politics of economic development in the frame of 'cooperation' and 'development aid' – generated, with their statist and economic partners of the West, the riposte of the so-called Islamic Revolution (see what follows on *Jihad* versus *McWorld*), supported by marginalized social strata which were badly integrated in enclaves of modernity too narrow, and dispossessed (even in the case of rural villagers and forcibly sedentarized nomads) of their languages, cultures, ecological equilibria, customary codes and traditional solidarities – just as the European peasantry had been dispossessed under mounting pressures of industrialization, but in its case with long transitions and effectively integrated institutions. Globalization deploys on a planetary scale the strategies of market conquest and multiplication of consumers and their loyalties without any regard for the cultural regression, intellectual misery, political oppression, social tragedy and individual enslavement brought about by this 'unequal exchange' which for so long has been denounced in vain. We know how the strategies of globalization bring about, on the one hand *interstate* agreements and diplomacy for the flow of goods in exchange for the importation of raw materials, and on the other hand the media which denounce the totalitarian, fanatical and regressive policies of those very states recognized officially as respectable partners and interlocutors.

Let us note here an important political notion rarely highlighted by analysts and almost never included in the themes of electoral campaigns in the most advanced democratic regimes. It concerns the systematic ignorance in which citizens are kept about everything pertaining to interstate diplomacy. That which is called popular sovereignty is unable to exercise any type of control over diplomatic relations, which lie in the exclusive competence of the heads of states and their ministers for foreign affairs. Thus, the responsibilities incurred in conflicts such as those of Algeria, Rwanda, Zaire, Iran, Sudan, Bosnia, etc., are not only dissimulated to those citizens most capable of undertaking juridical, historical and ethical analysis, but are knowingly distorted by the easy indignation generated against the crimes, assassinations and destruction stigmatized every day by the media. On this level, the most pertinent analyses and the most legitimate critiques are brushed aside with repeated appeals to the 'reason' of state security against the 'chattering' of idealist intellectuals.

This functioning of democracy is accepted particularly by civil societies as they are inclined in the first place to defending the 'social gains' which are in themselves brought about by globalization. This accounts for the development within the European Union of the notion and practice of strikes by proxy – the strike by every sector or professional category, supported unconditionally by all the workers who feel equally threatened with losing the advantages gained, and above all their jobs. One is far from the simplistic frontiers charted by class conflict; but the selfishness of civil societies, necessarily supported by their states, replaces that of the former classes, and it exacerbates the situation of those very people who are at the same time exploited and excluded by the forces of globalization, especially when delocalization is involved. One thus finds, once again, a relation of forces comparable to that between the colonizing nations-states and the peoples colonized until 1945.

It must be admitted that in the current state of the world, the relentless march of globalization generates more ruptures, tensions, contradictions and collective conflicts than did the exportation of fragments of material modernity to colonies in the 19th and 20th centuries. Neither the researchers and theoreticians with the highest competence and know-how, nor the expanding armies of managers of large multinational firms, nor the politicians who monopolize the use of 'legal violence' (as Max Weber would say) integrate into their analyses, expectations and strategies of development the real problems, the needs and hopes of those peoples who are deprived of adequate representation, as well as possibilities of direct expression and emancipation. The philosophical implications of this global process of change, which relate as much to scientific research as to technological innovation and economic expansion, are not even evoked as one of the decisive parameters which ought to inform decisions at all levels and in every sphere of activity. This is because philosophical thought itself is hardly mobilized by the urgent need to rethink the essential connections which bind together philosophy and democracy. I refer here to the very suggestive report entitled *Philosophie et démocratie dans le monde*, compiled by Roger Pol Droit at the request of UNESCO, on the present state of the teaching of philosophy in member countries. Rare are the countries which have introduced or maintained any serious teaching of philosophy at the high school level. In the Islamic context, the rich philosophical tradition that was developed from the 8th century until the death of Ibn Rushd (Averroes) in 1198 has, since the 13th century, been lost. Here is how Droit defines the traits of 'the common space' fundamental to philosophy and democracy: both bring about a *'founding relationship'* with the following features:

1. *Speech:* for a thought exists only when it is stated, expounded, submitted to discussion, criticism and arguments of others; this remark applies to philosophical thought as well as political positions in a democracy.
2. *Equality:* for one does not ask others 'by what right' they intervene in the debate; one does not require by any means that they be provided with any authority or authorization; it is sufficient that they should speak and argue. [I modify Droit's remark as follows: In the perspective of globalization, it is no longer only the citizens of one particular nation who take part in the political debate; for the first time, and in philosophy since the ancient Greeks, the entire human race is concerned as much with the political as with the philosophical debate on the subject, notably the founding conditions of political legitimacy in local regimes and the *governance* – in English, governability – of the inhabited planet.]
3. *Doubt:* since immediate certitudes have wavered, in order to

ensure that the research of the true as well as general discussion of the subject is open, it is necessary for one to be no longer in a universe of answers and beliefs, but of questions and research.

4. *Self-institution:* for no external decision comes to create the philosophical stage or the democratic community, no authority legitimates it 'from outside', nothing guarantees it 'from above'; they receive their power only from themselves and are not subjected to any authority whose source they would not be.'¹

I shall return to the critical examination of these definitions when I compare the status of the theologico-political implied by R.P. Droit to that of the philosophico-political which is inseparable from our modernity. This comparison is indispensable for demonstrating the incoherencies, anachronisms and illusions of the contemporary Islamic discourse on Islam and democracy. But first I will put forward three preliminary remarks:

1. On 25 February 1795, the French Revolution was defined by Joseph Lakanal as this 'educative utopia' aiming 'to put an end to the inequalities of development affecting the citizens' capacity to judge.'² In fact, philosophical teaching organized by the Republic was and still is offered in public and private establishments subsidized by the state. This French tradition may have been able to generate a taste for theoretical speculations; yet one cannot say that political thought in France and the current traits of French- style democracy are more marked than elsewhere by a philosophical attitude as just defined. The original harm comes, without doubt, from the tight control exercised by the secular republican state in the French sense, ever since the foundation of technical schools and high schools. In the 17th century, Benedict Spinoza defended rather the right for all men 'to teach [philosophy] publicly, at their own expense and at the peril of their reputation.'³

2. In the perspective of *political reason*, called upon to manage all the processes of globalization in the real, constant interest of every *person-individual-citizen*, it becomes necessary for the society and the regime, where this reason is called upon, to deploy its existence and redefine the conditions for a concretely universalizable philosophical attitude. It is in this sense that I

shall examine the contribution that critical thought can make to this project in concrete Islamic contexts.

3. The concept of *person-individual-citizen* which I have just introduced deserves to be elaborated in the perspectives opened up by anthropology for the exploration and critical analysis of all cultures, and no longer only the 'great' cultures which, at various times in history, exercised or still exercise a hegemony. In other words, the classical philosophical attitude is no longer sufficient for rethinking, with all the *descriptive and explicative adequacy* required by globalization, the status of the *person*, the *individual* and the *citizen* in a political, juridical and cultural space – a space which is no longer only that of the nation-states and still less that of religious communities such as the *umma* which the Islamist movements are trying to set up as a universal model of historical action.

It is to be feared that the call to philosophy, cultural anthropology and critical history of cultures, beyond all the hegemonical frames of realization of human existence, will draw little attention, even less than in the context of the nation-state, from the economic, monetary and political establishments, from official representatives in large international conferences, and from the variegated protagonists who contribute to the accelerated pace of globalization. All these actors are generally little prepared to accord a just place to the philosophical implications of the responsibilities that they prefer to exercise as *effective* experts. One follows in them less the historical project of promoting and extending democratic values to all peoples and societies in the world than the conquest of new markets for consumer goods which no longer find enough buyers in glutted markets.

Even if one were to agree to a philosophical and anthropological examination of the problems raised by the expansion of *McWorld*, it would still be necessary in the first place to work towards an indispensable intellectual overtaking of the frame of thought inherited from classical metaphysics. The latter has long remained a prisoner of recurrent interferences, in spite of efforts at distinction which are always invalidated by polemical tensions between theological themes and philosophical categories. What sociologists call the 'return of the religious' contributes, even in the most secularized societies, to the obstruction of efforts to elucidate the stakes peculiar to a theology and a philosophy that can be cultivated without polemics, without mimetic rivalry, in accordance with the new scientific spirit and new cognitive systems proposed by biology, linguistics, semiology, psychology, socio-anthropology and the study of historical problems. In other words, the process of economic, technological and monetary globalization is being deployed in a climate of 'disposable thought', where the crises in the study of man and society stand in sharp contrast to the spectacular advances of technological knowledge which are readily appropriated by the desire for power and profit.

All this shows the need to express clearly the philosophical attitude and the type of cognitive activity which must accompany present-day globalization as a concrete historical practice. Without minimizing, and much less ignoring, either the Greek references of philosophical thought or their journey and expansion in the European historical sphere, one will recognize the distances separating positions linked to precise socio-cultural and political spaces and those related to visions of the world too hastily proclaimed universal. Grammarians, logicians and linguists have long reflected upon this tension: from the famous *disputatio* (*munazara*) between the grammarian al-Sirafi and the logician Matta b. Yunus in 10th-century Baghdad, to the enlightening analysis of E. Benvéniste of the Aristotelian categories articulated in Greek and the linguistic categories, one will grasp the idea that a universalizable philosophical attitude is precisely that which cultivates systematically the aporia of tension between the local and the global. The implantation in the local of the sense of the universal is inscribed, in a more or less insistent manner, in every linguistic experience. This tension has been cultivated as a speculative theme, like the humanism of the lettered which nourished beautiful literary compositions until the Second World War. Only modern social and cultural anthropology furnishes the concrete data peculiar to every socio-cultural construction in a precise time and space, while situating every local type in a global context of political, social, cultural and religious facts. It so happens that, as philosophy and anthropology continue to be taught and practised as distinct and specialized disciplines, the many incursions of philosophers into anthropology remain incidental and cursory, while anthropologists are not always able to go beyond the ethnographic stage of their scientific practice.[4] We also cover here the important question of the reform of education systems in order to adapt them everywhere to the exigencies of globalization.

2. IS PRESENT-DAY ISLAM IMPERVIOUS TO GLOBALIZATION?

An American political scientist, Benjamin R. Barber, has recently promoted the Qur'anic and Islamic concept of *Jihad* to the rank of a polar figure of contemporary history, dialectically linked to *McWorld*, that is to say, to ongoing globalization, viewed from the perspective of the United States and Western Europe.[5] The author is not at all interested in *Jihad* in order to denounce the expansion of Islam through 'holy war', or to propose a new theory of 'just war', a theological concept elaborated long ago by St. Augustine and raised again in the early 1990s by Presidents Bush and Mitterrand during the Gulf War. He considers, correctly, that the violence which tears apart many societies called Muslim (I prefer to use, in contradistinction to the custom of all Islamic studies and political science literature, the expression 'societies moulded by the Islamic fact', which I shall explain later) is a manifestation of not only serious internal crises, but the protest common to all societies, including those of the West, against the blind forces of globalization called *McWorld*, characterized by its market economy, monetary system, technology, media and revolution in informatics which affect work and leisure, genetic engineering, etc. This protest opposes the structural violence spread in the world by incomprehensible, anonymous decision-makers with ethically irresponsible, murderous, physical violence; it is a radical rejection in the name of traditional and religious values, not exclusive of the means of effective action obtained by material modernity. *Jihad* and *McWorld* convey much irrational and semantic disorder which remains to be analysed within the critical and cognitive perspectives defined above; they confront each other with very unequal weapons, but with different objectives, both succeeding in perverting the democratic project of emancipation of the human condition. In order to defend democracy, Barber forces the opposition between *Jihad* and *McWorld*:

the first wants to resuscitate the obscure forces of the pre-modern world such as 'religious mysteries, hierarchic communities, suffo- cating traditions, historical torpor', whereas the second goes beyond modernity by insisting upon the promotion of the market over the rights and spiritual aspirations of mankind.

In qualifying negatively the two poles, the political scientist stays in the epistemological frame of the reason of the Enlightenment, whereas globalization obliges us to revise the cognitive systems bequeathed by all types of reason which respect the rules of criti- cal historical epistemology. Thus, the qualifications applied to the pre-modern world are pertinent if one sticks to the discourse of contemporary fundamentalist movements, but historically incor- rect if one refers to the humanist culture (*adab*) of the urban milieux of the Islamic world in the 9th–11th centuries. The rea- son at work in this culture anticipated many critiques and cognitive postures, which developed much later the humanism of the Ren- aissance and subsequently amplified the reason of the Enlightenment in Europe. The latter instrumentalized the Per- sians, Turks and the Muslims in general, not for enlarging significantly their cognitive field, but in the first place to lead its battle against the main enemy of that time: clericalism. The colo- nial 19th century developed a historiography, ethnography, sociology and psychology, largely marked by an epistemology which present-day anthropology depicts as an ideology of domi- nation. The argumentation of *Jihad vs. McWorld*, although seductive in its resolute option for a universalizable humanist de- mocracy, cannot be retained for the project of a critical history of thought in the Mediterranean space, encompassing the stakes-of- meaning and the wills-to-power which became manifested there since the first emergence of the Islamic fact in Arabia in 610– 632. Present-day Islam, in effect, needs to go beyond the sterile and often dangerous protestations of *Jihad* to integrate at the same time the positive gains of modernity and the new opportunities of political, economic, social and cultural emancipation opened up by globalization – the latter to be understood as an extension of the historical project of modernity and also a correction of its errors and injustices.

If modernity is an incomplete project consisting of a determi- nation to push back ever further the limits of the human condition, it must orient globalization towards a better integration of values made discordant by the systematic opposition between the visions of traditional religions and the ideological categorizations of secular religions. As a result of this conflict, the secular voices of the prophets, saints, theologians, philosophers, artists, poets and heroes have been relentlessly marginalized, disqualified and driven back to a past relegated to erudite historiography or to definitive oblivion. Our societies produce great captains of industry, bankers who work in secrecy, sports champions and stars who generate ephemeral enthusiasm, and highly specialized scientific researchers; but these people have neither the time nor the sources of inspiration necessary for generating intellectual and spiritual values to mobilize at the level where the economic system of production and exchange engages the ecological future of the planet and the quality of human life. I have deliberately refrained from mentioning politicians here because everywhere they continue to disappoint the people they are supposed to lead – not to mention the corrupt and corrupting leaders, bloodthirsty tyrants and oppressors, obscurantists and absolutists, who enjoy the honours and consideration due to 'heads of state.'

In these observations there is neither a desire to moralize nor nostalgia for a past to be compared with the present in developed or developing societies; they are meant, rather, to define with precision the new functions which the irresistible forces of *McWorld* assign to present-day Islam. The latter continues to guarantee to the social masses, excluded from the liberties and comforts reserved for limited privileged groups, a hope mixed with the traditional expectation of eternal salvation, the possibility of attaining moral dignity in intimate encounter with the Just and Merciful God of the Qur'an, a belief in a promise of imminent justice to be accomplished by their charismatic leader, a 'modern' substitute for the ancient Imam-Mahdi. Or it demands obedience to the divine injunction to eliminate by a just and holy war (*jihad*) all the 'Pharaohs' who sow disorder and corruption on earth.

The historian-sociologist-anthropologist will not enumerate, as I have just done, all these psycho-socio-political components of what one no longer calls *hope*, but representations of the social *imaginaire*. For the politico-religious vocabulary familiar to the believers of yesterday and today, one substitutes that of the critical analyst for whom *societies produce religions* like ideologies which, once systematized in normative codes, act in their turn upon societies. This epistemological postulate doubtless allows one to deconstruct a joint psychological configuration of the rational, the *imaginaire* and the remembered truths, which are for the most part memorized but not written and are confused in the expressions of belief and conduct. However, in so far as such explicative analysis does not reach the actors to the point of provoking in each of them a better reconstruction controlled by the psychological configuration bound to religious systems through *beliefs and non-beliefs*, the 'scientific' theory of religion will merely act as a mental, cultural and political frontier in societies where it is erected implicitly (as in secular republics) or explicitly as a doctrine of state (as in socialist and popular atheistic republics). One understands, consequently, why the liberal secular state loses in philosophical flexibility that which it gains in juridical neutrality, whereas the religious state despises both. The exclusion in French public establishments of all teaching of the comparative history of religions and theological thought illustrates clearly what I mean by philosophical and scientific flexibility. It is significant that this question of philosophical and political essence is not yet being discussed within the European Union with a view to proposing new academic programmes to reflect, simultaneously, the needs of multicultural societies and the exigencies of scientific knowledge adapted to the progress of globalization.

But the perverse effects of the latter must not distract us from the historical advances founded upon the positive experience of intellectual modernity. If the great religions and philosophies have long taught that man is spirit, one must not forget that spiritualism, ontologism, transcendentalism, theologism, essentialism and substantialism are as much rationalizing derivatives or dangerous *imaginaires* as those of present-day globalization, on the real nature of mankind. Drawing on contemporary Islam, I shall attempt to show that the work prescribed by the historical conjuncture of globalization consists in going philosophically, ethically, juridically and institutionally beyond all the systems of beliefs and non-beliefs inherited variously from the past, towards a better mastery of powers available to man for changing man.

3. RETHINKING ISLAM FACING ITS TRADITION

Raising the Islamic concept of *Jihad* to the rank of a historical figure of resistance to *McWorld* cannot be the basis of present-day Islam if it is to fulfil, as it claims, the role of an alternative model to that of the West for producing more just regimes and better integrated societies. The claim of the West to remain the unique model of reference for all contemporary regimes and societies is equally not acceptable so long as the conditions defined above are not strictly fulfilled to the point of creating, among all the observers and actors of our world, the feeling of a restraining *debt-of-meaning*. Now, one can contract a *debt-of-meaning* only towards the social actors who, like the prophets, saints, heroes, thinkers and artists, are able to demonstrate in their behaviour, and articulate in a discourse accessible to the greatest number, the existential paradigms which encourage free emulation by others. In the democratic and secular Western milieu, the individual, protected by the state of law coupled with a welfare state, tends to be his or her own model, increasingly incapable of recognizing a *debt-of-meaning* to a religion, philosophy, nation, community, hero-liberator, thinker or poet. In Muslim contexts, the *debt-of-meaning* towards the Qur'an as the word of God, towards the Prophet as the messenger of God, and towards the 'pious forefathers' (*al-salaf al-salih*) who have ensured the faithful collection and transmission of the founding messages of all truths, of all valid thoughts and all correct norms, continues to play a role so preponderant that there remains no place for the adoption of, or even the mere respect for, an idea, institution, innovation or personality that cannot be integrated into the system of identification and evaluation through which the *debt-of-meaning* is perpetuated. The social and political dialectic which has prevailed since independence from colonial rule has, despite the interlude of the years 1950-60, reinforced the psychological configuration postulated by this *debt-of-meaning*. The politics of traditionalization and the celebration of Islam as a component of national identities have thwarted the possibilities of modernizing tools of thought and institutions for the benefit of a religion which is cut off from both its historical origins and contemporary scientific contexts. It is not rare, therefore, to encounter 'intellectuals', academics and managers of large enterprises, banks and complex administrations, who shelter from all critical intervention in the 'sacred' and sacralizing domain of founding texts and beliefs of this *debt-of-meaning* without which social order would collapse.

The critical analyst will explain that all discourse is the bearer of the will-to-power because it seeks to share with others the proposition of meaning that every interlocutor articulates. The more my proposition infringes upon the sphere of meaning already occupied by other social actors, the more the conflict will become rough and lead to violence; and if I enter the mythical and symbolic sphere of their foundational accounts, then a 'holy', 'sacred', 'just', 'legitimate' war becomes inevitable. Consequently, even the most secular republics have their foundational accounts, their symbolic politics, their 'places of memory' constructed by historiography, which are officially and periodically celebrated. It is in these collective representations sacralized by time that national identity takes root; it is here that the 'values' which legitimize patriotic fervour, supreme sacrifices and heroic conduct take shape. I deliberately use this ethico-political vocabulary, from which sermons and official discourses are woven, to recall that at this level of production and consumption of meaning, the interferences between the religious and the political, the sacred and the profane, the spiritual and the temporal, are so constant, so inseminating, that it is misleading to stick to the juridical and institutional theme of the separation between church and state.

This deconstructive analysis of current terminology also shows another piece of evidence, hardly familiar even to cultivated minds, about what is called *truth* in the functional trilogy of *violence, sacred* and *truth*. In the ordinary sense, truth is an immediate sentiment of perfect equivalence between words and deeds, between a statement and its *objective referents*, or more generally between current language and the empirical experience which everyone has of reality. Religions and metaphysics represent this truth as unique, intangible, transcendent and divine. But for the critical analyst, truth is defined as the sum of the *effects of meaning* which authorizes for every individual or collective subject the system of connotations represented in its language; it is the totality of representations retained in the living tradition of a group, confessional community or nation which is more or less unified by a common political and cultural history.

These two definitions of *truth* draw an increasingly distinct mental cleavage between two postures of reason itself: the *classical metaphysical posture*, amply described by historians of philosophy, continues to resist the rise of the *new posture* of the so-called exact sciences, the biological and social sciences, which are themselves in disarray by the information revolution. Historians have clearly distinguished between several postures of reason in past epochs which continue to coexist in contemporary discourse without the knowledge of their authors. Clerics, essayists, ideologues, sermonizers and experts, highly specialized experts in activities which do not require know-how grounded in historical culture, express themselves on general problems without regard for the postures of reason and cognitive systems which they use. One finds in them a confusion between theological attitudes and philosophical reasoning, between ideological argument for the invocation of a belief and the historical fact; an ingenious striving to find in the founding religious texts (Bible, Gospels, Qur'an) or the medieval exegeses consecrated as orthodox, teachings on human rights, social justice, democracy, human dignity, etc. Inversely, the pressing needs for ethical principles to regulate, in however small a measure, the confusion and anguish brought about by discoveries in the life-sciences, force us to speak again about the status of the individual, the spiritual vocation of being human, and the inalienable values which underpin the ethics of conviction and responsibility. One thus perceives that the reason of the Enlightenment has opened up horizons which it had practically abandoned or badly explored, and that theological reason seeks to regain credibility in a context of a generalized crisis of thought. On the other hand, rather than harnessing itself to the conquest of an epistemological status adapted to the pressing challenges of history at the threshold of the third millennium, the reason which claims to be post-modern even indulges in a do-it-yourself kind of individualism and militantism

All this distances us from the definition of present-day Islam. To approach the latter, I want to break as radically as possible from the epistemological attitude and the so-called scientific practice which treat Islam as a domain apart from the history of religions, cultures and civilizations. One cannot deal with present-day Islam by simply repeating the linear chronological account of its historical spread, the theologico-juridical frames of its articulation as a *system of beliefs and non-beliefs* fixed by God, dedicated to the pious observance of the faithful, and the no less conformist and repetitive transcriptions of the Islamicists which have been adopted by political scientists to describe present-day Islam. It has been shown to what extent Islam is subjected, like all living traditions of thought, culture and beliefs, to the irresistible hurricane of globalization. There is no need to reinforce ritual expressions extended to an impressive number of the faithful; no need to mobilize and inspire armies of young militants, ready for all sacrifice; no need to retain the attention of all the political strategists who are themselves surrounded by experts more or less sagacious, or by charlatans. The fact remains that the historical test through which Islam has been passing as a religion since the 1970s has already created an irreversible situation which affects all living religions, and beyond religions, the conditions of production, transmission and consumption of meaning in human societies. One understands, therefore, why I have devoted such a long preamble to the question of the metamorphoses of meaning and of what continues to be called the *truth* under the pressures of globalization.

To encompass the historical situation of what I call present-day Islam, chronology has its importance. Innumerable works, dating back to the 19th century, have dealt with Islamic modernity, modern Islam and Islam facing modernity. Under these titles, the authors are interested, in fact, in the intellectuals and researchers who have tried to apply to the history of societies shaped by the *Islamic fact* decontextualized fragments of modernity from the classical age as they were translated especially in the historiographical and philological works of the 19th century. The orientalists then praised the relative successes of their pupils such as Taha Hussein, Zaki Mubarak, Bishr Faris, Salama Musa and others, who reproduced their methodologies. But Islam and its tradition have been very little affected by those initial, modest essays, even when they gave rise to violent condemnations on the part of the guardians of an obscurantist orthodoxy; the examples of Taha Hussein and 'Ali 'Abd al-Raziq are repeated today by other authors with writings no less soothing. Present-day Islam would not have turned to fundamentalist excesses at the end of the 20th century if modernity, even of a historicist and philological kind, had really succeeded in penetrating the frames of traditional thought as it did for Christianity. With the advent of the Muslim Brotherhood movement in the 1930s, intellectual modernists rushed to make concessions to apologetic tendencies such as those manifested in the writings of al-Aqqad, Hussein Haykal and even Taha Hussein.

After 1945, the political movements of liberation were able to harness to their advantage the mobilizing power of Islam, while maintaining a general secular and social orientation, because of the presence of militants inspired by communism, or converts to the political philosophy of the Third French Republic such as Bourguiba, Ferhat Abbas and their disciples. The nationalistic fever, the priority unanimously accorded to political freedom, and the geopolitical strategies used by the two super powers of the time (the United States and the Soviet Union) to attract the emerging nation-states to their spheres of influence, succeeded in maintaining Islamic militancy in a subsidiary role. One had to wait for the great defeat of the Arab armies in 1967, the failure and death of Gamal Abdel Nasser in 1970, the first symptoms of the demise of Soviet hegemony, the demographic growth which upset the social frames of knowledge and political expression, the revelation of the limits of oil as a weapon, the fallout of the euphoria generated by the independence that had been so dearly achieved and the subsequent erosion of ill-founded legitimacies, for there to emerge on the scene what is today called *radical Islam, Islamic radicalism, political Islam, Muslim rage* (these are typical titles of books or articles on the subject), which assumed power spectacularly in Iran in 1979, and has since then pursued a devastating struggle, ill-adapted to the magnitude and the real scope of the challenges of modernity complicated by those of globalization, as has been demonstrated.

Present-day Islam is witnessing the end of secular messianic ideologies and the certitudes of a conquering science;[6] it also witnesses the disarray of the legitimacies constructed by and for the nation-states and the concomitant awakening of peoples, ethnocultural minorities and regional communities long marginalized and oppressed by centralizing religious or secular states. It refuses nevertheless to record the numerous, repeated disappointments which the *internal* history of all societies called Muslim has inflicted upon the utopia of a 'revealed divine law' (*shari'a*), which continues to be proclaimed and imposed by clerics while political regimes are lacking in legitimacy and there is an upsurge of *populist* Islam claiming to be 'revolutionary'. To understand the reactivation in contemporary Islamic contexts of a contradiction common to all great religions, we must pause here to reflect on the internal history of the Islamic utopia and the sociology of its current expressions. But how can one proceed without repeating the many exposés which rehash relentlessly the frozen data, lacking critical objectives or explicative intentions?

If one aims to be exhaustive, informative, explicative and critical, one would require a proper frame for further research in a domain as vast and complex as the map of the world. One can obtain an idea of this complexity and its extent by going through the chronological and genealogical survey of the dynasties in the land of Islam, recently published by C.E. Bosworth.[7] The author enumerates some 186 dynasties scattered over the globe from the Philippines to Morocco and from Central Asia to South Africa. I do not mean, of course, that it is sufficient to go through the chronological history of the dynasties from their origins to our days in order to understand present-day Islam. I propose, rather, to begin with a sociology of contemporary expressions of this Islam to show how, in every socio-cultural and political context, the history of Islam has been solicited and interpreted according to the needs of ongoing struggles. This procedure allows us to distinguish clearly the imaginary productions of contemporary societies, with their manipulations of a multidimensional object which all the actors confusedly call Islam, from the critical, scientific knowledge of the different domains (spiritual, ritual, theological, juridical, political, artistic, etc.) which make up the historical realization of the same object. There is no question here of conflicts, in the manner of defensive or apologetic theologies, between an ideally constructed 'true Islam' and an imaginary Islam manipulated by actors and therefore *false*. The objective of our analysis remains scientific in both cases. In effect, religions, like all great mobilizing ideologies, structure the *imaginaire* of all social groups and thereby contribute to what C. Castoriadis has aptly described as 'the imaginary production of society'. In the case of present-day Islam, the projection of its 'values' and salutary hopes towards an inaugurating age, not just as part of an Islamic era but of a universalizable *existential paradigm*, takes on a psycho-social and political significance in the horizons opened up by the liberation struggles of the years 1950–60. The strong recurrence of the paradigm of historical action put in place already by the Qur'an, together with the teachings and normative conduct of the Prophet, are in themselves a fact which lead us to think about the links between religious and political hope in the historical evolution of societies.

To bring together all these data, I shall now introduce the concept of the dialectic of the local and the global, richly illustrated in the works of Clifford Geertz,[8] which from 1967 inaugurated, in contrast to the writings of the Islamicists, an anthropological problematic that has been insufficiently exploited.

The dialectic of the local and the global

The Islamic fact emerged in the most circumscribed locale: the modest city of Mecca, which after ten years was replaced by the yet more humble agglomeration of Yathrib/Medina. Receiving support, successively, in these two centres, a Meccan, Muhammad b. 'Abd Allah, with some disciples, was able to activate the most pertinent elements of a social, political and cultural dialectic which was sufficiently intense to generate an *existential paradigm* whose expansion raised the unrelenting hostility of some, and the fervent adhesion and inexhaustible hope of others. The Christian fact began in the same manner with Jesus of Nazareth. The passage of the two religions from the local to the global recognized neither the same rhythms nor the same vicissitudes; but in both cases, the same distinction asserts itself between a *prophetic moment* and an *imperial moment*. I reserve the case of Judaism which also inaugurated a prophetic function, but was not linked to an independent state before the creation of the state of Israel.

I call the *prophetic moment* the conjunction of a local historical dialectic with a discourse of mythical structure which transfigures ordinary actors and channels in educative spiritual tensions between man who is called to the exercise of a responsible freedom, and a God who is given to interiorize as a living counterpart, transcendent, demanding judge, merciful, protector, benefactor, etc.

This definition has no theological objective; it is programmatic in the sense that it introduces tools of analysis and understanding for the linguist, historian, psychologist, psycho-socio-linguist and anthropologist for the purpose of interpreting mythical accounts and identifying the evolving structures of the social *imaginaire*. I have demonstrated elsewhere,[9] with the example of the *Sura* 18 of the Qur'an how three ancient accounts – the Seven Sleepers or the 'People of the Cave' (*ahl al-kahf*), the Epic of Gilgamesh and the Romance of Alexander – illustrate the following three equally programmatic definitions of language, myth and scientific activity:

'Language is in the first instance a categorization, a creation of objects and relations between these objects.' (E. Benvéniste)

'Myth is an ideological palace constructed with the rubble of an ancient social discourse.' (Cl. Lévi-Strauss)

'Scientific activity is not a blind accumulation of truths; science is selective and seeks truths which matter most, either by their intrinsic interest or as tools for confronting the world.' (W. Van O. Quine)

The type of thought and the epistemological engagement of reason required by these definitions remain inaccessible to all those who have not made the methodological and conceptual journey peculiar to every discipline invoked. The difference between a *mental object* created by language and a *physical object*, whose existence does not depend either on the perception or the name given to it, remains *unthinkable* for all those who perceive, think and express themselves in the cognitive frame established by this verse of the Bible and reiterated by the Qur'an: 'God taught Adam all the names.' Naming possesses not only a power of *existentiation* (*ijad*) of the named objects, but also an ontological guarantee included in the names taught by God. This onto-psycho-linguistic mechanism is a main characteristic of what I call the *prophetic discourse* as embodied in its linguistic manifestations in the Hebrew Bible, the discourse of Jesus of Nazareth articulated in Aramaic and later transcribed in Greek, and the Qur'an, together with their respective expansions in living Traditions. The reconquest of the *prophetic discourse* as *linguistic fact* contextualized by the historian-anthropologist is in itself an educative operation that is difficult to achieve, even politically impossible in certain cases, because of the pressures exercised by religious orthodoxy, which is the basis of the legitimacy of power and of the representations which the community of the faithful itself gives to the founding moment of its religion. In the case of Islam, the work of misrepresentation is seen in the transfiguration of the historical actor Muhammad into the prophet-mediator of the 'Word of God', which is conceived as transcendent, normative and immutable revelation, *uncreated* according to the 'orthodox' position that eliminated the Mu'tazili theory of the *created* Qur'an.

These observations have nothing theoretical or speculative about them; they result from my personal experience with the most diverse Jewish, Christian and Muslim groups. The most patient pedagogical procedures and the most simplified explanations come up against either the opposition of the dogmatic minds, or an *unthinkable* linked to two diametrically opposite formations but leading to the same psycho-linguistic blockage. The 'orthodox' religious formation uses a strategy of refusal to rid itself of all the attitudes of thought which would compromise the ideal knowledge of what, without any critical examination, is called faith. In the democratic context, where every citizen is perfectly entitled to his own 'different' view, particularly when it is connected to the sacred region of faith, we are witnessing, in Europe notably, an intellectually exasperating and dangerous use of this strategy of refusal. No less exasperating and dangerous is the attitude of minds trained in the *culture* – which is termed modern and secular – of *unbelief*, the dogmatic cult of 'the death of God', the rejection not only of the dogmas and catechisms perpetuated by all types of 'church', but more seriously of the religious dimensions of all the cultures manifested in history. In this connection, the word of Voltaire is still very enlightening today: to those who were already worried about the void, nay of the ruins, caused by the success of the battles fought by the reason of the Enlightenment, he would reply, 'I deliver you from a ferocious beast and you are asking me with what I shall replace it!' Assuredly, the reason worrying about its autonomy in relation to external dogmas could not fight against an all-powerful and obscurantist clericalism and at the same time construct values of substitution. But it is a historical fact that the nation-state, representative democracy, universal suffrage and political philosophy managed by the state, are today showing their exhaustion, just as religious regimes did prior to modern revolutions.

One understands in these circumstances why the rare, innovating works on the major questions handed down by the prophetic discourse and its diverse articulations, piously collected and transmitted in every community under the name of a *living tradition*, do not have any *target public* capable of understanding it and making any contributions to it through fruitful debates. Look at the electoral campaigns in democratic societies: the problem of the production, management and functions of meaning and of the effects of meaning are never on the agenda. To say that the average elector would not understand anything of it is incorrect and unjust; the blinding and more frightening socio-cultural truth is that in their great majority, the 'representatives' of the people themselves do not have any interest in engaging in such debates. In the case of societies which claim affinity to 'Islam', researchers, thinkers, writers and artists who would think of transgressing, however little, the *orthodox living tradition*, are simply forbidden to delve into religious questions. I know a significant number of 'intellectuals' and colleagues who contribute to the maintenance of such taboos.

Considering everything that has been said so far, it will be noted that the prophetic moment does not escape the burden of history; it represents the stage of emergence, the socio-political and linguistic construction of a *system of beliefs and non-beliefs* not yet fixed in ritual, ethical, juridical and institutional codes which will intervene in the subsequent stage of the *imperial moment* when a state apparatus brings religion under its control. In the early Qur'anic stage, the relationship between men who hear the call and God is expressed in the context of an oral culture, outside the intervention of clerics who exercise a power of interpretation in favour of, or in opposition to, the state. Besides, what will later become the *Mushaf* or *Closed Official Corpus* and the orthodox collections of *hadith*, set up equally in the *Closed Official Corpus*, exist and function in this stage only as a form of oral statements open to the questioning and immediate reactions of the actors. I insist upon these historical data, which the normative discourse of belief will efface very quickly by projecting on the prophetic moment

of the inaugurating age all the operations of sacralization and
mythologization effected during the imperial moment.

I call the *imperial moment* the period of formation and rapid
expansion of the caliphal state which institutionally lasts from 661
to 1258, despite the political vicissitudes it witnessed from the
intervention of the Buyids (932), and then the Saljuqs,(1040).
The caliphal state is characterized by the construction and maintenance of a politico-religious legitimacy accepted by the Sunnis,
but rejected by the Kharijis and the various Shi'i branches. The
entire Muslim historiography, following orientalist scholarship
since the 19th century, has maintained these political and doctrinal facts without burdening itself with the problems raised by the
passage from the prophetic moment to the imperial moment; and
of the mythical construction of the former by the latter on the
one hand, and by the constant dialectic between the stakes-of-
meaning and the wills-to-power engaged in theologico-political
debates and confrontations for power in all the spaces administered by the caliphal state, on the other. I am not overlooking the
contribution of modern historians to the critical analysis of ancient texts, particularly since the orientalists are more open to
the enquiries of the social sciences. But the fact remains that the
prejudice of rationality continues to prevail over considerations
of the role of the *imaginaire* in the construction of legitimacies,
the formation and expansion of orthodoxies, the representations
of religious truth, and the discursive strategies of Islamic thought
to cover with a sacred divine veil the ethical, juridical, political
and economic norms which bring into relief all the activities and
profane struggles of the social actors.

It is thus that past and present historical writings, reinforced
by the literature of political science, have imposed a rigid, immutable, artificially sacralized image of an hypostatic Islam which
ignores the local, historical, sociological, psychological, linguistic
and mythological factors and assigns a legal status of divine essence to all thoughts, initiatives and productions of men in society.
One rarely finds in the most critical writings – in the sense of the
social sciences – about this Islam, written with a capital letter, the
concepts of state control over religion, sacralization,
transcendentalization, spiritualization, ontologization and mythologization of religion. All this has made it necessary today for

the analyst to undertake the reverse process of de-sacralization, etc. – in other words: *unveiling, deconstruction, de-historicization*; laying bare the reality which has been constructed by and for the social *imaginaire*, under the cover of a discourse formally critical and rationalized such as that of the *usul al-din* and *usul al-fiqh*; a critique of *hadith* (the 'authentic' collections including the *asbab al-nuzul*), and more generally the *akhbar*, the history of the Qur'anic text and Qur'anic exegesis, the elaboration of juridical norms (*istinbat al-ahkam*), the putting in 'historical' form of the *Sira* of the Prophet, 'Ali, the Imams, etc. That is the entire history of Islamic thought and the imperial context where it fulfilled, *simultaneously*, functions of ideation and ideologization/ mythologization – a history that must be rewritten for two main reasons: to acquire a better descriptive and explicative understanding of a domain that is still badly included in the tasks of theoretization undertaken by the social sciences; and to respond to the vital intellectual and cultural needs of all societies which today depend on false representations and illusory beliefs conveyed by the state-controlled and ritualized Islam, dangerously manipulated in the new contexts of flourishing populism and the disintegration of popular as well as urban cultural codes.

Present-day Islam provides neither the educative and cultural resources nor the political and sociological liberties which are indispensable for dealing successfully with the immense edifice of the 'orthodox' islams bequeathed by the imperial moment; the great historical ruptures with their exhaustive traditions and geopolitical and geohistoric environments (the Mediterranean world and modern Europe); and the increasingly more decisive challenges of science and technology, and of economies linked to the revolution in information technology. The long historical period which extends from the 13th to the end of the 18th century is described by historians in terms of *decadence, lethargy* and the *retreat of underdeveloped societies*, in contrast to the European societies which, from the same 13th century, commence an irresistible, uninterrupted march towards modernity with its still ongoing developments under the name of globalization. If we come back to our dialectic of the local and the global, one can speak of the revenge of the local upon the global after the gradual weakening and final demise of the caliphal state. Doubtless, one must take into account what is called the Ottoman Empire. In the frame of analysis which I have chosen – the dialectic of the local and the global, of the stakes-of-meaning and wills-to-power in the Mediterranean world, including the most dynamic part of Europe, from the 15th to 18th centuries – one can speak of a shrinking of the intellectual and cultural horizons of scholarly Islam, of its ritualization, its immersion in symbolic and customary local codes with, notably, the wide proliferation of religious brotherhoods to compensate for local deficiencies in different political centres which are too far away or too weak to exercise an effective control upon all ethno-cultural groups and regions. The depredation of meaning and intellectual diligence, the insignificance of literary creativity and scientific innovation, the disappearance of doctrinal pluralism and the humanist attitude (philosophical *adab* of the 10th century), are linked to several facts which dominated the Ottoman period: the imposition of a single official juridical school (the Hanafi) throughout the empire, the total elimination of philosophy, the widespread emergence of a subservient scholastic class which glossed indefinitely over some classical manuals selected to serve their orthodoxy, the absence of doctrinal disputations (*munazara*) between scholars belonging to different schools, and the obliviousness to currents of fruitful thought as well as significant works and authors of the classical period. On the other hand, the Ottoman state always favoured certain works and institutions, such as architecture and the army, which were more directly linked to the glory of the empire, the deployment of its power and the maintenance of its legitimacy. One will note, however, an instance of resistance by the *'ulama* who refused to grant to the sultans the coveted title of caliph.

Can one then speak of a 'renaissance' (*Nahda*) as have the 'Arabs' – the Arabic-speaking domain of the Ottoman Empire – who suffered a rehabilitated domination afterwards, notably in Algeria, to extol the Turks as the 'protectors of Islam' against the colonizing enterprises of Christian Europe? This question has introduced a huge problem of historical knowledge: we are, in effect, far from an objective definition of the role and place of the Ottoman period in the wider perspective of a global history of peoples, cultures, religions and hegemonies in the Mediterranean space. This objective implies the renunciation by European peoples and nation-states of a unilateral, self-centred historiography which mentions the Muslims in general and the Turks in particular as negative forces opposed to their expansion. Similarly, the colonized peoples and the party-nation-states which have taken charge of them after independence must cease to write and teach their history in terms of moralizing, apologetic and militant categories, which explain their historical stagnation in relation to modern Europe and all their present-day difficulties as a product of savage colonial domination, thus dispensing with the need to examine much older structural mechanisms.

There is a renaissance from the 19th century to the extent that there is a reactivation of the intellectual field, an opening up of cultural creativity and sensibility to the material progress of civilization on account of a mode of knowledge ignored until then in Islamic contexts. The scientific curiosity for the classical period (the *imperial moment*) welcomes for the first time the methods of philology and the frame of historicist enquiry; one is interested in the critical edition of ancient texts after the manner of the European Renaissance of Graeco-Latin texts. The modern political and juridical institutions are subjected to scrutiny, but not to the point of triggering a current of critical revision of the methodological and cognitive foundations of Islamic thought. Albert Hourani rightly designated this period as the *liberal age*.[10] But from the perspective of present-day Islamist discourse and the return to a disguised locality under the pretext of universality, the *Nahda* and even the Salafi thought were more charged with hope, with overtures to intellectual, political and juridical modernity, than the Arab Socialist Revolution of Nasser which was too aligned to a communism without critical Marxists, or the present-day Islamic Revolution in Iran which is too dominated by clerics closer to *populist* religion than to an intellectually demanding spirituality.

Many will reject this proposition because it seems to neglect the colonial domination which weighed until 1945 over all societies with Islamic references. This point is important, because it allows us to measure the responsibility of 'organic' intellectuals who, in order to benefit from the privileges of the new *Nomenklatura*, supported ideologies which were as much foreign to the Islamic tradition – considered obsolete and without political relevance – as to the customary and cultural codes of the rural and nomadic worlds. The 'proletariat' were the only driving force of a revolution which one can today only denounce for its horrors without relegating it to the camp of absolute evil, that is, colonialism and imperialism. This politico-Manichaean division, which has long affected the social link in post-war Europe, is being raised again today with more *anti-intellectual* radicalism by the militants of the Islamic Revolution. That is because the sociological bases of the socialist-communist ideology of the years 1950–70 have been considerably enlarged since then by population explosions, while the uprooting of rural populations and nomads has led to the expansion of cities which were conceived at the beginning of the century, or even in the 19th century, for more limited urban classes. The rapid development of a populist social force is explained by the conjugation of these factors, to which must be added the system of education conceived and imposed by party-nation-states.

The separation between the sciences of the engineer and the sciences of man and society has been more radical and even more harmful than in the model systems of the West. If engineers trained in the new faculties of sciences commit themselves more readily to Islamist movements, it is because they are even more deprived than their peers at the faculties of law and social sciences of the tools of thought which are indispensable for receiving or producing the reasoning of a historian, sociologist, linguist, psychologist or anthropologist. These domains of reality are lived and interpreted through the categories of beliefs and non-beliefs taught by religion, with the ideological reappropriation effected by scholarly discourse, which is itself modelled by the official discourse of national construction (the ministers of education work with their colleagues at the ministries of interior, 'national orientation', religious affairs and information in the line fixed by the party-state). Thus, the *populist* ideological Maquis find themselves spread in all strata and sectors of society; but it is in the great urban centres that they manifest themselves with the greatest political potency and social pressure. That certain regimes succeed better than others in regulating, diverting and containing these forces of protest and change is undeniable; the fact remains that populism is a structural, sociological phenomenon generated during the course of the years 1960–80 in all societies of the former Third World.

This fact conditions the demagogical discourse of the states, weighs upon the manipulation of religious 'values', and reduces the chances of diffusion of critical and disalienating modes of thought.

I have remarked on the scientific distances, the psychological postures, the objectives of meaning and power, which separate present-day Islam from the historical islams which the critical historian tries to reconstruct. The most valuable lesson of this brief journey concerns not only Islam and its faithful; it also touches the *status of meaning* and of *what makes meaning* in human society. One will recognize, however, an important difference between, on the one hand, the situation of Islam as a *model of historical action* and those Muslims who lay claim to it today, and on the other hand, modernity, its producers and its users. In the first case, at least since the 13th century, generations of social actors allowed an immense *unthought* to accumulate, generating *unthinkables* which have become more and more burdensome to handle today; in the second, one makes perilous jumps beyond the values, stakes, works, signs and symbols which one has not taken the time to evaluate and integrate into the successive 'paradigms' which only political battles have made to prevail. These paradigms are from then on possessed of philosophical contingence and political arbitrariness; they go even as far as favouring the consumption of what Pierre Bourdieu has recently called 'discardable thought'. Will one take the time to rethink it and eventually reintegrate it in the more complete, legible and enriching map of the cultures of the world? In other words, modernity has also generated unthoughts and unthinkables by putting the quest for meaning at the service of the will-to-power, whereas it ought to be careful not to bind human destiny to short-lived *effects of meaning*. Julia Kristéva spoke of '*the destructive genesis of meaning*' at a time when semiotics cultivated the ambition of introducing more effective cognitive strategies for better mastering the conditions of production and consumption of meaning.

Having said all this, it is necessary to elaborate further the concept to avoid reinforcing the idea, already too widespread, that Islam is a substantial entity which generates itself from its founding texts and imposes its brand upon societies and cultures which have accepted it. Present-day Islam, like classical Islam and the nascent Islam of the Qur'an and the action of Muhammad, are the evolving and changing products of social actors so diverse and under historical conditions so complex through time and space, that we prefer to speak of a hypostasized Islam of texts and believers rather than one moulded doctrinally and ideologically by concrete forces. Today these forces are termed populism; the uprooting of rural populations and nomads; the disintegration of urban mercantile and cultured milieux – in the sense of the learned written culture[11] – under the combined pressures of demography, the influx of unemployed rural populations, the destruction of cultural codes and systems of traditional solidarity; party-nation-states more concerned with monopolizing legal violence than constructing modern legitimacies; social and economic disparities between islets of supra-modernity; the middle classes maintained below their most legitimate ambitions, and the masses doomed to uncertainty, frustration, exclusion and unemployment, that is, to the constitutive situations of the *imaginaire* of revolt. I speak of revolt rather than revolution, because I prefer to reserve this latter concept for popular uprisings supported and legitimized by an ideology heralding imminent and lasting emancipation. That was the case of the Qur'anic discourse which accompanied the concrete organizing action of Muhammad while opening horizons of meaning which would allow future generations – particularly those who produced classical Islam under the great Abbasid caliphs – to construct the ideal sacred figure of the mediating-prophet and of a founding revelation as the indispensable reference for the actions and conduct of the faithful.

The Qur'anic discourse has neither the same cognitive status nor the same discursive strategies as that which I call the *prophetic discourse*. The latter is not to be confused with the sayings of the Prophet collected in the great 'closed official corpus' of *hadith*; for in the orthodox belief the *hadith* cannot be identified with the Qur'anic discourse which is divine. The *prophetic discourse* is that which is memorized, perceived, meditated, commented upon and put to advantage in a vast semantic expansion through sacralization, transfiguration, mythologization, transcendentalization and ontologization of the interpreting community in the course of centuries. It is the product of the collective *imaginaire* of various social groups; in return, it nourishes, galvanizes, stirs up and inflames this very same *imaginaire* which believers call faith. By its enunciation, every believer liberates himself from his ordinary in-dividual self, and from profane time and space, to make himself a contemporary of the Prophet, a witness to the descent of the Word of God; the pious ancients transfigured like the Prophet as mod-els of faithfulness, transmitters by word and action of all the teachings which come to inflate the living tradition and enrich the efficacy of the prophetic discourse. The latter is a homog-enous space of articulation of a necessarily true intangible meaning, which applies to all times and places but is itself inde-pendent of time and place. It combines the citations of the Qur'anic verses, the *hadith*, the edifying accounts of the lives and deeds of other recognized prophets, and saints who have attained proximity to God with the intercession of the Prophet, and the founder-imams of schools acknowledged as orthodox. It excludes, on the other hand, all other human discourses which are not au-thentically derived from the source-foundation-discourse. The recurrence of this discourse in the most diverse socio-cultural milieux and diverse historical conjunctures is explained by its mythical structure, paradigmatic nature, and its power of inter-cession, purification and spiritual elevation of the believer. This definition applies, of course, to all monotheistic religious tradi-tions which link all their discursive productions, and their conducts orientated towards salvation, to their foundational sacred texts (Bible, Gospels, Qur'an)[12] and to their expansion in the living tradition, through complex mechanisms of integration, selection and rejection.

The revolutionary secularist discourse in the English, American and French Revolutions of the age of the Enlightenment breaks totally with the postulates and religious representations of the pro-phetic discourse; but it retains of the latter several common traits. It also presents itself as the founder of a new departure of existen-tial code; it sets up a principle of hope for all mankind, paradigms and definitions which inform and govern all productions of hu-man existence. At the same time, it detaches ethics, law and spirituality from explicit references to a living God, revealing Him-self to men in history; and it confers to a sovereign and responsible reason the task of defining and evaluating all legitimacies. The rupture with the metaphysical vision of spiritual theologies is there-fore not total; there is a substitution of a secularist spiritual power for the power of divine law – it is in this sense that I speak of secularist (laic) discourse. The rivalry between the two discourses has continued until our day; and although the second has had a shorter life span and fewer instances of application than the first, one must recognize that the existential fecundity and promises of emancipation of both have not yet been exhausted. The destiny reserved by history for the Bolshevik Revolution of October 1917 confirms *a contrario* the validity of the comparative analysis which I have outlined here for better evaluating the status of what is called today, since the rise of Khomeini to power, the Islamic Revolution. One cannot, in fact, speak of present-day Islam without reflecting on the significance, scope and limits of this great event.[13]

Before examining the case of the Islamic Revolution, it is useful to insist upon the ideological derivatives of the two discourses I have just presented as two existential codes which are, at the same time, discontinuous, rival and intricate. The passage from prophetic discourse to theological, juridical and political codifications is comparable to the passage of the revolutionary discourse of the Enlightenment to the philosophical, juridical and institutional codifications which still function in the democratic societies of the West. The believers speak of degradation of the divine revelation in the perverse usages which men make of it in societies; the laic citizens speak of crises, corruption and infidelity to the principles of 1789 (in the French case). It is a fact that the Christian empires of Byzantium and the West, the Muslim empires under the caliphate and then the Ottoman sultanate, developed oppressive clerical systems which obliterated the emancipatory visions of the prophetic discourse and action. There is progress and a new departure of code with the reason of the Enlightenment because it liberated the intellectual field from false knowledge, as well as arbitrary political and juridical orders, accumulated by the clerical institutions of all religions. But in its turn, this liberating reason quickly exhausted its ethical and spiritual ethos by becoming conquering, dominating and dogmatic. Particularly in France, the anti-clerical struggle, which was so necessary and fruitful but also violent and radical, engendered a secularist religion that reveals its dogmatism and incapacity to manage cultural pluralism after two centuries of rich and powerful experiences.

Present-day Islam is engaged in demonstrating the intellectual and cultural limits of the revolutionary discourse initiated and nourished by the *Aufklärung*. I do not mean to say that present-day Islamic thought launches intellectual challenges, hitherto unknown, to the reason of the Enlightenment. The Christian counterpart has already made the most of all types and degrees of resistance, rejection and claims which can emanate from a religion of the Book before the rise of modernity in Europe. In any case, the Islamic thought of today is too unprepared in the face of modernity to serve as a fruitful dialectical partner in the ongoing debate on the functions of religion in the context of globalization. The challenge of present-day Islam to the societies of the West resides essentially in its semiological and sociological presence, which is visible enough to bring forth reactions of fear and rejection in populations reputed to be educated by the Enlightenment. It is a fact that in France the declaration of the rights of man and of the citizen was not followed by women's right to vote until 1945!

Can it be said that the Islamic Revolution, which sustains the political audacities and claims of *Jihad vs. McWorld*, has introduced new elements to enrich the typology just outlined by a third type? In the absence of any intellectual challenge on the part of Islamic thought, there would thus exist a historical challenge of paradigmatic scope which would imply stakes- of-meaning not only for the reason of the Enlightenment but, more decisively, for a new, emerging reason.

This question returns under a more programmatic form, but always with a radical and comprehensive critical intention, as I have already said, on the irreversible situation created for Islam and its tradition by the historical test of the 1970s. This time, Islam will not be able to elude, as it did with the alibi of liberation struggles, the major intellectual revolution which bears upon the conditions of production, transmission and consumption of meaning in human societies. At this point in our analytical and critical journey, it is necessary to introduce the problems raised by the attitude of present-day Islam towards its tradition.

The approach of tradition in the Islamic context

For this part of the exposé, I shall content myself with resuming a long study which I devoted to tradition in 1984 and which was published in 1985 under a title resembling the one I have adopted here by integrating the new data of globalization and taking into account *Jihad* as an ongoing figure of history.[14] One may notice that the critical and constructive objective of my earlier reflections imposes itself with more pertinence and urgency in the present-day context of political and social tensions culminating in the Algerian civil war.

At this juncture, I would like to introduce some keys by defining more clearly concepts which have become indispensable tools for any serious contribution to the project of a critique of the Islamic reason, which I have been developing for some forty odd years.[15] I distinguish between two frames of the cognitive activity of this reason, corresponding to two moments in the history of thought: *the frame of the intermediate civilization* as S.D. Goitein has defined it,[16] and *the frame of modernity* as presented historically and philosophically by F. Braudel and J. Habermas.[17] In the first frame, we have the closed sphere of a reason which is at once theocentric and logocentric but whose sovereignty is exercised in the limits fixed by God; in the second, the open sphere of modernity, an incomplete project in which reason remains logocentric but arrogates to itself a sovereignty whose limits are fixed or raised by its own decisions alone. Between the two frames, there is neither a chronological partition nor an impervious cognitive partition. It is, therefore, very important to be able to identify in the first frame certain postures already anticipated by pre-modern reason, which will be fully deployed only subsequently; inversely, the postures peculiar to pre-modern reason continue to resist all the disappointments raised by modern critical analysis. One witnesses even the failure of this latter before political progress and the social expansion of an aggressive, obscurantist religion because it ignores even the elementary critical preoccupations of pre-modern reason.

To illustrate these quick historical glimpses, it would be appropriate to resume here the analysis of concepts which I have often used elsewhere in the perspective of a critique of religious reason on the basis of the Islamic example. I shall mention the following concepts and say a few words about the first: *Qur'anic fact and Islamic fact; societies of the Book/books; holy, sacred, sacrilege, sacrifice; orthodoxy and heresy; exegesis, interpretation and critique of discourses; existential; myth, mythify, mythologize, mystify; ideation, ideologization and critical relation.*

The concept of the *Qur'anic fact* has been generally understood by my readers as the expression of a fideistic view to preserve the dogma of the divine authenticity of the Qur'an from the reach of modern critique; one can, on the other hand, concentrate upon the *Islamic fact* which is more directly the product of the ideological strategies of social actors. This common misunderstanding informs us more about the cognitive system of the readers who close themselves in positivist historicism than the epistemological posture which I am trying to apply in a new critique of religious reason from beyond the example of the Qur'an and its theological expansions. Lately, Malek Bennabi has used the expression *phénomène coranique* (*Qur'anic phenomenon*) in an apologetic perspective which assures great success for his book in the Islamist circles of today. That is why the conquest of a critical operational concept regarding the Qur'an is doomed to failure, for opposite reasons, from the Islamic side as well as from the side of the historians, guardians and administrators of the positivist historicist orthodoxy.

By the *Qur'anic fact* I mean the historical manifestation, at a time and in precise socio-cultural milieu, of an oral discourse which accompanied, for a period of twenty years, the concrete historical action of a social actor called Muhammad ibn 'Abd Allah. One sees that this concept aims not to defend or discard the religious dimension of the discourse, but to fix the attention, within a first methodological time-period, on the linguistic, cultural and social conditions of articulation of the discourse by an interlocutor and of its reception by various, explicitly targeted addressees. There is in it a project of investigation which claims to be simultaneously linguistic, semiotic, sociological, psychological and anthropological. All these dimensions are, in fact, present in all units of the discourse which exegetical literature and modern philology have tried to identify. Separating these dimensions, under the pretext of respecting the independence of various disciplines as they are defined by university scholars, amounts to imposing a first choice-reducing agent which is no less dangerous than that of the theologians, jurists and, even more so, the fundamentalist militants of today who only know the arbitrary projections of the oral discourse into text (the famous *Mushaf* which I call the *Closed Official Corpus*).

The linguistic and historical jump from the stage of the oral discourse, articulated in changing situations in the course of twenty years, to that of *Closed Official Corpus* has been considered until now neither by the literature on the juridical objectives of the discourse (the *asbab al-nuzul*, circumstances of the revelation), nor by the historicist and applied philological scholarship which shares with traditional exegesis the reading of the discourse as a sacralized and transfigured text as believers do. I have never come across the concept, however essential, of the *Closed Official Corpus* in the works of any of the most eminent 'modern' Qur'an scholars. The traditional term *Mushaf* is unanimously accepted without commentaries, other than those of textual philology. Under the circumstances, one understands that the concept of the *Qur'anic fact* is not only disdained but interpreted in a 'scientifically' disqualifying sense.

The concept of oral discourse, transformed into written discourse and then consigned to a *Closed Official Corpus* by a long series of complex manipulations – which philological enquiry clarified within the limits of its own problematics – is all the more fruitful as it allows us to open up a site of theoretical analysis where all the founding religious texts, and in the first place the Bible and the Gospels, can be taken into account. And one will no longer aim to enquire separately about the authenticity of textual fragments, or even words in a given corpus, which was the object of philological critique. What is at stake in the passage from the oral discourse to a *Closed Official Corpus* (one will note that I never say just 'corpus' because then I would be disregarding, as with the term *Mushaf*, all the problems relating to the notions of corpus, official and closure) is the cognitive status of meaning produced at the linguistic and historical stage of the oral discourse, taking into account all the real situations of discourse and the effects of meaning constructed by the successive exegeses in ideologically difficult contexts, and particularly the exclusive status of a *Closed*

Official Corpus resulting in an irreversible fact which can be dated to the orthodox *Commentary* of al-Tabari (d. 923).

Islam and its tradition have until now encountered modernity as a cultural aggression (*al-ghazw al-fikri*), not as a historical phenomenon local and universal at the same time. It remains to be explained why the intellectual, scientific, cultural and economic advances of the area moulded by the Islamic fact from the 7th to the 13th centuries have given way to the set of regressive forces which have detached the southern and eastern shores of the Mediterranean from all the historical activities of modernity to the point that at the end of the current century, the rejection of the West has assumed the dimensions of a pole of contemporary history and the rank of a symbolical figure dialectically opposed to the rival figure of *McWorld* in the new historical stage opened by the failure of international communism and the triumph of unbridled libertarianism. Although *McWorld* and *Jihad* translate the eternal dialectic of the dominators and the dominated, they are now united in fettering the very spirit to works which alienate and destroy it.

While sharing the arguments of B.R. Barber on the subject of political, economic and juridical strategies of *McWorld* and the phantasmical proclamations of *Jihad*, I would like to go further than him by taking into account the stakes-of-meaning and culture engaged in the irrational, suicidal confrontation of the two monsters of our contemporary history. I find a theoretical advantage in reflecting upon present-day Islam facing its tradition no longer only from within this tradition, which has been tried too often since at least the *Ihya 'ulum al-din* of al-Ghazali, but from the forces which subvert, for the first time in its history and in an irreversible manner, this very interior, this resistant nucleus upon which *Jihad* is believed to lean, and even to seize many tools of *McWorld*, while declaring them to be satanical in its dialectical opposite. In this confrontation with unequal arms, Islam–*Jihad*, like yesterday's nationalist discourse of liberation, presents itself as an innocent victim and a saviour-depositary of divine law and promise before an atheistic, materialistic, dominating and radically immoral West. The colonized peoples were promised only civil liberties and social justice in the frame of scientific socialism perfected in popular democracies, the inheritors of the revolution of the Enlightenment. In the confrontation between *Jihad* and *McWorld*, one returns to the Manichaean struggle between light and darkness after the apparent defeats and irremediable disqualifications of theologies, theocracies, empires and monarchies, as much as that of modern revolutions founded upon the secular cult of sovereign reason.

Who will take charge of all these sites in ruin? Who will inaugurate the new history after the proclaimed end of a certain history? Will it be religious reason, purified of the errancy, false hopes and oppressive violence of the scientific atheistic reason, at last re-enthroned as in Iran, Afghanistan and the Sudan, in its rank and functions of the 'vicar of God on earth' (*khalifat Allah fi'l-ard*)? That is the ambition set into motion by *Jihad*. Or will the reason of the Enlightenment, correcting its excesses, contradictions, false knowledge and theoretical dogmatism, restart on bases more solid and principles better mastered? That is the thesis of the more or less competent and convinced defenders of post-modern reason. But once again, thought as it is exercised in contemporary Islamic contexts is too caught up in semantic disorder, as generated and widely perpetrated by the conjugated violence of *Jihad* and *McWorld*, too handicapped by the unthoughts accumulated since the 16th century, to contribute to the great open debate on a world scale, other than through the violence of the poor and the excluded, and the support extended to *McWorld* by a greater number of consumers. Participation in the debate at the more essential level of intellectual responsibility is, to a large degree, conditioned by the orientations of philosophical thought within the crisis which moulds *McWorld*.

How do we think about this crisis that includes the radical changes which science and technology impose on all societies as well as the problems peculiar to societies dominated by Islam, be it dogmatic and ritualistic, conservative and traditionalist, or liberal within the non-transgressible limits fixed and supervised by the managers of orthodoxy? The politics of religion pursued in a large number of societies called Muslim make too many concessions to the forces of traditionalism, while favouring the adoption of all the benefits of material civilization. This results in dangerous mental cleavages, increasing backwardness in the systems of education, fruitless self-censorship, and the impoverishment of creativity in various domains of intellectual and cultural life. Whereas divisions, contradictions and conflicts, individual and collective, become the common lot of numerous populations, there remain few workers capable of assuming the indispensable tasks of an emancipation which is always aspired, always deferred and sometimes openly rejected (I think of the condition of women and the rights of children). Who is concerned with mastering the frames and tools of thought of the hegemonical powers that set all the agendas of historical outcome, as well as the modes of interpretation of the various epochs, so as to avoid being trapped again by false knowledge, false conscience, mental objects (such as the East, the West, Islam, development, the rights of man, the right to self-determination, etc.), constructed by and for the centres of homologation of 'true' knowledge and meaning which support their wills-to-power? Where are the institutions for training researchers and teachers who would widen the fields of investigation of the human and social sciences, and radicalize their critical questioning of the problems bequeathed to us by the unknown, mutilated and unthought pasts and presents, which blur or smash our visions of the future?

I have long shared the prevailing opinion which reclaims the elaboration of a 'modern theology' of Islam, after the manner of what the Catholics and Protestants have continued to do in the Western milieu since the beginning of what historians call the 'modernist crisis'. The collapse of all ideologies, added to the challenges posed by experimental sciences to the political, juridical, ethical and philosophical reason, have surely increased the demand for solutions in the direction of traditional theologies; but these remain too imprisoned by medievalist cognitive frames and tools to assume with any success the delicate tasks imposed by the ongoing exit of the religious *imaginaires*. With regard to Islam, the discourse of *Jihad* has practically reduced to silence, or struck with derision, every voice which attempts to reactivate theological, philosophical, ethical and juridical thinking, capable of integrating in the same critical movement all the tasks prescribed by the specific historical development which I have called the exhaustive Islamic tradition. An historical outline is necessary here to render more intelligibly these observations on the adventures of meaning in Islamic contexts.

1. The system of thought elaborated in the Islamic context during the phase of emergence and the classical period (661–1258) is totally closed in the antique and medieval cognitive, or pre-modern, space.

2. The long period which extends from the 13th to the beginning of the 19th century has long been passed over in silence, superficially evoked in school textbooks under the headings of decadence, lethargy, oblivion, conservatism and return to popular superstitions. The Turks can pride themselves in the initial success of a vast empire, but they are obliged to lower the tone in view of the irresistible rise of Europe after the defeat of Lepanto in 1571. Now, it was during this crucial historical phase that were programmed the factors, politically, sociologically and culturally important, of the crises, tensions, explosions, state formations and ruptures which characterize the contemporary evolution of all the societies subjected to hasty, arbitrary and uncontrollable reconstructions. It was then, in effect, that two major ruptures were accomplished in these societies which prescribe specific tasks for us today: the internal rupture of Islamic thought with regard to doctrinal pluralism, ethno-cultural cosmopolitism and incipient humanism, which constituted the richness of the classical period; and the rupture with the outside, that is to say with Europe, where the great changes and constitutive discoveries of modernity occurred.

3. When the intellectual and cultural movement of the *Nahda* engaged in the work of reactivation of the precious legacy of the classical period under the names of *Turath*, the golden age of Islamic civilization, the two ruptures just mentioned had already created a profound gulf between the revolutionary, euphoric Europe of the Enlightenment and the societies which could no longer benefit either from the tools bequeathed by classical thought, or still less from those proposed in the 19th–20th centuries (1850–1940) in Europe by the practitioners of historicist historiography and the philological reading of the major texts. Thus, the promising efforts of three generations of intellectuals, researchers, writers and artists has instigated, since the 1920s, a rejection leading to more radical political battles during the wars of liberation (1945–1970) and today to *Jihad* versus *McWorld*. Since the 1960s, demography has upset

the sociological conditions of political expression, dissemination of learning and manipulation of social *imaginaires*. One can speculate that in these circumstances an unforeseen subterranean evolution will operate towards the worst or the best. The visibility of the nearest horizon, the year 2010 for example, remains blurred so much so that the social sciences confine themselves to the almost journalistic description of superficial events by depending upon the discourse of the most active actors, most directly engaged in the conquest of political and religious power.

I shall end with these brief observations. I know they demand more clarification, critical examination and debate; but this is not possible so long as the great tasks involved in the general history of thought, of all the traditions of thought which seek to take their place and appointment with the generalized quest for one reliable, lasting and universalizable meaning, mobilize only a limited number of exceptional researcher-thinkers.

NOTES

1. Roger Pol Droit, *Philosopie et démocratie dans le monde* (Paris, 1995), p. 22.

2. Ibid., p. 24.

3. Ibid.

4. On connections between philosophy, anthropology and other social sciences, see the works of P. Bourdieu, notably his latest title, *Méditations Pascaliennes* (Seuil, 1997).

5. Benjamin R. Barber, *Jihad vs. McWorld: How Globalism and Tribalism are Reshaping the World* (New York, 1996); French trans. *Djihad vs. McWorld: Mondialisation et intégrisme contre la démocratie* (Paris, 1996).

6. I refer to the works of Ilya Prigogine, *La fin des certitudes* (Paris, 1995), Claude Allègre, *La Défaite de Platon* (Paris, 1996) and Alain Finkelkraut, *La Défaite de la pensée* (Paris, 1988). The abundant literature on this theme expresses at the same time the anguish of our time in face of the errancy of our history and the will to clarify new conditions of reflection to prevent as much as possible other totalitarian adventures.

7. C. Edmund Bosworth, *The New Islamic Dynasties: A Chronological*

and Genealogical Manual (Edinburgh, 1996).

8. See especially C. Geertz, *Islam Observed* (Chicago, 1968).

9. Mohammed Arkoun, *Lectures du Coran* (Paris, 1982), pp. 69–86.

10. Albert Hourani, *Arabic Thought in the Liberal Age, 1798–1939* (Oxford, 1962).

11. I evoke here a distinction of anthropological scope between learned written culture and oral culture termed 'popular'; the first is linked to all statist formations from the appearance of writing, the second applies particularly to segmentary societies in tension with centralizing powers. The bibliography on the subject is vast; the best introduction remains the work of J. Goody, *The Interface Between the Oral and the Written* (Cambridge, 1987). See the application which I make of it in 'Transgresser, déplacer, dépasser,' *Arabica*, 43 (1996), pp. 28–70.

12. I do not overlook the great religions of Asia; but due to a lack of sufficient competence, I cannot pronounce on the linguistic status of their founding discourses.

13. My friend Daryush Shayegan has already reflected upon the general problem of religious revolution in *Qu'est-ce qu'une révolution religieuse?* (Paris, 1982).

14. Mohammed Arkoun, 'L'Islam actuel devant sa tradition,' in *Aspects de la foi de l'Islam* (Brussels, 1985); also in M. Arkoun, *Penser l'Islam aujourd'hui* (Algiers, 1993).

15. I published in the Tunisian periodical *al-Fikr* in 1957 a first programmatic text entitled *Maghza ta'rikh shamal Ifrikiya*. Morocco and Tunisia had just regained their independence and the Algerians pursued a tragic struggle which was to last until March 1962. I had already the naïvety to believe that the rights of critical knowledge, bearing on vital subjects which the ideology of battle seizes upon, ought to be respected and integrated in the liberation struggle which derived its better legitimacy in the promises of liberty lavished on intellectuals, artists, creators and thinkers. All North Africans of my generation shared enthusiastically this naïve vision. Today the destiny of liberties and rights of the spirit in all societies moulded by the Islamic fact is such that there is no longer any place for naïve projects driven by plausible utopia; but the ever current project of a critical re-reading of the entire North African past inseparable from its African and Mediterranean dimensions, does not allow us to dispose either the social frames capable of supporting and putting it to

advantage, or the research duly formed for conducting several sites of exploration and writing with the tools of thought and scientific competency required by what I have called the emerging reason, different from all types of reason bequeathed by all types of tradition, including the reason of the Enlightenment.

16. Solomon D. Goitein, *Studies in Islamic History and Institutions* (Leiden, 1966).

17. F. Braudel, *Civilization and Capitalism, 15th to 18th Century* (London, 1981–84), and J. Habermas, *The Philosophical Discourse of Modernity*, tr. F. Lawrence (Cambridge, 1987).

Glossary

Note: Listings in the glossary are selected terms and names appearing frequently in the individual chapters.

ahl al-bayt: lit., people of the house; members of the household of the Prophet Muḥammad.

'aqīda (pl. *'aqā'id*): compendium of doctrines.

'Alids: descendants of 'Alī b. Abī Ṭālib, cousin and son-in-law of the Prophet and also the first Shī'ī imam.

'ālim (pl., *'ulamā'*): a scholar in Islamic religious sciences.

'aql: intellect, reason, reasoning in law.

āya (pl., *āyāt*): lit., sign, symbol; a single verse in the Qur'anic text.

bāṭin: the inward, hidden, or esoteric meaning behind the literal wording of sacred texts and religious prescriptions, notably the Qur'an and the *sharī'a* (q.v.), in distinction from the *ẓāhir* (q.v.).

dā'ī (pl., *du'āt*): lit., summoner; a religious missionary or propagandist, especially among the Ismailis.

da'wa: mission; in the religio-political sense, *da'wa* is the invitation or call to adopt the cause of an individual or family claiming the right to the imamate; it also refers to the hierarchy of ranks within the particular religious organization developed for this purpose.

dīwān: collected works of a poet; also a public financial register.

faqīh (pl., *fuqahā'*): an exponent of *fiqh* (q.v.); a Muslim jurist in general.

fatwā (pl., *fatāwā*): an opinion on Islamic law given by a *faqīh* (q.v.); collected legal opinions.

fiqh: the technical term for Islamic jurisprudence; the discipline of elucidating the *sharī'a* (q.v.).

ḥadīth: a report, sometimes translated as Tradition, relating an action or saying of the Prophet, or the corpus of such reports collectively, constituting a major source of Islamic law, second in importance only to the Qur'an. For Shī'ī communities, *ḥadīth* also refers to the actions and sayings of their imams. The Shī'īs also use the term *khabar* (pl., *akhbār*) as synonymous of *ḥadīth*.

ḥajj: the annual pilgrimage to Mecca, required of every Muslim at least once in his lifetime if possible.

ḥakīm: a person learned in medical, philosophic or scientific disciplines.

ḥaqīqa (pl., *ḥaqā'iq*): truth, spiritual reality.

ḥikma: wisdom; theosophy; also esoteric Ismaili doctrine.

'ilm: religious knowledge.

'irfān: gnosis; mystical knowledge.

'ishq: love.

jihād: lit., striving; effort directed toward inner religious perfection and also toward holy war of the Muslims against the infidels.

kalām: theology, sometimes called scholastic theology; the subject dealing with the problems of divine unity, attributes, human free will vs. determinism, etc.

khabar: see *ḥadīth*.

madhhab: a system or school of religious law in Islam.

madrasa: a college or seminary of higher Muslim learning, often attached to a mosque.

Mahdi: the rightly guided one; a name applied to the restorer of religion and justice who will appear and rule before the end of the world. Belief in the coming of the eschatalogical Mahdi from the *ahl al-bayt* (q.v.) became a central aspect of early Shī'ī teachings.

mujtahid: a person qualified to exercise *ijtihād* and give authoritative opinions on Islamic law.

nafs: soul, universal soul.

pīr: the Persian equivalent of the Arabic word *shaykh* in the sense of a spiritual guide or Sufi master, qualified to lead disciples (*murīds*).

qāḍī (pl., *quḍāt*): a religious judge administering the *sharī'a* (q.v.).

ṣadr: originally an Arabic honorific, *ṣadr* was especially used in Safawid
   Persia for a high religious dignitary whose function (*ṣadāra*) was
   concerned essentially with administering religious affairs of the
   realm.

sharī'a: the divinely revealed sacred law of Islam; the whole body of
   rules guiding the life of a Muslim.

sīra: biography; particularly the life of the Prophet.

Sufi: an exponent of Sufism (*taṣawwuf*), the commonest term for that
   aspect of Islam that is based on the mystical life.

sunna: custom, practice; particularly that associated with the exem-
   plary life of the Prophet, comprising his deeds, utterances, etc.; it
   is embodied in *ḥadīth* (q.v.).

sūra: a group of Qur'anic verses collected in a single chapter.

tafsīr: lit., explanation, commentary; particularly the commentaries
   on the Qur'an; the external philological exegesis of the Qur'an,
   in distinction from *ta'wīl* (q.v.).

ṭahāra: ritual purification; a necessary condition for the performance
   of prayer in Islam.

taqiyya: precautionary dissimulation of one's true religious beliefs,
   especially in time of danger; used especially by the Ismaili and
   Twelver Shī'īs.

ṭarīqa: path; the mystical, spiritual path followed by Sufis (q.v.); also
   any one of the organized Sufi orders.

taṣawwuf: see Sufi.

ta'wīl: the educing of the inner, original meaning from the literal
   wording or apparent meaning of a text or ritual religious prescrip-
   tion; among the Shī'īs, it denotes the method of educing the *bāṭin*
   (q.v.) from the *ẓāhir* (q.v.). Translated also as esoteric or spiritual
   exegesis, *ta'wīl* may be distinguished from *tafsīr* (q.v.).

umma: any people as followers of a particular religion or prophet; in
   particular, the Muslims as forming a religious community.

waḥdat al-wujūd: unity of being, existential monism.

wājib al-wujūd: necessary existent.

ẓāhir: the outward, literal, or exoteric meaning of sacred texts and
   religious prescriptions, notably the Qur'an and the *sharī'a* (q.v.),
   in distinction from the *bāṭin* (q.v.).

Select Bibliography

The bibliography includes some basic works of reference and a selection of sources and studies cited in the individual chapters.

'Abduh, Muḥammad. *Risālat al-tawḥīd*, ed. M. Abū Rayya. Cairo, 1977. French trans., *Risālat al-Tawḥīd: Exposé de la religion Musulmane*, tr. B. Michel and M. Abdel Raziq. Paris, 1978. English trans., *The Theology of Unity*, tr. I. Musa'ad and K. Cragg. London, 1966.

Abrahamov, Binyamin. *Islamic Theology: Traditionalism and Rationalism*. Edinburgh, 1998.

Adams, Charles C. *Islam and Modernism in Egypt: A Study of the Modern Reform Movement Inaugurated by Muḥammad 'Abduh*. London, 1933.

Amir-Moezzi, Mohammad Ali. *The Divine Guide in Early Shi'ism: The Sources of Esotericism in Islam*, tr. D. Streight. Albany, N.Y., 1994.

Amoretti, Biancamaria Scarcia. *Sciiti nel mondo*. Rome, 1994.

Arberry, Arthur J. *The Koran Interpreted*. London, 1955.

——. *Revelation and Reason in Islam*. London, 1957.

Arjomand, Said Amir. *The Shadow of God and the Hidden Imam*. Chicago, 1984.

——, ed. *Authority and Political Culture in Shi'ism*. Albany, N.Y., 1988.

Arkoun, Mohammed. *Aspects de la pensée Musulmane classique*. Paris, 1963.

——. *L'Ethique musulmanne d'après Mawardi.* Paris, 1964.

——. *L'Humanisme Arabe au IVe/Xe siècle.* 2nd ed., Paris, 1982.

——. *Lectures du Coran.* Paris, 1982.

——. *Pour une critique de la raison Islamique.* Paris, 1984.

——. *La pensée Arabe.* 4th ed., Paris, 1991.

——. *Ouvertures sur l'Islam.* 2nd ed., Paris, 1992.

——. *Rethinking Islam: Common Questions, Uncommon Answers,* tr. R.D. Lee. Boulder, 1994.

Arkoun, Mohammed and Borrmans, M. *L'Islam, religion et société.* Paris, 1982.

al-Ash'arī, Abu'l-Ḥasan 'Alī b. Ismā'īl. *Kitāb maqālāt al-Islāmiyyīn,* ed. H. Ritter. Istanbul, 1929–30.

Al-Azmeh, Aziz. *Islams and Modernities.* 2nd ed., London, 1996.

al-Baghdādī, Abū Manṣūr 'Abd al-Qāhir b. Ṭāhir. *al-Farq bayn al-firaq,* ed. M. Badr. Cairo, 1328/1910. English trans., *Moslem Schisms and Sects,* part I, tr. K.C. Seelye. New York, 1919; part II, tr. A.S. Halkin. Tel Aviv, 1935.

Baldick, Julian, *Mystical Islam.* London, 1989.

Barber, Benjamin R. *Jihad vs. McWorld: How Globalism and Tribalism are Reshaping the World.* New York, 1996.

Bausani, Alessandro. *L'Enciclopedia dei Fratelli della Purità.* Naples, 1978.

al-Bayḍawī, 'Abd Allāh b. 'Umar. *Anwār al-tanzīl wa-asrār al-ta'wīl.* Cairo, 1939. Partial English trans., *The Light of Inspiration and Secret of Interpretation,* tr. E.F.F. Bishop and M. Kaddal. Glasgow, 1957.

Bello, Iysa A. *The Medieval Islamic Controversy between Philosophy and Orthodoxy.* Leiden, 1989.

Berthels, Andrei E. *Nasir-i Khosrov i ismailizm.* Moscow, 1959. Persian trans., *Nāṣir-i Khusraw wa Ismā'īliyān,* tr. Y. Āriyanpūr. Tehran, 1346/1967.

Bosworth, C. Edmund. *Medieval Arabic Culture and Administration.* London, 1982.

——. *The New Islamic Dynasties: A Chronological and Genealogical Manual.* Edinburgh, 1996.

——. 'Abbasid Caliphate,' *Encyclopaedia Iranica,* vol. 1, pp. 89–95.

Bosworth, C. Edmund et al., ed. *The Islamic World: From Classical to Modern Times.* Princeton, 1989.

Böwering, Gerhard. *The Mystical Vision of Existence in Classical Islam.* Berlin and New York, 1980.

Browne, Edward G. *A Literary History of Persia.* Cambridge, 1928.

al-Bukhārī, Muḥammad b. Ismā'īl. *Kitāb jāmi' al-ṣaḥīḥ,* ed. L. Krenl and W. Juynboll. Leiden, 1862–1908. English trans., *The Translation of the Meanings of Ṣaḥīḥ al-Bukhārī*, tr. Muḥammad M. Khān. New Delhi, 1984.

Bulliet, Richard W. *Conversion to Islam in the Medieval Period: An Essay in Quantitative History*. Cambridge, Mass., 1979.

——. *Islam: The View from the Edge*. New York, 1994.

Butterworth, Charles E., ed. *The Political Aspects of Islamic Philosophy: Essays in Honor of Muhsin S. Mahdi*. Cambridge, Mass., 1992.

Cahen, Claude. *Les Peuples Musulmans dans l'histoire médiévale*. Damascus, 1977.

Calder, Norman. *Studies in Early Muslim Jurisprudence*. Oxford, 1993.

——. 'Law,' in Nasr and Leaman, ed., *History of Islamic Philosophy*, pp. 979–98.

——. 'History and Nostalgia: Reflections on John Wansbrough's *The Sectarian Milieu*,' *Method and Theory in the Study of Religion*, 9 (1997), pp. 47–73.

The Cambridge History of Arabic Literature: Arabic Literature to the End of the Umayyad Period, ed. A.F.L. Beeston et al. Cambridge, 1983.

The Cambridge History of Arabic Literature: Religion, Learning and Science in the 'Abbasid Period, ed. M.J.L. Young et al. Cambridge, 1990.

Canard, Marius. 'Fāṭimids,' *The Encyclopaedia of Islam*, new ed., vol. 2, pp. 850–62.

Chittick, William C. *The Sufi Path of Knowledge: Ibn al-'Arabī's Metaphysics of Imagination*. Albany, N.Y., 1989.

——. *The Self-Disclosure of God: Principles of Ibn al-'Arabī's Cosmology*. Albany, N.Y., 1998.

Chodkiewicz, Michel. *Le Sceau des saints: Prophétie et sainteté dans la doctrine d'Ibn 'Arabī*. Paris, 1986. English trans., *Seal of the Saints: Prophethood and Sainthood in the Doctrine of Ibn 'Arabi*, tr. L. Sherrard. Cambridge, 1993.

Cooper, John. 'From al-Ṭūsī to the School of Iṣfahān,' in Nasr and Leaman, ed., *History of Islamic Philosophy*, pp. 585–96.

Cooper, John et al., ed. *Islam and Modernity: Muslim Intellectuals Respond*. London, 1998.

Corbin, Henry. *Avicenne et le récit visionnaire*. Tehran, 1952–54. English trans., *Avicenna and the Visionary Recital*, tr. W.R. Trask. New York, 1960.

——. *Creative Imagination in the Ṣūfism of Ibn 'Arabī*, tr. R. Manheim. Princeton, 1969.

——. *En Islam Iranien: Aspects spirituels et philosophiques*. Paris, 1971–

72.

——. 'Nāṣir-i Khusrau and Iranian Ismāʿīlism,' in *The Cambridge History of Iran*: Volume 4, *The Period from the Arab Invasion to the Saljuqs*, ed. R.N. Frye. Cambridge, 1975, pp. 520–42.

——. *Cyclical Time and Ismaili Gnosis*, tr. R. Manheim and J.W. Morris. London, 1983.

——. *History of Islamic Philosophy*, tr. L. Sherrard. London, 1993.

Coulson, Noel J. *A History of Islamic Law*. Edinburgh, 1964.

——. *Conflicts and Tensions in Islamic Jurisprudence*. Chicago, 1969.

Crone, Patricia. *Meccan Trade and the Rise of Islam*. Princeton, 1987.

——. *Roman, Provincial and Islamic Law: The Origins of the Islamic Patronate*. Cambridge, 1987.

Crone, Patricia and Hinds, Martin. *God's Caliph: Religious Authority in the First Centuries of Islam*. Cambridge, 1986.

Dabashi, Hamid. *Authority in Islam*. New Brunswick, N.J., 1989.

——. *Theology of Discontent: The Ideological Foundations of the Islamic Revolution in Iran*. New York, 1993.

Daftary, Farhad. *The Ismāʿīlīs: Their History and Doctrines*. Cambridge, 1990.

——, ed. *Mediaeval Ismaʿili History and Thought*. Cambridge, 1996.

——. 'Diversity in Islam: Communities of Interpretation,' in Nanji, ed., *The Muslim Almanac*, pp. 161–73.

——. *A Short History of the Ismailis: Traditions of a Muslim Community*. Edinburgh, 1998.

——. 'Ismāʿīliyya,' in *Dāʾirat al-maʿārif-i buzurg-i Islāmī* (*The Great Islamic Encyclopaedia*), ed. K. Musavi Bojnurdi. Tehran, 1367–/1989–, vol. 8, pp. 681–702.

Daiber, Hans. 'Abū Ḥātim ar-Rāzī (10th Century AD) on the Unity and Diversity of Religions,' in J. Gort et al., ed., *Dialogue and Syncretism: An Interdisciplinary Approach*. Grand Rapids, Michigan, 1989, pp. 87–104.

Davidson, Herbert A. *Alfarabi, Avicenna, and Averroes on Intellect*. Oxford, 1992.

Denny, Frederick M. *An Introduction to Islam*. New York, 1985.

Derrida, Jacques. *Margins of Philosophy*, tr. A. Bass. Chicago, 1982.

Droit, Roger Pol. *Philosophie et démocratie dans le monde*. Paris, 1995.

Enayat, Hamid. *Modern Islamic Political Thought: The Response of the Shīʿī and Sunnī Muslims to the Twentieth Century*. London, 1982.

Encyclopaedia Iranica, ed. E. Yarshater. London, 1982– .

The Encyclopaedia of Islam, ed. H.A.R. Gibb et al. New ed., Leiden and

London, 1960– .

Encyclopaedia of Arabic Literature, ed. Julie Scott Meisami and P. Starkey. London, 1998.

The Encyclopedia of Religion, ed. M. Eliade. London and New York, 1987.

Esmail, Aziz. The Poetics of Religious Experience: The Islamic Context. London, 1998.

Ess, Josef van. 'The Logical Structure of Islamic Theology,' in G.E. von Grunebaum, ed., Logic in Classical Islamic Culture. Wiesbaden, 1970, pp. 21–50.

——. Theologie und Gesellschaft im 2. und 3. Jahrhundert Hidschra: Eine Geschichte des religiösen Denkens im frühen Islam. Berlin, 1991–97.

Fakhry, Majid. A History of Islamic Philosophy. 2nd ed., London and New York, 1983.

——. Ethical Theories in Islam. Leiden, 1991.

——. A Short Introduction to Islamic Philosophy, Theology and Mysticism. Oxford, 1997.

Foucault, Michel. Madness and Civilization: A History of Insanity in the Age of Reason, tr. R. Howard. London, 1989.

Fyzee, Asaf A.A. Outlines of Muhammadan Law, 4th ed., Delhi, 1974.

Garcin, Jean Claude et al. États, sociétés et cultures du monde Musulman médiéval, Xe–XVe siècle, vol. 1. Paris, 1995.

Gardet, Louis. Dieu et la destinée de l'homme. Paris, 1967.

Gardet, Louis and Anwati, M.M. Introduction à la théologie Musulmane. 2nd ed., Paris, 1970.

Gätje, Helmut. The Qur'ān and its Exegesis, tr. A.T. Welch. London, 1976.

Geertz, Clifford. Islam Observed: Religious Development in Morocco and Indonesia. Chicago, 1968.

Gellner, Ernest. Postmodernism, Reason and Religion. London, 1992.

Gibb, Hamilton A.R. Studies on the Civilization of Islam, ed. S.J. Shaw and W.R. Polk. Boston, 1962.

Giese, Alma and Bürgel, J.C., ed. Gott ist schön und Er liebt die Schönheit/ God is beautiful and He loves beauty: Festschrift in honor of Annemarie Schimmel. Bern and Berlin, 1994.

Gilsenen, Michael. Recognizing Islam: An Anthropologist's Introduction. London, 1982.

Gimaret, Daniel. Théories de l'acte humain en théologie Musulmane. Paris, 1980.

——. La Doctrine d'al-Ash'arī. Paris, 1990.

Goitein, Solomon D. *Studies in Islamic History and Institutions.* Leiden, 1966.

Goldziher, Ignaz. *Muslim Studies,* ed. and tr. S.M. Stern and C.R. Barber. London, 1967–71.

——. *Introduction to Islamic Theology and Law,* tr. A. and R. Hamori. Princeton, 1981.

Graham, William A. *Divine Word and Prophetic Word in Early Islam.* The Hague, 1977.

——. *Beyond the Written Word: Oral Aspects of Scripture in the History of Religion.* Cambridge, 1987.

Grunebaum, Gustave E. von. *Modern Islam: The Search for Cultural Identity.* Berkeley, 1962.

——. *Classical Islam: A History, 600–1258,* tr. K. Watson. London, 1970.

——, ed. *Theology and Law in Islam.* Wiesbaden, 1971.

Gutas, Dimitri. *Avicenna and the Aristotelian Tradition.* Leiden, 1988.

——. *Greek Thought, Arabic Culture.* London, 1998.

Gutas, Dimitri et al. 'Fārābī,' *Encyclopaedia Iranica,* vol. 9, pp. 208–29.

Haarmann, Ulrich, ed., *Geschichte der arabischen Welt.* 2nd ed., Munich, 1991.

Habermas, Jürgen. *The Philosophical Discourse of Modernity: Twelve Lectures,* tr. F. Lawrence. Cambridge, 1987.

Hallaq, Wael B. *Ibn Taymiyya against the Greek Logicians.* Oxford, 1993.

——. *Law and Legal Theory in Classical and Medieval Islam.* Aldershot, 1995.

——. *A History of Islamic Legal Theories.* Cambridge, 1997.

Halm, Heinz. *Kosmologie und Heilslehre der frühen Ismāʿīlīya.* Wiesbaden, 1978.

——. *Die islamische Gnosis.* Zürich and Munich, 1982.

——. *Shiism,* tr. J. Watson. Edinburgh, 1991.

——. *The Fatimids and their Traditions of Learning.* London, 1997.

Hinds, Martin. *Studies in Early Islamic History,* ed. J. Bacharach et al. Princeton, 1996.

Hodgson, Marshall G.S. *The Order of Assassins: The Struggle of the Early Nizārī Ismāʿīlīs against the Islamic World.* The Hague, 1955.

——. 'The Ismāʿīlī State,' in *The Cambridge History of Iran: Volume 5, The Saljuq and Mongol Periods,* ed. J.A. Boyle. Cambridge, 1968, pp. 422–82.

——. *The Venture of Islam: Conscience and History in a World Civilization.* Chicago, 1974.

Hourani, Albert. *Arabic Thought in the Liberal Age, 1798–1939.* Oxford,

1962.
———. *A History of the Arab Peoples.* London, 1991.
Hourani, George F. *Averroes on the Harmony of Religion and Philosophy.* London, 1961.
———. *Reason and Tradition in Islamic Ethics.* Cambridge, 1985.
Hovannisian, Richard G. and Sabagh, G., ed. *The Persian Presence in the Islamic World.* Cambridge, 1998.
Hunsberger, Alice C. *Nasir Khusraw: The Ruby of Badakhshan.* London, 2000.
Ibn al-'Arabī, Muḥyi al-Dīn. *Fuṣūṣ al-ḥikam,* ed. A. 'Affifi. Cairo, 1946. English trans., *The Bezels of Wisdom,* tr. R.W.J. Austin. London, 1980.
———. *Kitāb al-futūḥat al-Makkiyya.* Cairo, 1329/1911; ed. 'Uthmān Yaḥyā, Cairo, 1972–78. Abridged trans., *Les Illuminations de la Mecque (The Meccan Illuminations),* tr. M. Chodkiewicz et al. Paris, 1988.
Ibn Ḥazm, Abū Muḥammad 'Alī b. Aḥmad. *Kitāb al-fiṣal fi'l-milal.* Cairo, 1317–21/1899–1903.
Ibn al-Qutayba, Abū Muḥammad 'Abd Allāh. *Kitāb al-ma'ārif,* ed. T. 'Ukāsha. 2nd ed., Cairo, 1388/1969; ed. M.I. 'Abd Allāh al-Ṣāwī. 2nd ed., Beirut, 1970.
Iqbal, Muhammad. *Payām-i Mashriq.* Lahore, 1923.
———. *The Reconstruction of Religious Thought in Islam.* Lahore, 1930.
———. *Javidnāma.* Lahore, 1932. English trans., *Javid-Nama,* tr. A.J. Arberry. London, 1966.
al-Iṣfahānī, Abu'l-Faraj 'Alī b. al-Ḥusayn. *Kitāb al-aghānī.* Bulāq, 1284–85/1867–89; ed. 'A. Aḥmad Farrāj et al. Beirut, 1955–61.
Ivanow, Wladimir. *Nasir-i Khusraw and Ismailism.* Bombay, 1948.
———. *Ismaili Literature: A Bibliographical Survey.* Tehran, 1963.
Izutsu, Toshihiko. *God and Man in the Koran.* Tokyo, 1964.
———. *The Concept of Belief in Islamic Theology.* Tokyo, 1965.
———. *Ethico-religious Concepts in the Qur'ān.* Montreal, 1966.
Jambet, Christian. *La Grande résurrection d'Alamût.* Lagrasse, 1990.
Juwaynī, 'Alā' al-Dīn 'Aṭā-Malik. *Ta'rīkh-i jahān-gushā,* ed. M. Qazwīnī. Leiden and London, 1912–37. English trans., *The History of the World-Conqueror,* tr. J.A. Boyle. Manchester, 1958; reprinted, Manchester and Paris, 1997.
Juynboll, G.H.A. *Studies on the Origins and Uses of Islamic Ḥadīth.* Aldershot, 1996.
Kāshānī, Fatḥ Allāh. *Minhāj al-ṣādiqīn fī ilzām al-mukhālifīn.* Tehran, 1969.

232   INTELLECTUAL TRADITIONS IN ISLAM

Keddie, Nikki R. *An Islamic Response to Imperialism: Political and Religious Writings of Sayyid Jamāl ad-Dīn 'al-Afghānī'*. Berkeley, 1968.
——. *Sayyid Jamāl ad-Dīn 'al-Afghānī': A Political Biography*. Berkeley, 1972.
Kedouri, Elie. *Afghani and 'Abduh: An Essay on Religious Unbelief and Political Activism in Modern Islam*. London, 1966.
Kennedy, Hugh. *The Early Abbasid Caliphate: A Political History*. London, 1981.
——. *The Prophet and the Age of the Caliphates*. London, 1986.
Khadduri, Majid. *The Islamic Conception of Justice*. Baltimore, 1984.
Khalidi, Tarif. *Arabic Historical Thought in the Classical Period*. Cambridge, 1994.
King, David A. *Islamic Mathematical Astronomy*. London, 1986.
al-Kirmānī, Ḥamīd al-Dīn Aḥmad b. 'Abd Allāh. *Rāḥat al-'aql*, ed. M. Kāmil Ḥusayn and M. Muṣṭafā Ḥilmī. Cairo, 1953; ed. M. Ghālib. Beirut, 1967. Russian trans., *Uspokoenie Razuma*, tr. A.V. Smirnov. Moscow, 1995.
Kohlberg, Etan. *Belief and Law in Imāmī Shī'ism*. Aldershot, 1991.
Köhler, Bärbel. *Die Wissenschaft unter den ägyptischen Fatimiden*. Hildesheim, 1994.
Kraemer, Joel L. *Humanism in the Renaissance of Islam*. Leiden, 1986.
Kraus, Paul, ed. *Rasā'il falsafiyya li-Abī Bakr Muḥammad b. Zakariyyā' al-Rāzī*. Cairo, 1939.
——. 'Plotin chez les Arabes,' *Bulletin de l'Institut d'Égypte*, 23 (1940–41), pp. 263–95, reprinted in his *Alchemie, Ketzerei, Apokryphen im frühen Islam*, ed. R. Brague. Hildesheim, 1994, pp. 313–45.
al-Kulaynī, Abū Ja'far Muḥammad b. Ya'qūb. *al-Uṣūl min al-kāfī*, ed. 'A.A. al-Ghaffārī. Tehran, 1388/1968.
Laoust, Henri. *Les Schismes dans l'Islam*. 2nd ed., Paris, 1977.
Lapidus, Ira M. *A History of Islamic Societies*. Cambridge, 1988.
Leaman, Oliver. *An Introduction to Medieval Islamic Philosophy*. Cambridge, 1985.
——. *Averroes and his Philosophy*. Oxford, 1988.
——. 'Islamic Philosophy since Avicenna,' in *Companion Encyclopaedia of Asian Philosophy*, ed. B. Carr and I. Mahalingam. London, 1997, pp. 69–82.
——. 'Islamic Humanism,' in Nasr and Leaman, ed., *History of Islamic Philosophy*, pp. 155–64.
Leith, Vincent B. *Deconstructive Criticism: An Advanced Introduction*. New York, 1983.

Lerner, Ralph and Mahdi, Muhsin, ed. *Medieval Political Philosophy: A Sourcebook*. Ithaca, N.Y., 1972.

Lewis, Bernard. *Studies in Classical and Ottoman Islam (7th-16th Centuries)*. London, 1976.

Lewis, Bernard and Holt, Peter M. *Historians of the Middle East*. London, 1964.

Lewisohn, Leonard, ed. *Classical Persian Sufism: From its Origins to Rumi*. London and New York, 1993.

Lory, Pierre. *Les Commentaires ésotériques du Coran*. Paris, 1980.

Madelung, Wilferd. 'Das Imamat in der frühen ismailitischen Lehre,' *Der Islam*, 37 (1961), pp. 43-135.

——. *Der Imam al-Qāsim ibn Ibrāhīm und die Glaubenslehre der Zaiditen*. Berlin, 1965.

——. *Religious Schools and Sects in Medieval Islam*. London, 1985.

——. *Religious Trends in Early Islamic Iran*. Albany, N.Y., 1988.

——. *The Succession to Muḥammad: A Study of the Early Caliphate*. Cambridge, 1997.

——. 'Ismā'īliyya,' *The Encyclopaedia of Islam*, new ed., vol. 4, pp. 198-206.

Mahdi, Muhsin. *Al-Fārābī's Philosophy of Plato and Aristotle*. Rev. ed., Ithaca, 1969.

——. *Ibn Khaldūn's Philosophy of History*. London, 1957.

——. *Orientalism and the Study of Islamic Philosophy*. Oxford, 1990.

Mahdi, Muhsin et al. 'Avicenna,' *Encyclopaedia Iranica*, vol. 3, pp. 66-110.

Makdisi, George. *The Rise of Colleges: Institutions of Learning in Islam and the West*. Edinburgh, 1981.

——. *The Rise of Humanism in Classical Islam and the Christian West*. Edinburgh, 1990.

al-Maqrīzī, Taqī al-Dīn Aḥmad b. 'Alī. *Kitāb al-mawā'iẓ wa'l-i'tibār fī dhikr al-khiṭaṭ wa'l-āthār*, ed. A. Fu'ād Sayyid. London, 1995.

Marquet, Yves. *La Philosophie des Iḥwān al-Ṣafā'*. Algiers, 1975.

Massignon, Louis. *The Passion of al-Hallāj: Mystic and Martyr of Islam*, tr. H. Mason. Princeton, 1982.

Meisami, Julie Scott. *Medieval Persian Court Poetry*. Princeton, N.J., 1987.

——. *Persian Historiography to the End of the Twelfth Century*. Edinburgh, 1999.

Modarressi Tabātabā'i, Hossein. *An Introduction to Shī'ī Law: A Bibliographical Study*. London, 1984.

Momen, Moojan. *An Introduction to Shi'i Islam: The History and Doctrines of Twelver Shi'ism.* New Haven, 1985.

Morewedge, Parviz, ed. *Islamic Philosophical Theology.* Albany, N.Y., 1979.

——, ed. *Islamic Philosophy and Mysticism.* Delmar, N.Y., 1981.

Morris, James W. *The Wisdom of the Throne: An Introduction to the Philosophy of Mulla Sadra.* Princeton, 1981.

Mottahedeh, Roy P. *Loyalty and Leadership in an Islamic Society.* Princeton, 1980.

——. *The Mantle of the Prophet.* London, 1986.

Mullā Ṣadrā Shīrāzī, Ṣadr al-Dīn Muḥammad. *Asfār al-arba'a*, ed. R. Luṭfī. Qumm, 1378–89/1958–69.

Nanji, Azim A. *The Nizārī Ismā'īlī Tradition in the Indo-Pakistan Subcontinent.* Delmar, N.Y., 1978.

——, ed. *The Muslim Almanac: A Reference Work on the History, Faith, Culture, and Peoples of Islam.* Detroit, 1996.

——, ed. *Mapping Islamic Studies.* Berlin and New York, 1997.

Nasir Khusraw. *Dīwān*, ed. N. Taqavī et al. Tehran, 1304–7/1925–28; ed. M. Mīnuvī and M. Mohaghegh. Tehran, 1353/1974. Partial English trans., *Make a Shield from Wisdom*, tr. Annemarie Schimmel. London, 1993.

——. *Gushāyish wa rahāyish*, ed. and tr. F.M. Hunzai under the title *Knowledge and Liberation.* London, 1998.

——. *Jāmi' al-ḥikmatayn*, ed. H. Corbin and M. Mu'īn. Tehran and Paris, 1953. French trans., *Le Livre réunissant les deux sagesses*, tr. Isabelle de Gastines. Paris, 1990.

——. *Safar-nāma*, ed. M. Dabīr Siyāqī. Tehran, 1356/1977. English trans., *Nāṣer-e Khosraw's Book of Travels (Safarnāma)*, tr. W.M. Thackston, Jr. Albany, N.Y., 1986.

Nasr, S. Hossein. *Three Muslim Sages.* Cambridge, Mass., 1964.

——. *Science and Civilization in Islam.* Cambridge, Mass., 1968.

——, ed. *Ismā'īlī Contributions to Islamic Culture.* Tehran, 1977.

——. *An Introduction to Islamic Cosmological Doctrines.* 2nd ed., London, 1978.

——, ed. *Islamic Spirituality.* London, 1987–91.

——. *Ideals and Realities of Islam.* Rev. ed., London, 1994.

Nasr, S. Hossein and Leaman, Oliver, ed. *History of Islamic Philosophy.* London, 1996.

al-Nawbakhtī, al-Ḥasan b. Mūsā. *Kitāb firaq al-Shī'a*, ed. H. Ritter. Istanbul, 1931.

Netton, Ian R. *Muslim Neoplatonists: An Introduction to the Thought of the Brethren of Purity (Ikhwān al-Ṣafā')*. London, 1982.

———. *Allāh Transcendent: Studies in the Structure and Semiotics of Islamic Philosophy, Theology and Cosmology*. London, 1989.

———. *Al-Fārābī and his School*. London and New York, 1992.

Nicholson, Reynold A. *Studies in Islamic Mysticism*. Cambridge, 1921.

———. *A Literary History of the Arabs*. Cambridge, 1930.

al-Nuʿmān b. Muḥammad, al-Qāḍī Abū Ḥanīfa. *Daʿāʾim al-Islām*, ed. A.A.A. Fyzee. Cairo, 1951–61. Partial English trans., *The Book of Faith*, tr. A.A.A. Fyzee. Bombay, 1974.

———. *Taʾwīl al-daʿāʾim*, ed. M. Ḥasan al-Aʿẓamī. Cairo, 1967–72.

Nwyia, Paul. *Exégèse coranique et langage mystique*. Beirut, 1970.

The Oxford Encyclopedia of the Modern Islamic World, ed. John L. Esposito. Oxford, 1995.

Peters, Rudolph. *Islam and Colonialism: The Doctrine of Jihad in Modern History*. The Hague, 1979.

Piscatori, James P., ed. *Islam in the Political Process*. Cambridge, 1981.

Poonawala, Ismail K. *Biobibliography of Ismāʿīlī Literature*. Malibu, Calif., 1977.

———. 'Ismāʿīlī Taʾwīl of the Qurʾān,' in A. Rippin, ed., *Approaches to the History of the Interpretation of the Qurʾan*. Oxford, 1988, pp. 199–222.

———. 'Al-Qāḍī al-Nuʿmān and Ismaʿili Jurisprudence,' in Daftary, ed., *Mediaeval Ismaʿili History*, pp. 117–43.

Rahman, Fazlur. *The Philosophy of Mullā Ṣadrā*. Albany, N.Y., 1975.

———. *Islam and Modernity: Transformation of an Intellectual Tradition*. Chicago, 1982.

Rahnema, Ali, ed. *Pioneers of Islamic Revival*. London, 1994.

al-Rāzī, Abū Ḥātim Aḥmad b. Ḥamdān. *Aʿlām al-nubuwwa*, ed. Ṣ. al-Ṣāwī and G.R. Aʿvānī. Tehran, 1977.

Renan, Ernest. *Averroës et l'Averroïsme*. Paris, 1882.

Richard, Yann. *Shiʿite Islam*, tr. A. Nevill. Oxford, 1995.

Rosenthal, Franz. *The Classical Heritage in Islam*. London, 1975.

———. *Muslim Intellectual and Social History*. Aldershot, 1990.

Rūmī, Mawlānā Jalāl al-Dīn. *The Mathnawī*, ed. and tr. R.A. Nicholson. Leiden and London, 1925–40.

———. *Dīwān-i kabīr yā kulliyyāt-i Shams*, ed. Badīʿ al-Zamān Furūzānfar. Tehran, 1957–75.

Ruthven, Malise. *Islam: A Very Short Introduction*. Oxford, 1997.

Rypka, Jan. *History of Iranian Literature*, ed. K. Jahn. Dordrecht, 1968.

Sachedina, Abdulaziz. *Islamic Messianism: The Idea of Mahdi in Twelver Shi'ism.* Albany, N.Y., 1981.

——. *The Just Ruler (al-sulṭān al-'ādil) in Shī'ite Islam.* Oxford, 1988.

——. *The Islamic Roots of Democratic Pluralism.* Oxford, 1999.

Ṣafā, Zabīḥ Allāh. *Ta'rīkh-i adabiyyāt dar Īrān.* Various editions, Tehran, 1342– / 1963–.

Schacht, Joseph. *The Origins of Muhammadan Jurisprudence.* Oxford, 1950.

——. *An Introduction to Islamic Law.* Oxford, 1964.

Schimmel, Annemarie. *Gabriel's Wing: A Study into the Religious Ideas of Sir Muhammad Iqbal.* Leiden, 1963.

——. *Mystical Dimensions of Islam.* Chapel Hill, 1975.

——. *The Triumphal Sun: A Study of the Works of Jalāloddin Rumi.* London, 1978.

——. *Islam in the Indian Subcontinent.* Leiden, 1980.

——. *As Through a Veil: Mystical Poetry in Islam.* New York, 1982.

——. *And Muhammad is His Messenger.* Chapel Hill, 1985.

——. *A Two-Colored Brocade: The Imagery of Persian Poetry.* Chapel Hill, 1992.

——. *Deciphering the Signs of God: A Phenomenological Approach to Islam.* Edinburgh and Albany, N.Y., 1994.

Schmidtke, Sabine. *The Theology of al-'Allāma al-Ḥillī (d. 726/1325).* Berlin, 1991.

Schuon, Frithjof. *Understanding Islam,* tr. D.M. Matheson. London, 1963.

——. *Dimensions of Islam,* tr. P.N. Townsend. London, 1970.

al-Shahrastānī, Abu'l-Fatḥ Muḥammad b. 'Abd al-Karīm. *Kitāb al-milal wa'l-niḥal,* ed. W. Cureton. London, 1842–46. French trans., *Livre des religions et des sectes,* tr. D. Gimaret et al. Louvain, 1986–93. Partial English trans., *Muslim Sects and Divisions,* tr. A.K. Kazi and J.G. Flynn. London, 1984.

Sharif, M.M., ed. *A History of Muslim Philosophy.* Wiesbaden, 1963–66.

Shayegan, Daryush. *Qu'est-ce qu'une révolution religieuse?* Paris, 1982.

al-Shushtarī, al-Qāḍī Nūr Allāh. *Majālis al-mu'minīn.* Tehran, 1365/1986.

Sībawayhī, Abū Bishr 'Amr b. 'Uthmān. *Le Livre de Sībawaihi, traité de grammaire Arabe,* ed. H. Derenbourg, Paris, 1881–89; reprinted, Hildesheim, 1970.

al-Sijistānī, Abū Ya'qūb Isḥāq b. Aḥmad. *Kitāb al-yanābī',* ed. and French trans. H. Corbin, in his *Trilogie Ismaélienne.* Tehran and

Paris, 1961, text pp. 1–97, translation pp. 1–127. English trans., *The Book of Wellsprings*, tr. P.E. Walker, in his *The Wellsprings of Wisdom*. Salt Lake City, 1994, pp. 37–111.

Smet, Daniel de. *La Quiétude de l'intellect: Néoplatonisme et gnose Ismaélienne dans l'oeuvre de Hamîd ad-Dîn al-Kîrmânî (Xᵉ/XIᵉs)*. Louvain, 1995.

Smith, Wilfred Cantwell. *Islam in Modern History*. Princeton, 1957.

Stern, Samuel M. *Studies in Early Ismāʿilism*. Jerusalem and Leiden, 1983.

al-Suhrawardī, Shihāb al-Dīn Yahyā. *Opera metaphysica et mystica*, ed. H. Corbin and S.H. Nasr. Istanbul and Tehran, 1945–70.

——. *The Mystical and Visionary Treatises of Shihabuddin Yahya Suhrawardi*, tr. W.M. Thackston, Jr. London, 1982.

al-Tabarī, Abū Jaʿfar Muhammad b. Jarīr. *Taʾrīkh al-rusul waʾl-mulūk*, ed. M.J. de Goeje et al., 3 series. Leiden, 1879–1901. English trans. by various scholars under the title *The History of al-Tabarī*. Albany, N.Y., 1985–99.

——. *Jāmiʿ al-bayān fī tafsīr al-Qurʾān*. Beirut, 1972. Partial English trans., *The Commentary on the Qurʾān*, vol. 1, tr. John Cooper. Oxford, 1987.

al-Tabarsī, Abū ʿAlī al-Fadl b. al-Hasan. *Majmaʿ al-bayān fī tafsīr al-Qurʾān*. Beirut, 1959.

Tibi, Bassam. *The Crisis of Modern Islam: A Preindustrial Culture in the Scientific-Technological Age*, tr. J. von Sivers. Salt Lake City. 1988.

Trimingham, J. Spencer. *The Sufi Orders in Islam*. Oxford, 1971.

al-Tūsī, Abū Jaʿfar Muhammad b. al-Hasan. *al-Tibyān fī tafsīr al-Qurʾān*. Najaf, 1957.

al-Tūsī, Nasīr al-Dīn Muhammad. *Akhlāq-i Nāsirī*, ed. M. Mīnuvī and ʿA. Haydarī. Tehran, 1356/1977. English trans., *The Nasirean Ethics*, tr. G.M. Wickens. London, 1964.

——. *Rawdat al-taslīm*, ed. and tr. W. Ivanow. Leiden, 1950. French trans., *La Convocation d'Alamût: Somme de philosophie Ismaélienne*, tr. Ch. Jambet. Lagrasse, 1996.

Ullmann, Manfred. *Islamic Medicine*. Edinburgh, 1978.

Walker, Paul E. *Early Philosophical Shiism: The Ismaili Neoplatonism of Abū Yaʿqūb al-Sijistānī*. Cambridge, 1993.

——. *Abū Yaʿqūb al-Sijistānī: Intellectual Missionary*. London, 1996.

——. *Hamīd al-Dīn al-Kirmānī: Ismaili Thought in the Age of al-Hākim*. London, 1999.

Walzer, Richard. *Greek into Arabic: Essays on Islamic Philosophy*. Oxford,

1962.

Wansbrough, John. *Quranic Studies: Sources and Methods of Scriptural Interpretation*. Oxford, 1977.

——. *The Sectarian Milieu: Content and Composition of Islamic Salvation History*. Oxford, 1978.

Watt, W. Montgomery. *The Formative Period of Islamic Thought*. Edinburgh, 1973.

——. *Islamic Philosophy and Theology*. 2nd ed., Edinburgh, 1985.

——. *Early Islam: Collected Articles*. Edinburgh, 1990.

Wolfson, Harry A. *The Philosophy of the Kalam*. Cambridge, Mass., 1976.

Yarshater, Ehsan, ed. *Persian Literature*. Albany, N.Y., 1988.

al-Zamakhsharī, Abu'l-Qāsim Maḥmūd b. 'Umar. *al-Kashshāf 'an ḥaqā'iq al-tanzīl*. Cairo, 1948.

Ziai, Hossein. 'Shihāb al-Dīn Suhrawardī: Founder of the Illuminationist School,' in Nasr and Leaman, ed., *History of Islamic Philosophy*, pp. 434–64.

Index

pir 106, 149, 152 *see also*
   murshid
Plato 12, 13, 34, 35, 36, 39, 50,
   58, 95, 132, 149
Plotinus (al-Shaykh al-Yunani)
   34, 49, 52, 95, 125 *see also*
   Neoplatonism
poetry 22, 23, 135, 136
prophecy (*nubuwwa*) 15, 48,
   51, 52, 53, 54
Prophetic traditions *see hadith*
Protestants, Protestantism 15,
   46, 64, 217
psychology 187, 189
Ptolemy 28

Qadi Qadan 140
Qadiris, Sufis 156
qalam (pen) 96
Qarmatis 92, 116
qisas al-anbiya 74, 76
qiyama (resurrection) 103, 104,
   105, 124
Quhistan, south-eastern
   Khurasan 106
Quhistani, Abu Ishaq 106
Quine, W. Van O. 199
Qumm, Persia 156, 162
Qur'an 11, 12, 18, 20, 21, 22,
   23, 25, 28, 29, 35, 41, 50,
   68, 70, 73, 74, 75, 76, 77,
   78, 79, 81, 85, 89, 90, 91,
   92, 93, 94, 96, 98, 100, 102,
   118, 120, 124, 127, 131,
   134, 137, 140, 141, 143,
   144, 147, 160, 164, 165,
   167, 168, 169, 170, 171,
   172, 173, 174, 175, 176,
   177, 178, 188, 190, 192,
   194, 198, 199, 200, 201,

   203, 207, 208, 209, 213, 214
Quraysh, Meccan tribe 12
al-Qushayri 82

Rahat al-'aql (al-Kirmani) 97
Rahman, Fazlur 64
Rashid al-Din Fadl Allah,
   historian 105
Rashidun caliphs 19
rationalism 44–6, 48, 52, 53,
   54, 55, 56, 97
Rawdat al-taslim (al-Tusi) 104
al-Razi (Rhazes), Abu Bakr
   Muhammad, philospher and
   physician 51, 52, 55
al-Razi, Abu Hatim Ahmad,
   Ismaili *da'i* and author 51,
   95, 97–8
al-Razi, Fakhr al-Din, theologian
   69, 76, 80, 81
*The Reconstruction of Religious
   Thought in Islam* (Iqbal) 61–
   2, 63
Reformation 10, 13
Renaissance 10, 63, 189
Renan, Ernest 60
revelation 10, 12, 42, 44, 48,
   51, 52, 53, 56, 60, 71, 72,
   73, 74, 75, 77, 78, 88, 90,
   91, 92, 96, 97, 134, 140,
   165, 170, 174, 176, 196,
   200, 208, 210, 214
Rida, Rashid 60, 61
Roman Catholic Church *see*
   Catholics, Catholocism
Roman Empire 24
Rumi, Mawlana Jalal al-Din,
   mystical poet 130, 131, 132,
   133, 136, 137, 140, 144, 156
Russell, Bertrand 62